Poets and Poetry

Sadler/Hayllar/Powell

Illustrated by Carol Pelham-Thorman

First published 1992 by
MACMILLAN EDUCATION AUSTRALIA PTY LTD
107 Moray Street, South Melbourne 3205
6 Clarke Street, Crows Nest 2065
Reprinted 1993 (with corrections)

Associated companies and representatives
throughout the world

National Library of Australia
cataloguing in publication data

Sadler, R. K. (Rex Kevin).
   Poets and poetry.

   Includes index.
   ISBN 0 7329 1787 5.

   1. Australian poetry. 2. Australian poetry – Problems, exercises, etc.
   I. Hayllar, T. A. S. (Thomas Albert S.). II. Powell, C. J. (Clifford J.),
   III. Title.

A821.008

Typeset in Baskerville and Optima by
Superskill Graphics, Singapore
Printed in Hong Kong.

Cover design by Jan Schmoeger
Cover photograph: Australian Picture Library
Edited by Vivienne Perham

Contents

Preface

At a time when many are concerned about the proliferation of violence, sexual explicitness and morbidity in material on offer in our society, it has been totally refreshing to look again into the richness available in the writings of major poets of our time. One of the genuine delights of compiling *Poets and Poetry* has been the opportunity to select from the wealth of quality poetry available to us. Tacky special effects and gory sensationalism have nothing to compare with the depth and sensitivity on offer here.

Poetry has a special capacity to touch the soul. Well written, it connects with our finest human qualities – with compassion, empathy, wonder and appreciation of the beautiful. There are such poems here. Crafted with skill, it can also disturb us, shaking us out of our comfort zone and demanding an emotional response from us. Ground out of the agony or joy of the poet's experience, it can move us deeply. So many of the poems on offer here, by poets as diverse as Hopkins and Heaney, Dickinson and Dawe, Oodgeroo and Owen, have just such capacity. We confidently anticipate that everyone who uses this book will discover treasure of lasting value from the poems we have selected.

Poets and Poetry features separate chapters on thirteen major poets. While a significant number are Australian, there are also poets from Ireland, England, and the USA. Each of these chapters begins with an account of the poet's life and background. The poems chosen to represent each poet offer a significant encounter with the diversity and uniqueness of his or her work. Questions are provided to help students 'break open' the poems in search of gold. A number of appreciation essays, which serve as models for students, have also been included.

The first three chapters of *Poets and Poetry* pick up issues of central importance to the skill of appreciating poetry. These are 'The Poet's Purpose', 'Understanding the Poet's Craft' and 'A Love of Poetry'. Four chapters of thematically selected poems round out the book, offering us the opportunity to include a taste of the work of other gifted writers.

We have enjoyed putting this book together. Our hope is that others will share the pleasure that such a selection offers.

1 The Poet's Purpose

What Is the Purpose of Poetry?

The truth is that poets have many purposes. Pernaps we can summarise them by saying that poets seek to use words, sounds, rhythms and special structuring of language to help us to consider ideas that they think are worth our reflection. Sometimes the ideas will be serious; occasionally they will be humorous. Nevertheless, the poet wants us to encounter them, maybe to wrestle with them a little, and then, hopefully, be affected by them in some way. Usually the poet wants us to respond emotionally to his or her ideas, as they are presented in the poem.

Let's look at some of the specific purposes that poets may have.

Poets Paint Word Pictures

When poets set out to describe a scene, an object, or a bird or animal, they want us to be able to picture in our minds what they have seen. This is where the skill and artistry of poetry comes in. The poet must find words, sounds, rhythms and a structure that combine to stimulate our imagination so that we can 'see' what he or she has seen.

But a poem is not a photograph! It is important to remember that we do not 'see' an exact reproduction of what the poet has seen. Rather, we visualise a scene or situation that is stimulated into existence by the poet's words and skills, but is uniquely shaped and flavoured by *our* past experiences. Thus, the reception of the poet's offering is always partly a reflection of who we are and how we respond. That is why a poem may move one person to tears, while another person may find it superficial, or even boring.

Poets, like artists, often use colour to help touch our emotions. They use images or symbols to try to convey an important aspect of their subject. They use words that arouse emotion to try to re-create their experience for us.

'The Red Wheelbarrow' is a simple word picture. Notice the effect of the lack of normal punctuation, the detached phrases. The poet has chosen this structure so that we can more easily enter into this as a collection of little awarenesses that the poet is experiencing which, taken together, reflect his overall impression of this scene. Notice the importance of the colour words 'red' and 'white' and the contrast they bring to our minds. Be aware of the selection of the word 'glazed', and the picture of undisturbed smoothness it conveys. Notice the introductory phrase, 'So much depends'. The poet is alerting us to the fact that he wants us to take this seemingly unimportant scene seriously, and reflect upon it.

Red Wheelbarrow

So much depends
upon

a red wheel
barrow

glazed with rain
water

beside the white
chickens.
WILLIAM CARLOS WILLIAMS

Read through William Hart-Smith's delightful word picture of an otter experiencing the joy of being able to swim, and wanting to share this with his mate.

Otters

His wet fur, velvet-smooth, was sleek as reeds
stroked downstream by a river.
He did not run so much as undulate
down the long ramp from his nest when the keeper came
and turned the brass tap on for him
to fill the concrete water-trough. He flowed
into the water like water
entering water . . . and he swam
seal-like, eel-like, delighted.
Flowed out again, ran up the wooden ramp
to his sleeping mate
coiled warmly in the straw,
nudged her, nuzzled her,
thrust his nose in her lap—
'Come quickly, dear!
The keeper has turned on the tap!'
WILLIAM HART-SMITH

Otters under Observation

1 What impression of the otter does the poet create by the words 'sleek as reeds'?
2 'He did not run so much as undulate'. How does this cause you to picture the otter? Why is the word 'undulate' such a good choice here?
3 ' . . . He flowed/into the water'. What does the word 'flowed' add to our picture of the otter?

4 How effective is the simile 'like water entering water'? What does it convey to you?
5 'Seal-like, eel-like, delighted'. What does the poet achieve for us by this playing with the sounds of words?
6 What overall impression of the otter has the poet created by this word picture?

Carl Sandburg has written a little word picture called 'Soup'. In it he shares an experience of his, seeking to convey by the poem's structure and word selection an aspect of a famous person that we might not normally think about.

Soup

I saw a famous man eating soup.
I say he was lifting a fat broth
Into his mouth with a spoon.
His name was in the newspapers that day
Spelled out in tall black headlines
And thousands of people were talking about him.

　When I saw him.
He sat bending his head over a plate
Putting soup in his mouth with a spoon.

CARL SANDBURG

'Girls in a Factory' describes a scene that has impressed the poet in some way. He wants to share it with us, but especially he wants to share his reflections about this scene. He uses the image of sewing to describe what the women may be thinking of as they work.

Girls in a Factory

Seated in rows at the machines
Their heads are bent; the tacking needle
Stitches along the hours, along the seams.

What thoughts follow the needle
Over the fields of cloth,
Stitching into the seams
Perhaps a scarlet thread of love.
A daisy-chain of dreams?

DENNIS GLOVER

'On Frosty Days' builds a word picture around a memory of the past. The poet recalls the feelings, sounds and sights that make this scene vivid in his memory.

On Frosty Days

On frosty days, when I was young,
I rode out early with the men
And mustered cattle till their long
Blue shadows covered half the plain;

And when we turned our horses round,
Only the homestead's point of light,
Men's voices, and the bridles' sound,
Were left in the enormous night.

And now again the sun has set
All yellow and a greening sky
Sucks up the colour from the wheat—
And here's my horse, my dog and I.

DAVID CAMPBELL

Word Pictures in On Frosty Days

1 Read through the first verse and notice the rhythm. What does this contribute to the word picture the poet is creating?
2 ' . . . their long/Blue shadows'. Why is the word 'blue' so appropriate in this poem?
3 What was the only sight as they turned for home?
4 What sounds does the poet recall, as they headed for home?
5 The last stanza tells us why the poet has recalled this picture from the past. Why has he?
6 What techniques has the poet used that have helped create the word picture for you?

Poets Appeal to the Senses

Poets often attempt to create for us a sensory experience — an experience that involves one or more of our five senses of sight, sound, taste, touch and smell. Once again, they rely on their poetic technique to achieve this. Obviously, they cannot *really* re-create a smell for us! But by careful selection of words they may touch our memories or imaginations so that we can share in the smell by recalling it. Images, sounds, rhythm and the structure of the poem, if used well, will all add to this effect.

Laurie Lee's poem 'Apples' appeals to our senses of sight and taste, as we are invited to 'Behold the apples' rounded worlds'.

Apples

Behold the apples' rounded worlds:
juice-green of July rain,
the black polestar of flower, the rind
mapped with its crimson stain.

The russet, crab and cottage red
burn to the sun's hot brass,
then drop like sweat from every branch
and bubble in the grass.

They lie as wanton as they fall,
and where they fall and break,
the stallion clamps his crunching jaws,
the starling stabs his beak.

In each plump gourd the cidery bite
of boys' teeth tears the skin;
the waltzing wasp consumes his share,
the bent worm enters in.

I, with as easy hunger, take
entire my season's dole;
welcome the ripe, the sweet, the sour,
the hollow and the whole.

LAURIE LEE

Biting into Apples

1 What does the poet mean by 'the apples' rounded worlds'?
2 Explain how the sound of the words 'juice-green of July rain' appeals to our senses?
3 Why does the poet use the word 'mapped' to describe the crimson stain on the skin of apples?
4 '... the sun's hot brass'. What does the word 'brass' convey to us here?
5 Is 'drop like sweat' an effective simile? Why or why not?
6 '... bubble in the grass'. To which of our senses does the word 'bubble' appeal? What is the effect?
7 Why is the word 'plump' an effective one in touching our senses?
8 What picture is created for us by the listing of different creatures who feed off the apples?
9 How do you think the poet feels as he takes his share at the poem's end?

THE POET'S PURPOSE 7

10 What words and phrases can you identify in the last stanza that have a clear appeal to our senses? Give examples.

Poets Reveal Their Feelings

Poets often write about experiences that are deeply emotional for them. They may write about times of joy, or fear or sadness. They want to convey their feelings through the words, images, sounds, rhythm and structure of their poetry. If poets are skilful in the use of these techniques, we are able to share some of their emotions.

In 'The Lesson', the poet recounts an experience in his boyhood when he was engulfed in emotion after his father's death. While we expect sadness, he also reveals a mixture of other feelings at this time.

The Lesson

'Your father's gone,' my bald headmaster said.
His shiny dome and brown tobacco jar
Splintered at once in tears. It wasn't grief.
I cried for knowledge which was bitterer
Than any grief. For there and then I knew
That grief has uses—that a father dead
Could bind the bully's fist a week or two;
And then I cried for shame, then for relief.

I was a month past ten when I learnt this:
I still remember how the noise was stilled
In school-assembly when my grief came in.
Some goldfish in a bowl quietly sculled
Around their shining prison on its shelf.
They were indifferent. All the other eyes
Were turned towards me. Somewhere in myself
Pride, like a goldfish, flashed a sudden fin.

EDWARD LUCIE-SMITH

Learning from The Lesson

1 'Your father's gone'. What was the impact of this blunt statement on the young ten-year-old?
2 The headmaster's shiny bald head and his tobacco jar 'splintered at once in tears'. What does the word 'splintered' add to the description here?
3 The poet tells us his tears were not tears of grief, but of knowledge. What was it he knew?

4 What feelings did his tears express after this initial outpouring?
5 How did the school-assembly respond to news of his father's death?
6 What feeling did he identify in himself as everyone's eyes turned towards him?
7 At the end of the poem, what is used as an image of his emotional response?
8 How do you think the poet feels about these emotional responses now?
9 What techniques has the poet used to convey some of his feelings at the time of his father's death? Give examples.
10 What do you think 'the lesson' is that the poet refers to in the poem's title?

In 'Song of the Rain', the poet seeks to express a set of feelings quite different from those in 'The Lesson'.

Song of the Rain

Night,
And the yellow pleasure of candle-light . . .
Old brown books and the kind fine face of the clock
Fogged in the veils of the fire—its cuddling tock.

The cat,
Greening her eyes on the flame-litten mat;
Wickedly wakeful she yawns at the rain
Bending the roses over the pane,
And a bird in my heart begins to sing
Over and over the same sweet thing—

Safe in the house with my boyhood's love,
And our children asleep in the attic above.

HUGH McCRAE

Listening in to Song of the Rain

1 Why do you think the poet begins with the single-word line 'Night'?
2 'And the yellow pleasure of candle-light . . .' What feeling is the poet experiencing here?
3 'Old brown books and the kind fine face of the clock'. Which words here convey the poet's sense of peace and comfort?
4 '. . . its cuddling tock'. Why is 'tock' a better word in this description than 'tick'?
5 'Wickedly wakeful she yawns at the rain'. How is the cat feeling? What conveys this?
6 'And a bird in my heart begins to sing'. What feelings in the poet lie behind this experience?

7 What techniques has the poet used to convey his feelings? Give examples.
8 How successful do you think the poet has been in conveying his feelings in this poem? Explain your answer.

Poets Arouse Our Emotions

Poets try to bring about a response in the person who reads or hears their poetry. Often the response they seek is that of arousing our emotions. They know that if our feelings are touched in some way, then a more tangible response, even a change within, may occur.

In 'Foodless Children', the poet describes the sad plight of the children, then ends with an abrupt, jarring statement that is intended to arouse emotions in us.

Foodless Children

Foodless Children,
With stomachs puffed out,
Why have you no food to eat?
Why do you beg?

Foodless Children,
Suffering from starvation,
Why is your skin like paper?
Why do your bones poke out?

Foodless Children,
Eaten up by disease,
Why not see a doctor?
Why not?

Foodless Children,
You are so thin,
Your eyes are so appealing,
And you will soon be dead.
MALDWYN DAVIES

Poets Describe People

Many powerful poems have been written describing a person who is known to the poet, someone of significance in his or her life. Poems such as 'Felix Randal' by Gerard Manley Hopkins fit this classification.

Love poems, of course, also fit into this category. A love poem often describes someone who is particularly precious to the poet, and he or she seeks to enshrine in the poem some of this special person's qualities.

In 'To a Trainee Accountant' the poet sets out to describe a general vocational category — the accountant. The poet is particularly concerned to give a picture of the future for the trainee.

To a Trainee Accountant

You have traded your schooldesk for an office replica,
in two years time you will qualify—for what?
In four years you will marry
leaving your parents' home to buy a block of land
on which to place your square, orange brick home from home.
You will have three children, one motor car,
a twenty year mortgage and a weekly game of
cards with the people down the road.
On Saturday you will wash your car while listening to the football,
on Sunday mow the lawn and eat a barbecue lunch.
By fifty you will have left behind all aspirations dreams and hopes,
at sixty you will be made chief clerk—a man who is respected,
a man who is respectable,
a man to be listened to with nothing to say.
At sixty-five you will retire, a brief farewell speech,
a watch, a travelling rug and dinner on the company,
a clearing of desks and waving goodbyes,
and two weeks later someone will say,
'the place feels funny without old whatsisname,'
and no one there will ever think of you again.
Meanwhile you will go on that world trip,
to return, mind broadened, after a year
of ships, and buses, hotels and places where you mustn't drink
    the water.
Six months after returning you will die of
. a boredom induced heart attack.
Fifty-two people will attend your funeral, and
return to their houses already thinking of other things,
your wife will knit socks for your grandchildren,
watch T.V., make cups of tea for the neighbours
and occasionally wonder what you were really like.

MICHAEL DUGAN

Figuring Out the Trainee Accountant

1 'You have traded your schooldesk for an office replica'. What does this opening line convey about the change the trainee accountant has made?
2 What effect is created by the asking of the question 'for what?'
3 Why does the poet describe the home the trainee will build as 'square'?
4 What is the effect of listing people, possessions and activities in the lines beginning 'You will have three children . . .'?
5 'By fifty you will have left behind all aspirations dreams and hopes'. What does this description suggest about the accountant's future?
6 'A man to be listened to with nothing to say'. What emotional response do you have to this line? Why?
7 'The place feels funny without old whatsisname'. What aspect of the worklife of the accountant is the poet alerting us to here?
8 The poet describes the world trips by listing experiences, finishing with ' . . . and places where you mustn't drink the water'. What is he wanting to convey about the world trip?
9 What does the poet believe will probably bring on the fatal heart attack?
10 What impression is given by the list of things that the accountant's widow will do?
11 What feelings about the trainee accountant's world does this poem leave you with?
12 What was the poet's purpose in writing this poem?

Poets Describe the World of Nature

Many of our finest poets are known as nature poets. In this book you will find excellent examples of nature poems in the works of Emily Dickinson, Douglas Stewart and Judith Wright, as well as others. A good poet is always a keen observer, so that his or her description of some aspect of nature will often be a wonderful or powerful description. Sometimes the poet reflects on the subject he or she is describing and draws a message from it.

In 'To the Snake', Denise Levertov gives a powerful, sensual description of her experience when she allowed a snake to coil around her neck. Notice the life and energy in the descriptive words she has used.

To the Snake

Green Snake, when I hung you round my neck
and stroked your cold, pulsing throat
    as you hissed to me, glinting
arrowy gold scales, and I felt
    the weight of you on my shoulders,
and the whispering silver of your dryness
    sounded close at my ears—

Green Snake—I swore to my companions that certainly
   you were harmless! But truly
I had no certainty, and no hope, only desiring
   to hold you, for that joy,
                which left
a long wake of pleasure, as the leaves moved
and you faded into the pattern
of grass and shadows, and I returned
smiling and haunted, to a dark morning.

DENISE LEVERTOV

Poets Try to Change Our Attitudes

As already noted, poets frequently look for an emotional response in their readers. However, there are clearly times when poets look for an even more specific response. They want to challenge our complacency, they want to disturb our comfortableness, they want to change our attitudes about something.

In 'Five Ways to Kill a Man', the poet reflects on methods of killing through the ages. While all are gruesome, he finds the last method the most appalling.

Five Ways to Kill a Man

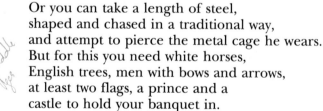

There are many cumbersome ways to kill a man:
you can make him carry a plank of wood
to the top of a hill and nail him to it. To do this
properly you require a crowd of people
wearing sandals, a cock that crows, a cloak
to dissect, a sponge, some vinegar and one
man to hammer the nails home.

Or you can take a length of steel,
shaped and chased in a traditional way,
and attempt to pierce the metal cage he wears.
But for this you need white horses,
English trees, men with bows and arrows,
at least two flags, a prince and a
castle to hold your banquet in.

Dispensing with nobility, you may, if the wind
allows, blow gas at him. But then you need
a mile of mud sliced through with ditches,
not to mention black boots, bomb craters,
more mud, a plague of rats, a dozen songs
and some round hats made of steel.

In an age of aeroplanes, you may fly
miles above your victim and dispose of him by
pressing one small switch. All you then
require is an ocean to separate you, two
(atomic) systems of government, a nation's scientists,
several factories, a psychopath and
land that no one needs for several years.

These are, as I began, cumbersome ways
to kill a man. Simpler, direct, and much more neat
is to see that he is living somewhere in the middle
of the twentieth century, and leave him there.

EDWIN BROCK

Thinking About Five Ways to Kill a Man

1 In the first line, how does the poet describe the 'ways to kill a man'?
2 Who does the poet have in mind as he describes the first method?
3 ' . . . and one/man to hammer the nails home'. What impression does this final line describing the first method leave with us?
4 What would we call the second method that the poet describes?
5 'Dispensing with nobility . . . ' Which method, presumably, had 'nobility'?
6 What is the poet describing in the third method? Where was this used?
7 What is the purpose of including both 'a mile of mud' and 'more mud' in this third description?
8 What is the fourth way of killing a man?
9 For the fourth method you need 'a psychopath'. What would his or her involvement presumably be?
10 In what ways is the final method seen as superior?
11 In your own words, what is the final method?
12 What attitude in us do you think the poet wants to change? Explain your answer.

2 Understanding the Poet's Craft

Similes

To make their images come alive, poets use all kinds of word patterns that are called figures of speech. One of the most important of these is the simile.

A simile makes a comparison between two unlike things, using the words 'like', 'as' or 'than'. All of the following comparisons are similes from everyday life.

- He ran *like the wind.*
- I am *as warm as toast.*
- Her kisses were sweeter *than wine.*

SIMILE SNAPSHOTS

Poets use similes to stimulate our imagination. Their similes enable us to see and experience what they are describing. For example, in her poem 'Striking Moon', Christina Rossetti delights us with the beautiful simile 'The dragon-fly hangs like a blue thread loosened from the sky'.

In each of the following poems there is a striking simile. Write down each simile and explain why you found it appealing or not.

Starlings

This cold grey winter afternoon
The starlings
On the television aerial
Look like sultanas
On a stalk.

LUCY HOSEGOOD

Lost

Desolate and lone
All night long on the lake
Where fog trails and mist creeps,
The whistle of a boat
Calls and cries unendingly,
Like some lost child
In tears and trouble
Hunting the harbour's breast
And the harbour's eyes.

CARL SANDBURG

A SIMILE POEM

The following poem depends on the development of a simile.

Sunset

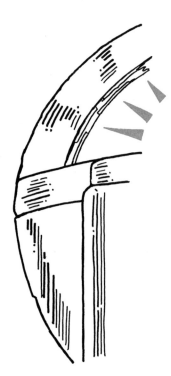

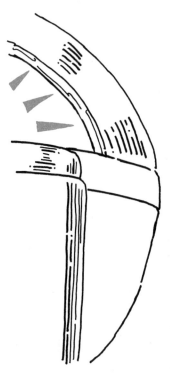

The sun spun like
a tossed coin.
It whirled on the azure sky,
it clattered into the horizon,
it clicked in the slot,
and neon lights popped
and blinked 'Time expired',
as on a parking meter.

MBUYISENI OSWALD MTSHALI

Simile Questions

1 Why do you think the poet compares the sun to 'a tossed coin'?
2 What does 'whirled' mean? Why is it an effective word to use here?
3 'It clattered into the horizon'. What is happening?
4 'It clicked in the slot'. What is the sun being compared to here?
5 'Time expired'. What has happened?
6 Do you think the simile running through the poem is effective? Why or why not?

Metaphors

The metaphor takes us one step further than the simile. Instead of asking us to picture one thing as *being like* another, we are asked to picture one thing as *being* another. For example:

• The hose *is like* a green snake on the lawn.   (simile)
• The hose *is* a green snake on the lawn.   (metaphor)

METAPHOR MOMENTS

By their use of metaphors in 'Signs' and 'Broken Sky', Max Fatchen and Carl Sandburg give us a clear picture of their experience of nature. Comment on the effectiveness of their metaphors.

Signs

The paths of my garden
Have silvery trails:
The lazy graffiti
Of wandering snails.

MAX FATCHEN

Broken Sky

The sky of grey is eaten in six places,
Rag holes stand out.
It is an army blanket and the sleeper
slept too near the fire.

CARL SANDBURG

A METAPHOR POEM

It is difficult to explain what time is. The poet Cindy Booth has succeeded admirably by comparing it to cars travelling along the road.

I Know Where
Yesterday Has Gone

Yesterday stopped at the traffic light.

As it sat, Today tore by in front of it,
At a life-threatening speed.

And Tomorrow turned the corner, following
Slowly behind Today. It would reach its
Destination all too soon for anyone's liking.

Yesterday sat, its engine idling slower and slower.
The light, never to be green again,
Stared at Yesterday with a baleful
Red eye.

The traffic light of the mind realised,
It had the power to hold Yesterday
On the corner of Memory Avenue . . . forever . . .

It grinned, strangely pleased with itself.

CINDY A. BOOTH

Metaphor Questions

1 'Yesterday stopped at the traffic light'. What is 'Yesterday' being compared to?
2 Why is 'stopped' a suitable word to use with 'Yesterday'?
3 '. . . Today tore by in front of it'. Why is 'tore by' an appropriate word to use with 'Today'?
4 What impression does the poet give of 'Tomorrow'?
5 Why is Yesterday's engine 'idling slower and slower'?
6 What is happening to 'Yesterday' in the last four lines of the poem?

Personification

Personification is a special kind of metaphor in which human characteristics are given to non-human things. Carefully look at the following examples.

• Blow wind, and crack your cheeks! rage! blow!

•   Busie old foole, unruly Sunne,
        Why dost thou thus,
  Through windowes, and through curtaines call on us?

• But look, the dawn, in russet mantle clad,
  Walks o'er the dew of yon high eastern hill.

You can see that the wind, the sun and the dawn have been given human qualities.

A PERSONIFICATION POEM

Sylvia Plath's poem gives a mirror's view of life.

Mirror

I am silver and exact, I have no preconceptions.
Whatever I see I swallow immediately
Just as it is, unmisted by love or dislike.
I am not cruel, only truthful—
The eye of a little god, four-cornered.
Most of the time, I meditate on the opposite wall.
It is pink, with speckles. I have looked at it so long
I think it is part of my heart. But it flickers.
Faces and darkness separate us over and over.

Now I am a lake. A woman bends over me,
Searching my reaches for what she really is.
Then she turns to those liars, the candles or the moon.
I see her back, and reflect it faithfully,
She rewards me with tears and an agitation of hands.
I am important to her. She comes and goes.
Each morning it is her face that replaces the darkness.
In me she has drowned a young girl, and in me an old woman
Rises toward her day after day, like a terrible fish.

SYLVIA PLATH

Reflecting on Personification

1 'Whatever I see I swallow immediately'. What is happening? What human characteristics does the mirror have?
2 'I am not cruel, only truthful'. Why does the mirror describe itself as 'truthful'?
3 Why do you think the mirror refers to itself as 'a little god, four-cornered'?
4 'Most of the time, I meditate on the opposite wall'. What human qualities does the mirror have?
5 'Faces and darkness separate us over and over'. What is happening?
6 'Now I am a lake'. Explain why the mirror compares itself to a lake?
7 'She rewards me with tears and an agitation of hands'. Why do you think the woman is behaving in this manner?
8 'I am important to her'. Why?
9 Explain the meaning of 'In me she has drowned a young girl'.
10 What is the meaning of ' . . . and in me an old woman/Rises toward her day after day'?
11 'Like a terrible fish'. Is this an effective simile? Why or why not?
12 What does the poet achieve by having the mirror talk personally to the reader?

Symbolism

Symbols are part of our daily lives. We are constantly coming into contact with symbols at the supermarket, at the airport, on the highway or going to a restaurant. Many symbols, such as a red cross, the big 'M' for McDonalds and a white flag are internationally famous.

A symbol is an object used to stand for one or more abstract ideas. The skull and crossbones, for example, symbolises evil, while the dove symbolises love and peace. In poetry, symbols are used to increase our awareness or deepen our understanding. We can actually judge what something symbolises by looking at the poem as a whole. Once we have done this, some things start to glow with symbolic meaning and this always adds a certain richness to the writing. Of course, one of the dangers for a poet using symbolism is that the symbols may be too complicated or remote for the reader to understand.

THE SYMBOL IN POETRY

In this poem the kangaroo sees itself as a symbol of the rugged Australian landscape.

The Kangaroo

I am the kangaroo,
Slate-grey, and red;
And when, as oft I do,
I lift my head
Against the far-off blue
Of sky and earth,
I am a symbol, too,
Of this land's birth.

I am the rock and tree,
The wide plains dry,
The gorges wild and free
The blue-hot sky,
The blue-grey greenery—
Gully and rise,
The Aboriginal,
And his far eyes.

The silences am I,
The granite peak,
The flood, the river high,
The dried-up creek,
The hot white clouds that lie
Before the sun,
The breeze that rustles by
Where grasses run.

I lift my head, and so
Time there is writ,
Ages of long ago
Are held in it.
I am a statue, oh,
As old as stone:
Grey boulder stooping low,
Standing, alone.

I am the dry, hot land.
The sand, the clay,
The burning wind that fanned
Some far-off day:
I, kangaroo, as planned,
Still, still unspent,
The breath, the bone, the strand
Of our continent.

JAMES HACKSTON

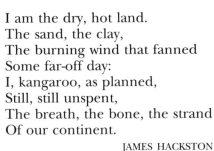

Symbolism Questions

1 What picture of the kangaroo does the poet present you with in the first stanza?
2 In the second stanza, what does the kangaroo symbolise?
3 What contrasting images of the Australian landscape does the kangaroo describe in the third stanza?
4 'I am a statue, oh,/As old as stone'. What does the kangaroo symbolise here?
5 How does the poet convey the sensation of heat in the last stanza?
6 'Still, still unspent'. What quality of Australia does the kangaroo represent?
7 What is the impression of Australia that the poet is trying to convey?
8 Do you think the poet's use of the kangaroo as a symbol of Australia is successful? Why or why not?

Parody

A parody is an imitation of a poem or piece of prose, written with the clear purpose of poking fun at the original. It is intended to be a humorous piece of writing and depends on the reader being familiar with the original poem, song or story. The parody usually copies the structure, metre and much of the language, but tends to replace the original subject with something much more trivial or frivolous. Nursery rhymes are often a good subject for parody as Paul Dehn shows in his poem 'Hey Diddle Diddle'.

Hey Diddle Diddle

Hey diddle diddle,
The physicists fiddle,
 The Bleep jumped over the moon.
The little dog laughed to see such fun
 And died the following June.

      PAUL DEHN

PARODY IN ACTION

'Clancy of the Overflow' is a famous poem that is often read in schools. The parody that follows it is called 'Clancy of the Underflow'. How does the parody make fun of the original?

Clancy of the Overflow

I had written him a letter which I had, for want of better
 Knowledge, sent to where I met him down the Lachlan, years ago;
He was shearing when I knew him, so I sent the letter to him,
 Just on spec, addressed as follows, 'Clancy, of The Overflow.'

And an answer came directed in a writing unexpected
 (And I think the same was written with a thumb-nail dipped in tar):
'Twas his shearing mate who wrote it, and *verbatim* I will quote it:
'Clancy's gone to Queensland droving, and we don't know where he are.'

In my wild erratic fancy visions come to me of Clancy
 Gone a-droving 'down the Cooper' where the Western drovers go:
As the stock are slowly stringing, Clancy rides behind them singing,
 For the drover's life has pleasures that the townsfolk never know.

And the bush has friends to meet him, and their kindly voices greet him
 In the murmur of the breezes and the river on its bars,
And he sees the vision splendid of the sunlit plains extended,
 And at night the wondrous glory of the everlasting stars.

I am sitting in my dingy little office, where a stingy
   Ray of sunlight struggles feebly down between the houses tall,
And the foetid air and gritty of the dusty, dirty city,
   Through the open window floating, spreads its foulness over all. . . .

And I somehow rather fancy that I'd like to change with Clancy,
   Like to take a turn at droving where the seasons come and go,
While he faced the round eternal of the cash-book and the journal—
   But I doubt he'd suit the office, Clancy of The Overflow.

A. B. ('BANJO') PATERSON

Clancy of the Underflow

Mister Clancy was a debtor, and I'd written him a letter
Bluntly asking for the fiver that I'd lent him long ago.
He was loafing when I lent it and was drinking when he spent it
And he painted things vermilion round about the Underflow.

And an answer quite expected came in ciphers disconnected
And I think the same was written with his pipestem dipped in beer,
It was Clancy's self that penned it, and he said, 'Old chap, I'll send it
When the Lachlan sheds have cut out in the twilight of the year.'

Often in my frenzied fancy curses hurl themselves at Clancy
Gone a-roving down the Cooper where the Western slopers go.
As the sun is slowly setting, Clancy rides along forgetting
All those little obligations due to men he used to know.

For the bush has friends to meet him, and they chuckle as they greet him
As they join the reckless skiting in the humble shanty bar,
For the views of beer extended, and the two ales nicely blended
And at night the amber radiance of Hennessy's Three Star.

And I somehow rather fancy that I'd like to damage Clancy,
Like to bash that burly figure till he couldn't come or go.
But then I think my turn'll never come while I am vernal,
For he knows the art of boxing, Clancy of the Underflow.

ANONYMOUS

Hyperbole

The hyperbole is a figure of speech that uses deliberate exaggeration for emphasis. For example, 'Wild horses wouldn't drag me away'. The hyperbole is a valuable tool for poets, enabling them to add emphasis, usually to the strength of someone's feelings or to the importance of a particular point being made.

HYPERBOLES IN ACTION

Here are two famous hyperboles from English literature. Read them through and comment on their impact.

from **To His Coy Mistress**

My vegetable love should grow
Vaster than empires, and more slow.
An hundred years should go to praise
Thine eyes, and on thy forehead gaze:
Two hundred to adore each breast:
But thirty thousand to the rest;
An age at least to every part,
And the last age should show your heart.
For, lady you deserve this state,
Nor would I love at a lower rate.

ANDREW MARVELL

from **Hamlet**

I lov'd Ophelia; forty thousand brothers
Could not, with all their quantity of love,
Make up my sum . . .

WILLIAM SHAKESPEARE

Apostrophe

Apostrophe is a direct address to a thing or person who is either dead or absent. Walt Whitman, a very popular American poet, uses the apostrophe to great effect in a number of his poems. His poem on the assassination of Abraham Lincoln begins with the famous apostrophe 'O Captain! my Captain!' In his poem 'To a Locomotive in Winter' he addresses the locomotive as:

Fierce-throated beauty!
Roll through my chant with all thy lawless music . . .

Paradox

A paradox is a statement that, although it seems to contradict itself, actually conveys a truth. For example, 'One must be cruel to be kind'. Because of its contradictory nature, the paradox tends to shock the reader initially.

In the following poem Richard Lovelace is convincing his mistress, Lucasta, that he loves her all the more because he is deserting her for another 'mistress', war.

To Lucasta,
Going to the Wars

Tell me not, Sweet, I am unkind,
    That from the nunnery
Of thy chaste breast and quiet mind
    To war and arms I fly.

True, a new mistress now I chase,
    The first foe in the field;
And with a stronger faith embrace
    A sword, a horse, a shield.

Yet this inconstancy is such
    As thou too shalt adore;
I could not love thee, Dear, so much,
    Loved I not honour more.

SIR RICHARD LOVELACE

Paradox Questions

1 'Tell me not, Sweet, I am unkind'. Why could Lucasta consider the poet to be unkind?
2 'True, a new mistress now I chase'. Who is the 'new mistress' the poet is chasing?
3 What is the paradox of the last two lines of the poem?

Onomatopoeia

There are many words in English that actually resemble the sounds they are describing. Everyday examples are 'bang', 'fizz', 'grunt', 'drip', 'rattle', 'splash' and 'shriek'. The use of sound-words in poetry is called onomatopoeia.

As you read through Alfred Lord Tennyson's description of a small brook moving over stones, you will also 'hear' it as well. How many onomatopoeic words are you able to find in this poem?

from **The Brook**

I chatter over stony ways,
    In little sharps and trebles,
I bubble into eddying bays,
    I babble on the pebbles.

ALFRED, LORD TENNYSON

ONOMATOPOEIA IN ACTION

Nancy Cato uses sound-words to energise the scene she is describing.

The Two Windmills

There are two windmills at the bottom of our garden.
One whistles like a rainbird as the dry rod squeaks,
The other groans like a camel as the snails drag round.
They stand lonely as giants by the little sheep,
Endlessly moving, never going anywhere,
Circular as the sun's days under the wheeling eagle.

Earth hardens, the drought is silent, sometimes
Whispering into dust, though the children shout as they bounce
Off the plank across the banks of the sandy creek-bed.

When the rain comes at last, at night the sound of rain,
The magpies all begin to sing and the galahs clang,
And sliding in the rain the two windmills are silent
As if joyful at water, water falling freely down,
Not heaved up groaning from the stubborn ground.

NANCY CATO

Onomatopoeia Questions

1 'One whistles like a rainbird'. What does the word 'whistles' indicate about the windmill?
2 '. . . the dry rod squeaks'. What does the word 'squeaks' reveal about the rod?
3 'The other groans like a camel'. What does the word 'groans' suggest about the windmill?
4 'Whispering into dust'. Why is 'whispering' an effective word?
5 '. . . the children shout as they bounce/Off the plank'. What sounds can you identify here?
6 'The galahs clang'. What is happening?

Alliteration

The repetition of the same consonant, especially at the beginning of words, is called alliteration. Some poets use it to create musical effects, while others use it to focus the reader's attention on certain qualities or attributes. For example, the alliteration of the letter 'm' in 'Five miles meandering with a mazy motion' (from Samuel Taylor Coleridge's poem 'Kubla Khan') suggests the slow, aimless winding of the river. In Wilfred Owen's poem 'Arms and the Boy', the alliteration of the letter 'b' in 'blind, blunt, bullet-heads' evokes the power of the bullets to maim and destroy.

APPRECIATING ALLITERATION

In his poem 'From My Diary, July 1914', Wilfred Owen has made extensive use of alliteration to convey his joyful feelings about his life in the French Pyrenees.

From My Diary, July 1914

Leaves
   Murmuring by myriads in the shimmering trees.
Lives
   Wakening with wonder in the Pyrenees.
Birds
   Cheerily chirping in the early day.
Bards
   Singing of summer, scything through the hay.
Bees
   Shaking the heavy dews from bloom and frond.
Boys
   Bursting the surface of the ebony pond.
Flashes
   Of swimmers carving through the sparkling cold.
Fleshes
   Gleaming with wetness to the morning gold.
A mead
   Bordered about with warbling waterbrooks.
A maid
   Laughing the love-laugh with me; proud of looks.
The heat
   Throbbing between the upland and the peak.
Her heart
   Quivering with passion to my pressèd cheek.
Braiding
   Of floating flames across the mountain brow.
Brooding
   Of stillness; and a sighing of the bough.
Stirs
   Of leaflets in the gloom; soft petal-showers;
Stars
   Expanding with the starr'd nocturnal flowers.

WILFRED OWEN

Alliteration Questions

1 What does the alliteration of the letter 'w' in 'Wakening with wonder' help to show about Owen's life in the Pyrenees?
2 What is the effect of the alliteration of the letters 'ch' in 'Cheerily chirping'.
3 Bards are poets. What does the alliteration of the letter 's' in 'Singing of summer, scything through the hay' help to suggest about life?
4 What does Owen achieve by his alliteration of the letter 'b' in 'Bursting the surface of the ebony pond'?
5 'Laughing the love-laugh with me; proud of looks'. What does the alliteration of the letter 'l' help to show about the feelings of Owen and a maid towards each other?
6 How many other examples of alliteration can you find? Write them down and say what Owen has achieved by using them.

Assonance

Assonance is the repetition of identical vowel sounds followed by different consonant sounds (as distinct from rhyme in which the same vowel sounds are followed by the same consonant sounds). Thus, for example, 'sun' and 'hut' is an example of assonance; 'sun' and 'fun' is an example of rhyme. Assonance is one of the techniques commonly used by poets to achieve a musical effect. Look at the first two lines of 'Ode on a Grecian Urn' by John Keats:

> Thou still unravished bride of quietness,
> Thou foster-child of silence and slow time.

The long 'i' sound in 'bride' which is repeated in 'quietness', 'child', 'silence' and 'time' suggests the peaceful passing of time. The short 'i' sound in 'still unravished' suggests a brisker movement to indicate present time.

ASSONANCE IN ACTION

Here is a famous piece of poetry that illustrates what can be achieved by the poet's use of assonance and alliteration. Notice as you read through the verse how the poet creates an effect of lethargy and tiredness. See how many examples of assonance you can find.

from **Choric Song**

There is sweet music here that softer falls
Than petals from blown roses on the grass,
Or night-dews on still waters between walls
Of shadowy granite, in a gleaming pass;
Music that gentlier on the spirit lies,
Than tir'd eyelids upon tir'd eyes;
Music that brings sweet sleep down from the blissful skies.
Here are cool mosses deep,
And thro' the moss the ivies creep,
And in the stream the long-leaved flowers weep,
And from the craggy ledge the poppy hangs in sleep . . .

ALFRED, LORD TENNYSON

Rhyme

END-RHYME

In poetry, rhyme is usually the similarity in the end-sounds of words at the end of lines. Two consecutive lines may rhyme, or alternate lines may rhyme, or even later lines. In the following examples each new end-rhyme is given a new letter of the alphabet (**a**, **b** etc.) to show the rhyming pattern of the poem.

The Next War

War's a joke for me and you,
While we know such dreams are true.

SIEGFRIED SASSOON

Out there, we've walked quite friendly up to Death;	**a**
Sat down and eaten with him, cool and bland,—	**b**
Pardoned his spilling mess-tins in our hand.	**b**
We've sniffed the green thick odour of his breath,—	**a**
Our eyes wept, but our courage didn't writhe.	**c**
He's spat at us with bullets and he's coughed	**d**
Shrapnel. We chorussed when he sang aloft;	**d**
We whistled while he shaved us with his scythe.	**c**

Oh, Death was never enemy of ours!   e
    We laughed at him, we leagued with him, old chum.   f
No soldier's paid to kick against his powers.   e
    We laughed, knowing that better men would come,   f
And greater wars; when each proud fighter brags   g
He wars on Death—for lives; not men—for flags.   g

WILFRED OWEN

Down by the Salley Gardens

Down by the salley gardens my love and I did meet;   a
She passed the salley gardens with little snow-white feet.   a
She bid me take love easy, as the leaves grow on the tree;   b
But I, being young and foolish, with her would not agree.   b

In a field by the river my love and I did stand,   c
And on my leaning shoulder she laid her snow-white hand.   c
She bid me take life easy, as the grass grows on the weirs; d
But I was young and foolish, and now am full of tears.   d

WILLIAM BUTLER YEATS

IDENTIFYING END-RHYME

Write out the end-line words from 'Killed in the Street'. Then identify each rhyme with a letter of the alphabet as shown in the previous examples.

Killed in the Street

He was so frail,
So small where he lay dead,
Hands at the trail,
And slack the little head;
They laid him in her lap
And still she did not weep,
But with his tattered cap
Fanned him asleep.
And then, 'O God!' she said,
And then, again, 'O God!'
And touched him where the shod
Hard hoof had marked his head.

MARY GILMORE

INTERNAL RHYME

Sometimes the rhyming pattern of a poem involves rhyming a word that occurs halfway through a line with the end-word of the same line. This is called internal rhyme. The following excerpt from 'Song of the Cattle Hunters' contains examples of internal rhyme, shown in *italics*.

from Song of the Cattle Hunters

While the morning light *beams* on the fern-matted *streams*,
And the water-pools flash in its glow,
Down the ridges we *fly*, with a loud ringing *cry*—
Down the ridges and gullies we go!
And the cattle we *hunt*, they are racing in *front*,
With a roar like the thunder of waves,

HENRY KENDALL

INDENTIFYING INTERNAL RHYME

The poem 'The Cloud' contains many examples of internal rhyme. From the excerpt below, write down the examples of internal rhyme.

from The Cloud

I bring fresh showers for the thirsting flowers,
    From the seas and the streams;
I bear light shade for the leaves when laid
    In their noonday dreams.
From my wings are shaken the dews that waken
    The sweet buds every one,
When rocked to rest on their mother's breast,
    As she dances about the sun.
I wield the flail of the lashing hail,
    And whiten the green plains under,
And then again I dissolve it in rain,
    And laugh as I pass in thunder.

PERCY BYSSHE SHELLEY

Rhythm

Rhythm refers to the beat, or the pattern of stresses, that occurs in poetry and music. It is a vital part of the poet's craft, for the rhythm can be used to indicate all kinds of sensations. It can evoke the galloping of horses, the working of a machine, the lazy motion of a river or the urgent rush of a sprinter. Usually, we can feel the rhythm of a poem best when we read it aloud. A small sloping dash symbol is often used to mark the beats or stresses and thus show the pattern created by the poet.

FEELING THE RHYTHM

Read through 'A Sea Song'. Explain how the rhythm matches the action of the poem.

A Sea Song

A wet sheet* and a flowing sea,
A wind that follows fast
And fills the white and rustling sail
And bends the gallant mast;
And bends the gallant mast, my boys,
While like the eagle free
Away the good ship flies, and leaves
Old England on the lee.

O for a soft and gentle wind!
I heard a fair one cry:
But give to me the snoring breeze
And white waves heaving high;
And white waves heaving high, my lads,
The good ship tight and free—
The world of waters is our home,
And merry men are we.

There's tempest in yon horned moon,
And lightning in yon cloud;
But hark the music, mariners!
The wind is piping loud;
The wind is piping loud, my boys,
The lightning flashes free—
While the hollow oak our palace is,
Our heritage the sea.

ALLAN CUNNINGHAM

* a rope

3 A Love of Poetry

Developing an Appreciation of Poetry

Often we speak of the experience of 'falling in love'. Wiser people will tell you that falling in love is really only one facet of the experience of love. It might be better named 'cardiac-respiratory love', since it is the first flush of emotion, involving romantic feelings and a quickening of our heartbeat and breathing rate.

'Falling in love' can get you started, but 'growing in love' is needed to sustain the experience of love over a lifetime. To grow in love we need to spend time with a person, we need to grow in our understanding of each other, we need to give a priority to the other person.

Developing a love for poetry requires this second part of the experience. We may 'fall in love' by experiencing a poem that we enjoy, or that touches our emotions in some way. But to develop a love for poetry we need to grow in our understanding of what makes good poetry, we need to give time to experiencing a wide range of poets and their work, we need to develop insight about what it is in a particular poem that we intuitively respond to.

In deepening our understanding of poetry we need to appreciate *what* the poet is trying to say, or describe. We also need to understand *how* she or he has gone about the task — what techniques or resources have been used to craft the poem. As we deepen our awareness of these aspects of the artistry of poem-crafting, so our appreciation grows and our love for poetry develops.

Consider the following aspects of poetry.

SUBJECT MATTER

This is the 'what' of poetry. We are always interested in trying to understand what the poet is sharing with us. What is the content of the poem and what is the poet's purpose in writing about this content? Does he or she want to share an experience with us? Does the poet want to entertain us, perhaps bring smiles to our faces? What theme, or message, is the poet trying to communicate?

TECHNIQUE

This is the 'how' of poetry. When we seek to increase our understanding of a poem, we are always interested in how the poet has written it, how she or he has achieved the impact that the poem has, what specific techniques have been used. A number of areas are important.

Language

The 'how' of poetry involves, primarily, the poet's language. We are interested in whether it is appropriate and vivid. Is the language full of emotion, or is it boring? Do the words, and their flow, enhance what the poet is trying to achieve, or do they jar things and diminish the impact? Is the language simple or complex, and how does this fit with the poet's purpose?

Imagery

The 'how' of poetry involves imagery. Here we are interested in the word pictures that the poet creates as part of technique, or the crafting of a poem. What is the effect achieved by the use of similes, metaphors, personification, symbols, and sustained images in the poem?

Sounds

This aspect of language is of particular importance in poetry. We are always interested in the sounds created by the poet's choice of words, and the way these sounds work in the poem to create emotion or a pleasing effect. Rhyme is, of course, a particular form of sound in a poem. Other forms include alliteration, assonance and onomatopoeia. Listen to Gerard Manley Hopkins as he plays with the sound of words to capture a feeling of celebration at harvest time:

> Summer ends now; now, barbarous in beauty, the stooks arise
> Around; up above, what wind-walks! what lovely behaviour
> Of silk-sack clouds! Has wilder, wilful-wavier
> Meal-drift moulded ever and melted across skies?

Rhythm

The effectiveness of many poems is enhanced by the rhythmic flow of the language. Sometimes rhythm may create a deliberate jarring effect, in keeping with a moment of shock in the poem. At other times it may flow smoothly, or copy a sound that is being described, such as bells pealing, a clock ticking, or horses galloping. Aptly used, rhythm adds to our sense of satisfaction at a poem's achievement. Here is Christopher Brennan using a distinct rhythm in his poem 'The Wanderer' to create a sense of the never-ending call to journey on.

> Go: tho' ye find it bitter, yet must ye be bare
> to the wind and the sea and the night and the wail of birds in the sky;
> go: tho' the going be hard and the goal blinded with rain
> yet the staying is a death that is never soften'd with sleep.

Mood

The mood of a poem is usually the product of specific words and rhythm. Thus, sadness will often be created by the use of emotionally 'sad' words, and a slow-moving rhythm. Joy may be evoked by a bright rhythm and 'happy' language. Here is Douglas Stewart creating a mood of joy and vitality through a description of the antics of birds in his poem 'Firetail Finches':

> Such flashing joy of flower and feather
> Over the rock and wild creek-water,
> Such ragged scrub and such confusion
> Of perching green and flying crimson.

'Spring Hail' is one of Les Murray's best-known and loved poems. In it he celebrates a childhood memory, a time when he and his pony took shelter from a spring hailstorm. He experiences the freshness of the world and the joy in everything, and finally feels the call to move on.

Spring Hail

This is for spring and hail, that you may remember:
for a boy long ago, and a pony that could fly.

We had huddled together a long time in the shed
in the scent of vanished corn and wild bush birds,
and then the hammering faltered, and the torn
cobwebs ceased their quivering and hung still
from the nested rafters. We became uneasy
at the silence that grew about us, and came out.

The beaded violence had ceased. Fresh-minted hills
smoked, and the heavens swirled and blew away.
The paddocks were endless again, and all around
leaves lay beneath their trees, and cakes of moss.
Sheep trotted and propped, and shook out ice from their wool.
The hard blue highway that had carried us there
fumed as we crossed it, and the hail I scooped
from underfoot still bore the taste of sky
and hurt my teeth, and crackled as we walked.

This is for spring and hail, that you may remember
a boy long ago, and a pony that could fly.

With the creak and stop of a gate, we started to trespass:
my pony bent his head and drank up grass
while I ate ice, and wandered, and ate ice.
There was a peach tree growing wild by a bank
and under it and round, sweet dented fruit
weeping pale juice amongst hail-shotten leaves,
and this I picked up and ate till I was filled.

I sat on a log then, listening with my skin
to the secret feast of the sun, to the long wet worms
at work in the earth, and, deeper down, the stones
beneath the earth, uneasy that their sleep
should be troubled by dreams of water soaking down,
and I heard with my ears the creek on its bed of mould
moving and passing with a mothering sound.

This is for spring and hail, that you may remember
a boy long ago on a pony that could fly.

My pony came up then and stood by me,
waiting to be gone. The sky was now
spotless from dome to earth, and balanced there
on the cutting-edge of mountains. It was time
to leap to the saddle and go, a thunderbolt whirling
sheep and saplings behind, and the rearing fence
that we took at a bound, and the old, abandoned shed
forgotten behind, and the paddock forgotten behind.
Time to shatter peace and lean into spring
as into a battering wind, and be rapidly gone.

It was time, high time, the highest and only time
to stand in the stirrups and shout out, blind with wind
for the height and clatter of ridges to be topped
and the racing downward after through the lands
of floating green and bridges and flickering trees.
It was time, as never again it was time
to pull the bridle up, so the racketing hooves
fell silent as we ascended from the hill
above the farms, far up to where the hail
formed and hung weightless in the upper air,
charting the birdless winds with silver roads
for us to follow and be utterly gone.

This is for spring and hail, that you may remember
a boy and a pony long ago who could fly.

LES MURRAY

Exploring the What and How of Spring Hail

1 In your own words describe the subject matter of this poem.
2 Most readers agree that the theme of 'Spring Hail' is the transition from childhood into adulthood. It is about leaving childhood behind. The hailstorm memory recalls two precious experiences of childhood — companionship and freedom. Notice the use of 'we' and 'us' to capture the companionship of the boy and his pony. Find a phrase from the early part of the poem that also reflects the closeness of this companionship.
3 'The beaded violence had ceased'. What is the assonance here contributing to the rhythm and speed of the poem? How is this appropriate to the subject matter at this point?

4 The aftermath of the hailstorm and the actions of the boy and pony represent childhood. Notice the effect of lines like:

> 'my pony bent his head and drank up grass
> while I ate ice, and wandered, and ate ice.'

What do these lines and the whole pace of the second stanza suggest about the boy's attitude to time during childhood?

5 Notice the marvellous sensual imagery of 'sweet dented fruit weeping pale juice'. What effect does this have for us?

6 'Listening with my skin'. Comment on the effect of this phrase.

7
> 'My pony came up then and stood by me,
> waiting to be gone. The sky was now
> spotless from dome to earth, and balanced there
> on the cutting-edge of mountains.'

This is almost a sacred moment. Pony and boy realise they have to leave. What point on the journey through life is symbolised here?

8 Find lines in the last stanza that illustrate a growing sense of urgency, of life speeded up. What is there in the poet's technique that builds the pace of the poem?

9 'It was time, high time, the highest and only time'. What is the effect of this repetition of 'time'?

10 At what point near the end does the rhythm slow again, and begin to build to finality?

11 Some readers have felt a sadness in this poem. What phrase near the end might contribute to this feeling? Do you agree that it is a sad poem? What other feelings does the poem arouse in you?

12 The poet has created a specific memory of a hailstorm during childhood and used it to symbolise the call to leave childhood behind. How would you judge the achievement of this poem? Why?

'He Was . . .' is a simple poem. John Cunliffe writes it to recall key memories of his father who is now dead. His technique centres on recalling specific, concrete aspects of his father's life to give a dimension of strong reality. He doesn't paint his father as a saint; he includes aspects that show his father's weakness.

He Was . . .

> He was . . .
> a boy who became
> a man
> a husband
> a father.

He was . . .
a good goalie,
a rotten batsman,
not bad at darts.

He was . . .
second cornet in the works band;
a man who brought his pay-packet straight home
without stopping at the pub;
a man who enjoyed his dinner.

He was . . .
forgetful,
rarely on time,
sometimes tongue-tied,
at a loss for what to say.

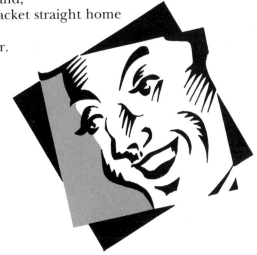

He was . . .
always honest,
never sober at Christmas,
often puzzled by the world.
He was . . .
. . . my dad.

JOHN CUNLIFFE

In 'One Parent Family', the poet expresses the wish for a deeper relationship with his father. Here John Kitching uses the image of 'a dad who shakes the dust of Sunday from his feet', to give us a sense of the father's disinterest. His choice of words such as 'sourly dumped' and 'mother's peeling five-day door' evoke for us some of the feelings of rejection and the emptiness in this boy's world, because of his father's physical and emotional absence.

One Parent Family

I wish that I had more than just
A weekend dad, a dad who shakes
The dust of Sunday from his feet
And makes his short drive home
When we've been sourly dumped
At mother's peeling five-day door.
It isn't only childish greed
That makes me want my father more.

JOHN KITCHING

In both of the following poems the poet focuses on a hedgehog. Anthony Thwaite's poem attempts to describe the creature, picking out interesting aspects of its being, while Roy Holland focuses on a specific encounter that he had with a hedgehog and the mystery that it left behind.

Hedgehog

Twitching the leaves just where the drainpipe clogs
In ivy leaves and mud, a purposeful
Creature at night about its business. Dogs
Fear its stiff seriousness. He chews away

At beetles, worms, slugs, frogs. Can kill a hen
With one snap of his jaws, can taunt a snake
To death on muscled spines. Old countrymen
Tell tales of hedgehogs sucking a cow dry.

But this one, cramped by houses, fences, walls,
Must have slept here all winter in that heap
Of compost, or have inched by intervals
Through tidy gardens to this ivy bed.

And here, dim-eyed, but ears so sensitive
A voice within the house can make him freeze,
He scuffs the edge of danger: yet can live
Happily in our nights and absences.

A country creature, wary, quiet and shrewd,
He takes the milk we give him, when we're gone.
At night, our slamming voices must seem crude
To one who sits and waits for silences.

ANTHONY THWAITE

Uncovering Hedgehog

1 How is the hedgehog's character depicted in the first two lines? What word does the poet use to give this impression?
2 '. . . Dogs/Fear its stiff seriousness'. Why is the word 'stiff' an appropriate word here?
3 What does the hedgehog feed on?
4 What evidence is there of the ruthless and dangerous qualities that the hedgehog possesses?
5 Do you think that the tales of the 'old countrymen' are believable? Why?
6 What is the effect of the word 'cramped' in the third stanza?
7 What effect has the poet created in the phrase 'inched by intervals'?
8 What information are we given about the senses of the hedgehog?

9 'He scuffs the edge of danger'. Comment on the use of the word 'scuffs'.
10 What is the 'edge of danger' for the hedgehog?
11 'He takes the milk we give him, when we're gone'. What does the phrase 'when we're gone' reinforce for us about the hedgehog's character?
12 In the phrase 'our slamming voices', what is the effect of the word 'slamming'?
13 Identify the alliteration in the last line, and comment on its effect.
14 How would you rate the achievement of this poem? Why?

Hedgehog

Suddenly, a dark amorphous
Shape in the middle of the road
Drowned in the splashed circle of the
Lamps. I stop the car and get out.

Some of his prickles look dry, their
Points bent or broken. Tiny dark
Lice glitter at their roots. A globe
Of weight and some warmth; pressed, a ball

Of agony balanced on nails
In my palms. I turn him over.
A dark eye flickers in the lights,
Then lids out. Put him in the boot.

I drive home. Placed on the dew-soaked grass,
He lies still as a coprolite.
Twenty-five minutes of silence.
And stillness and muteness and cold.
Then go in for an overcoat.

But when I come back he has gone
Off into the fragrant hedges of
Hawthorn and fallen leaves. I search
The garden with a torch. Nothing.

And I would give the hand that holds
This pen to know what fierce blaze of
Purpose took him off into the
Inscrutable, earthy dark.

ROY HOLLAND

Discovering Hedgehog

1 What is the impact of the first word in the poem?
2 We are not told specifically what has happened in the first stanza, yet we know. What has happened?
3 ' . . . I stop the car and get out'. Notice that each word is just one syllable in length. What is the effect of this?
4 ' . . . A globe/Of weight and some warmth'. Which word here suggests that the hedgehog may still be alive?
5 The poet describes the hedgehog as 'a ball of agony'. What impact does the word 'agony' have for the reader?
6 'Then lids out'. What effect does the poet achieve by using the noun 'lid' as a verb here?
7 What words does the writer use to suggest death when the hedgehog lies still for so long?
8 Why does the writer go inside for a coat?
9 ' . . . the fragrant hedges of/Hawthorn'. Why is 'fragrant' a good choice here?
10 'Nothing'. What is the impact of this single-word sentence?
11 How effective is the phrase 'what fierce blaze of purpose'?
12 What evidence is there that the poet has a powerful desire to know what drove the hedgehog to move back into life?
13 Why do you think the poet wrote this poem?
14 What strengths do you see in this poet's technique?

In 'Auto Wreck', the poet is shocked by an accident. He describes the aftermath, but wants to wrestle more with his feelings and the meaning, or lack of meaning, in this event.

Auto Wreck

Its quick soft silver bell beating, beating,
And down the dark one ruby flare
Pulsing out red light like an artery,
The ambulance at top speed floating down
Past beacons and illuminated clocks
Wings in a heavy curve, dips down,
And brakes speed, entering the crowd.
The doors leap open, emptying light;
Stretchers are laid out, the mangled lifted
And stowed into the little hospital.
Then the bell, breaking the hush, tolls once,
And the ambulance with its terrible cargo
Rocking, slightly rocking, moves away,
As the doors, an afterthought, are closed.

We are deranged, walking among the cops
Who sweep glass and are large and composed.
One is still making notes under the light.
One with a bucket douches ponds of blood
Into the street and gutter.
One hangs lanterns on the wrecks that cling,
Empty husks of locusts, to iron poles.

Our throats were tight as tourniquets,
Our feet were bound with splints, but now,
Like convalescents, intimate and gauche,
We speak through sickly smiles and warn
With the stubborn saw of common sense,
The grim joke and the banal resolution.
The traffic moves around with care,
But we remain, touching a wound
That opens to our richest horror.
Already old, the question Who shall die?
Becomes unspoken Who is innocent?
For death in war is done by hands;
Suicide has cause and stillbirth, logic;
And cancer, simple as a flower, blooms.

But this invites the occult mind,
Cancels our physics with a sneer,
And spatters all we knew of dénouement
Across the expedient and wicked stones.

KARL SHAPIRO

Witnesses of the Auto Wreck

1 The word 'beating' is an unusual one to describe an ambulance bell. What else
   does it remind us of that fits into this scene?
2 'Pulsing out red light like an artery'. Comment on the simile 'like an artery'
   used here.
3 Why do you think the ambulance is described as 'floating down'?
4 'The doors leap open, emptying light'. What is unusual about the description
   here? Is it effective?
5 Why is the ambulance's cargo described as 'terrible'?
6 Why is the closing of the doors almost overlooked?
7 'We are deranged'. What does the poet mean by the word 'deranged'?
8 What is the emotional impact of the scene with the police officer washing away
   blood with buckets of water?
9 The wrecks are described as 'Empty husks of locusts'. Is this an effective image?
   Why or why not?

10 Initially, the witnesses seem to feel frozen and numb. Which two lines describe this experience?
11 Why are people's smiles 'sickly'?
12 What evidence is there that the accident has had an effect on other drivers?
13 How does the poet appear to feel as a result of this accident? What evidence is there from the poem to support your answer?
14 What do you see as the strengths of this poem? Give evidence from the poem.

In 'Solitude', the poet recalls a car accident that almost took his life.

Solitude

Right here I was nearly killed one night in February.
My car slewed on the ice, sideways,
into the other lane. The oncoming cars—
their headlights—came nearer.

My name, my daughters, my job
slipped free and fell behind silently,
farther and farther back. I was anonymous,
like a schoolboy in a lot surrounded by enemies.

The approaching traffic had powerful lights.
They shone on me while I turned and turned
the wheel in a transparent fear that moved like eggwhite.
The seconds lengthened out—making more room—
they grew long as hospital buildings.

It felt as if you could just take it easy
and loaf a bit
before the smash came.

Then firm land appeared: a helping sandgrain
or a marvelous gust of wind. The car took hold
and fish-tailed back across the road.
A signpost shot up, snapped off—a ringing sound—
tossed into the dark.

Came all quiet. I sat there in my seatbelt
and watched someone tramp through the blowing snow
to see what had become of me.

TOMAS TRANSTROMER
(translated from the Swedish by Robert Bly)

Experiencing Solitude

1 'Right here I was nearly killed one night in February'. What effect does this opening line have? Why?
2 What caused the accident?
3 What was the main source of danger as the car spun out of control?
4 What is the effect of detailing the bits of life that slipped away in that moment?
5 'I was anonymous'. How did the writer feel at this moment?
6 '. . . while I turned and turned/the wheel'. What does the repetition of 'turned' contribute here?
7 '. . . in a transparent fear that moved like eggwhite'. Comment on the effect of this unexpected simile.
8 The seconds are described as growing 'long as hospital buildings'. Is this an effective simile? Why?
9 What stopped the car spinning?
10 Comment on the effect of the short sentence 'Came all quiet'.
11 Why do you think the poet has chosen the title 'Solitude'?
12 Why do you think the poet has written 'Solitude'?

Fragments of memories of magpies are the subject matter of this poem by R. G. Hay. Each fragment is quite specific, adding to the overall picture. Their unpredictability and aggression is captured in words such as 'fierce swoop and snap/chuck your hat at them/duck'. The last line plays on the black and white colour of magpies, as the poet describes them in words on paper — that is, 'in white and black'.

Magpies

Early morning fresh
breathe deep cool
yellow air
silver glint on dew and
leaves of bimble box
dappled shade on the road's white dust:
magpies carol,
transduce it all to sound.

But nesting
fierce swoop and snap
chuck your hat at them
duck
spill groceries
scramble to recover under that
relentless dive-bombing:
took a tuft of hair once
bloodied my scalp another time—
terrible furies.

That's magpies in white and black.

R. G. HAY

Judith Wright's description of magpies is an interesting contrast to the poem above. Here, the poet is more interested in capturing different facets of the character of magpies, using unexpected images and strong descriptive words.

Magpies

Along the road the magpies walk
with hands in pockets, left and right.
They tilt their heads, and stroll and talk.
In their well-fitted black and white

they look like certain gentlemen
who seem most nonchalant and wise
until their meal is served—and then
what clashing beaks, what greedy eyes!

But not one man that I have heard
throws back his head in such a song
of grace and praise—no man nor bird.
Their greed is brief; their joy is long,
for each is born with such a throat
as thanks his God with every note.

JUDITH WRIGHT

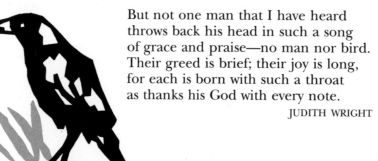

Richard Church laments the destruction of peaceful nature that accompanies the building of a new housing estate.

Housing Scheme

All summer through
The fields drank showers of larksong;
Offering in return
The hospitality of grasses,
And flowers kneedeep.

Over those wide acres
Trooped the plovers
Mourning and lamenting as evening fell.
From the deep hedgerows
Where the foam of meadowsweet broke,
The rabbits and mice
Peeped out, and boldly sat in the sun.

But when the oaks were bronzing,
Steamrollers and brickcarts
Broke through the hedges.
The white-haired grasses, and the seedpods
Disappeared into the mud,
And the larks were silent, the plovers gone.

Then over the newlaid roads
And the open trenches of drains,
Rose a hoarding to face the highway,
'Build your house in the country.'

RICHARD CHURCH

4 Judith Wright

Judith Wright's Life and Background

Judith Wright is one of the world's leading poets. She was born in 1915 at 'Wallumbi', her family property on the New England Tableland in New South Wales. In 'South of My Days' she describes this country:

> . . . high delicate outline
> of bony slopes wincing under the winter

She began writing poetry at the age of six. Her mother and her aunts supervised her primary education by correspondence. She was twelve years old when her mother died and she went to a boarding school in Armidale to complete her secondary education. After this she attended Sydney University where she had her poetry published in *Honi Soit*, the student newspaper.

After graduating from Sydney University, she travelled with a cousin throughout Europe two years before the outbreak of the Second World War. On her return to Sydney she undertook secretarial work.

When the War began, because her brothers had joined the army, she decided to return home to help her father, who was running the family property with the help of only one stockman. It was here, while she washed, milked, mustered and kept the books, that she began to see the New England countryside and its people through the eyes of a poet. Many of the poems of this period were published in her first book of poetry, *The Moving Image*, in 1948. This collection of poems was extremely well received and established her as a poet.

Her next book of poems, *Woman to Man*, published in 1949, examined love from a woman's point of view. She has gone on to publish a further eleven collections of poetry, a volume of short stories and important books about Australian history, poetry and the environment.

Judith Wright is vitally concerned about the natural world and society itself. Her book *The Coral Battleground* reveals her ideas for preserving the Great Barrier Reef. She is one of our foremost conservationists and has condemned the greed that is destroying our environment: 'We are still a frontier civilisation, still mowing the place down to make money from it.' Judith Wright is now living at Mongarlowe, between Canberra and the New South Wales coast.

Judith Wright's Poetry

In *The Moving Image*, Judith Wright was concerned to focus on the Australian landscape and its people. She has commented on her inspiration:

> My own poems in *The Moving Image* were the result of my discovery of Australian literature and of my sudden realisation that my country background, and the ties I had always felt to the Australian landscape and the people I had known in my childhood, could be a subject of poetry. I had at last begun to understand that before I could write good poetry, I must explore my own experience and find in it the meaning it had for me.

The subjects for these poems are people such as the bullocky, the Aborigines, old Dan, the remittance man, the surfer, and the brother and sisters.

In her second book of poems, *Woman to Man*, there was a change of direction. She continued to use beautiful natural images, but now she wove them into her personal descriptions of love and creation in poems such as 'Woman to Man' and 'Woman to Child'.

Her third book of poetry was *The Gateway* and it contained favourites such as 'The Cedars', 'The Cicadas' and 'Legend'. This collection was followed by *The Two Fires*, in which Judith Wright had become preoccupied with the destruction of humankind by the atomic bomb. She says of this: 'The atom bomb was really under my skin. Not because it was a bomb, but because it was an atom bomb.'

Her fifth book, *Birds*, was published in 1962. The poems are all about birds such as the peacock, the brush turkey and the blue wren. Her other collections of poetry are, *Five Senses, The Other Half, Collected Poems 1942–1970, Alive, Fourth Quarter and Other Poems, The Double Tree, Phantom Dwelling* and *A Human Pattern*.

Judith Wright herself has put forward some of the important reasons for her success:

> Those years from 1940 onwards gave me confidence in my own background and in the truth of my own experience, as well as the knowledge that in writing as an Australian, it was possible also to write as a poet on equal terms with other poets in all times and countries.

As Judith Wright looks south from her family property, she observes the country around her and reflects on old Dan and his memories.

South of My Days

South of my days' circle, part of my blood's country,
rises that tableland, high delicate outline
of bony slopes wincing under the winter;
low trees blue-leaved and olive; outcropping granite—
clean, lean, hungry country. The creek's leaf-silenced,
willow-choked, the slope a tangle of medlar and crab-apple,
branching over and under, blotched with a green lichen;
and the old cottage lurches in for shelter.

O cold the black-frost night. The walls draw in to the warmth
and the old roof cracks its joints; the slung kettle
hisses a leak on the fire. Hardly to be believed that summer
will turn up again some day in a wave of rambler roses,
thrust its hot face in here to tell another yarn—
a story old Dan can spin into a blanket against the winter.
Seventy years of stories he clutches round his bones.
Seventy summers are hived in him like old honey.

Droving that year, Charleville to the Hunter,
nineteen-one it was, and the drought beginning;
sixty head left at the McIntyre, the mud round them
hardened like iron; and the yellow boy died
in the sulky ahead with the gear, but the horse went on,
stopped at the Sandy Camp and waited in the evening.
It was the flies we seen first, swarming like bees.
Came to the Hunter, three hundred head of a thousand—
cruel to keep them alive—and the river was dust.

Or mustering up in the Bogongs in the autumn
when the blizzards came early. Brought them down; we brought them
down, what aren't there yet. Or driving for Cobb's on the run
up from Tamworth—Thunderbolt at the top of Hungry Hill,
and I give him a wink. I wouldn't wait long, Fred,
not if I was you; the troopers are just behind,
coming for that job at the Hillgrove. He went like a luny,
him on his big black horse.
          Oh, they slide and they vanish
as he shuffles the years like a pack of conjuror's cards.
True or not, it's all the same; and the frost on the roof
cracks like a whip, and the back-log breaks into ash.
Wake, old man. This is winter, and the yarns are over.
No one is listening.
        South of my days' circle
I know it dark against the stars, the high lean country
full of old stories that still go walking in my sleep.

                    JUDITH WRIGHT

Enjoying South of My Days

1 What does Judith Wright mean by 'my blood's country'?
2 'Bony slopes wincing under the winter'. What impression does the poet give of the land? How does she show the effect on the land of the cold of winter?
3 What impression does she give of the creek?
4 ' . . . the old roof cracks its joints'. Explain the poet's use of personification? What does she achieve by it?
5 'Thrust its hot face in here to tell another yarn'. What human qualities has the poet given to summer?
6 Why is 'hisses' an effective word?
7 What is the meaning of 'Seventy years of stories he clutches round his bones'?
8 In the third stanza, how do you know that Dan is telling one of his stories?
9 What harshness does Dan reveal about the Australian landscape?
10 'The flies are swarming like bees'. What has caused this? What is the poet showing about the flies?
11 What was old Dan's relationship with Thunderbolt?
12 'As he shuffles the years like a pack of conjuror's cards'. Is this an effective simile? Give reasons for your answer.
13 What effect has old Dan and his stories had on the poet?
14 What is your attitude to old Dan?
15 What is the poet's purpose in this poem?
16 Why has the poet called this poem 'South of My Days'?

In 'Sanctuary', Judith Wright shows us how civilisation brings about the destruction of nature. Not even in a sanctuary is the native wildlife safe from humans.

Sanctuary

The road beneath the giant original trees
sweeps on and cannot wait. Varnished by dew,
its darkness mimics mirrors and is bright
behind the panic eyes the driver sees
caught in headlights. Behind his wheels the night
takes over: only the road ahead is true.
It knows where it is going; we go too.

Sanctuary, the sign said. Sanctuary—
trees, not houses; flat skins pinned to the road
of possum and native-cat; and here the old tree stood
for how many thousand years? that old gnome-tree
some axe-new boy cut down. Sanctuary, it said:
but only the road has meaning here. It leads
into the world's cities like a long fuse laid.

Fuse, nerve, strand of a net, tense
bearer of messages, snap-tight violin-string,
dangerous knife-edge laid across the dark,
what has that sign to do with you? The immense
tower of antique forest and cliff, the rock
where years accumulate like leaves, the tree
where transient bird and mindless insect sing?
The word the board holds up is Sanctuary,
and the road knows that notice-boards make sense,

but has no time to pray. Only, up there,
morning sets doves upon the power-line.
Swung on that fatal voltage like a sign
and meaning love, perhaps they are a prayer.

JUDITH WRIGHT

Appreciating Sanctuary

1 'The giant original trees'. What does the word 'original' suggest?
2 What impression do the words 'sweeps on and cannot wait' give us of the road and civilisation?
3 ' . . . the panic eyes the driver sees/caught in headlights'. What is happening?
4 What is the effect of the repetition of the word 'Sanctuary'?
5 In the second stanza, how does the poet make you aware of the destructive power of the road?
6 What is the meaning of 'some axe-new boy'?
7 What contrast is there between the boy and the tree?
8 Why does the poet compare the road to 'a long fuse laid'? Do you think this is an effective comparison? Why or why not?
9 What impression of the road does the poet give you in the first three lines of the third stanza?
10 Why does the poet compare the road to a 'strand of a net'?
11 Why does the poet describe the road as a 'dangerous knife-edge laid across the dark'?
12 'What has that sign to do with you?' Why does the poet ask the road this question?
13 Why does the poet describe the forest as 'antique'?
14 In what ways is the power-line similar to the road?
15 'Morning sets doves upon the power-line'. The dove is a symbol of peace and love. What do you think is the poet's message at the end of the poem?
16 What is the poet's attitude to civilisation?
17 What is the poet's attitude to nature?
18 Why do you think the poet has written this poem?

This poem uses natural imagery to comment on the relationship between the sea and the surfer.

The Surfer

He thrust his joy against the weight of the sea,
climbed through, slid under those long banks of foam—
(hawthorn hedges in spring, thorns in the face stinging).
How his brown strength drove through the hollow and coil
of green-through weirs of water!
Muscle of arm thrust down long muscle of water.
And swimming so, went out of sight
where mortal, masterful, frail, the gulls went wheeling
in air, as he in water, with delight.

Turn home, the sun goes down; swimmer, turn home.
Last leaf of gold vanishes from the sea-curve.
Take the big roller's shoulder, speed and swerve.
Come to the long beach home like a gull diving.

For on the sand the grey-wolf sea lies snarling;
cold twilight wind splits the waves' hair and shows
the bones they worry in their wolf-teeth. O, wind blows,
and sea crouches on sand, fawning and mouthing;
drops there and snatches again, drops and again snatches
its broken toys, its whitened pebbles and shells.

JUDITH WRIGHT

Appreciating The Surfer

1 In the first stanza, what is the swimmer's attitude to the sea?
2 What words in the first stanza show the power of the sea?
3 'Hawthorn hedges in spring, thorns in the face stinging'. What does the poet compare the stinging of the waves to?
4 How does the poet suggest that the sea and the swimmer are opposed to each other?
5 In what ways are the gulls 'masterful'?
6 How does the swimmer also seem to be 'masterful' in the first stanza?
7 What other similarities can you see between the surfer and the gulls?
8 How does the poet create feelings of fear in the second stanza?
9 What is the meaning of 'Last leaf of gold vanishes from the sea-curve'?
10 How does the poet create a sense of action in 'Take the big roller's shoulder, speed and swerve'?
11 What impression does the simile 'like a gull diving' create?
12 What contrast in mood is there between the first and last stanza?
13 What impression of the sea does the poet create by comparing it to a grey wolf?
14 Using evidence from the poem, explain how the poet further develops the 'wolf' metaphor?
15 '. . . sea crouches on sand, fawning and mouthing'. What is happening?
16 What is the poet's aim in 'The Surfer'?

Here Judith Wright gives a woman's view of the wonder of love and creation.

Woman to Child

You who were darkness warmed by flesh
where out of darkness rose the seed.
Then all a world I made in me:
all the world you hear and see
hung upon my dreaming blood.

There moved the multitudinous stars,
and coloured birds and fishes moved.
There swam the sliding continents.
All time lay rolled in me, and sense,
and love that knew not its beloved.

O node and focus of the world—
I hold you deep within that well
you shall escape and not escape—
that mirrors still your sleeping shape,
that nurtures still your crescent cell.

I wither and you break from me;
yet though you dance in living light,
I am the earth, I am the root,
I am the stem that fed the fruit,
the link that joins you to the night.

JUDITH WRIGHT

In 'Brother and Sisters', Judith Wright shows the destructive qualities of time.

Brother and Sisters

The road turned out to be a cul-de-sac;
stopped like a lost intention at the gate
and never crossed the mountains to the coast.
But they stayed on. Years grew like grass and leaves
across the half-erased and dubious track,
until one day they knew the plans were lost,
the blue-print for the bridge was out of date,
and now their orchards never would be planted.
The saplings sprouted slyly; day by day
the bush moved one step nearer, wondering when.
The polished parlour grew distrait and haunted
where Millie, Lucy, John each night at ten
wound the gilt clock that leaked the year away.

The pianola—oh, listen to the mocking-bird—
wavers on Sundays and has lost a note.
The wrinkled ewes snatch pansies through the fence
and stare with shallow eyes into the garden
where Lucy shrivels waiting for a word,
and Millie's cameos loosen round her throat.
The bush comes near, the ranges grow immense.

Feeding the lambs deserted in early spring
Lucy looked up and saw the stockman's eye
telling her she was cracked and old.
                                        The wall
groans in the night and settles more awry.
O how they lie awake. Their thoughts go fluttering
from room to room like moths: 'Millie, are you asleep?'
'Oh John, I have been dreaming.' 'Lucy, do you cry?'
—meet tentative as moths. Antennae stroke a wing.
'There is nothing to be afraid of. Nothing at all.'

JUDITH WRIGHT

Judith Wright describes her encounter with a flying-fox that has been impaled on barbed wire.

Flying-fox on Barbed Wire

Little nightmare flying-fox
trapped on the cruel barbs of day
has no weapon but a wing
and a tiny scream.
Here's a patch of night, a thing
that looks by daylight like a hoax;
dawn wouldn't let it fly away
with its kin into its dream,
but stabbed with a pin its velvet hand
and hunt it in a hostile land.

Imp from the world of upside-down,
here's some darkness in a bag
to foil your frightened needle-bite.
Now we can untie
from the staring stake of pain
your black claw on its velvet rag.
Scramble, silent, out of the light
and hang by your feet in the kind-leaved tree.
Gargoyle, thief, forget your grief
and go to your country night; and we,
accomplice to day's enemy,
too must forget
that we and the Devil ever met.

JUDITH WRIGHT

Examining the Flying-fox

1 Why does the poet refer to the flying-fox as 'nightmare'?
2 What are 'cruel barbs of day'?
3 'That looks by daylight like a hoax'. What is the poet trying to show about the appearance of the flying-fox in daylight?
4 '. . . stabbed with a pin its velvet hand'. What has happened?
5 In what ways is the land 'hostile' towards the flying-fox?
6 'Imp from the world of upside-down'. What trait of the flying-fox is the poet drawing our attention to?
7 How does the poet remove the flying-fox from the barbed wire without being bitten?
8 What words emphasise the suffering of the flying-fox on the barbed wire?
9 Why does the poet consider the tree to be 'kind-leaved'?
10 What is the poet suggesting about the flying-fox's appearance when she describes it as a 'gargoyle'?
11 Why does the poet address the flying-fox as 'thief'?
12 '. . . go to your country night'. What does the poet want the flying-fox to do?
13 Why does the poet describe herself as an 'accomplice'?
14 Why do you think the poet has written this poem?
15 What is the poet's attitude to the flying-fox?
16 What does the poet reveal about herself in this poem?

Judith Wright sympathetically describes the cicadas' struggle to continue their life cycle.

The Cicadas

On yellow days in summer when the early heat
presses like hands hardening the sown earth
into stillness, when after sunrise birds fall quiet
and streams sink in their beds and in silence meet,
then underground the blind nymphs waken and move.
They must begin at last to struggle towards love.

For a whole life they have crouched alone and dumb,
in patient ugliness enduring the humble dark.
Nothing has shaken that world below the world
except the far-off thunder, the strain of roots in storm.
Sunk in an airless night they neither slept nor woke,
but hanging on the tree's blood dreamed vaguely the dreams
    of the tree,
and put on wavering leaves, wing-veined, too delicate to see.

But now in terror overhead their day of dying breaks.
The trumpet of the rising sun bursts into sound
and the implacable unborn stir and reply.
In the hard shell an unmade body wakes
and fights to break from its motherly-enclosing ground.
These dead must dig their upward grave in fear
to cast the living into the naked air.

Terrible is the pressure of light into the heart.
The womb is withered and cracked, the birth is begun,
and shuddering and groaning to break that iron grasp
the new is delivered as the old is torn apart.
Love whose unmerciful blade has pierced us through,
we struggle naked from our death in search of you.

This is the wild light that our dreams foretold
while unaware we prepared these eyes and wings—
while in our sleep we learned the song the world sings.
Sing now, my brothers; climb to that intolerable gold.

JUDITH WRIGHT

Understanding The Cicadas

1 Why does the poet describe the summer days as 'yellow'?
2 How does the poet create the impression of quietness in the first stanza?
3 What effect does the heat of summer have on the cicadas?

4 What does the poet mean by 'They must begin at last to struggle towards love'?
5 ' . . . they have crouched alone and dumb'. How has the poet made the cicadas seem human? What is the effect of this use of personification?
6 What do the words 'the far-off thunder' suggest about the world above?
7 How does the poet suggest that the tree is nurturing the cicadas?
8 They 'put on wavering leaves, wing-veined, too delicate to see'. What is happening to the cicadas?
9 What does the poet mean by 'their day of dying breaks'?
10 'The trumpet of the rising sun bursts into sound'. Why is this an unusual image? What does the poet mean?
11 Why does the poet refer to the cicadas as 'these dead'? What words continue this idea?
12 What words suggest the great struggle that the cicadas have to break out of their shells?
13 What does the poet mean by 'climb to that intolerable gold'?
14 The poet has portrayed the life cycle of the cicada. After reading the poem what are your feelings towards the cicada?
15 What do you think is the poet's message to the reader?

Judith Wright, through her poetry, has shown her great concern for the environment. In this poem she reveals how the beauty of the Peacock transcends the hostile environment created by humans.

The Peacock

Shame on the aldermen who locked
the Peacock in a dirty cage!
His blue and copper sheens are mocked
by habit, hopelessness and age.

The weary Sunday families
along their gravelled paths repeat
the pattern of monotonies
that he treads out with restless feet.

And yet the Peacock shines alone;
and if one metal feather fall
another grows where that was grown.
Love clothes him still, in spite of all.
How pure the hidden spring must rise
that time and custom cannot stain!
It speaks its joy again—again.
Perhaps the aldermen are wise.

JUDITH WRIGHT

5 Robert Frost

ROBERT FROST
Selected Poems

Signet Classic
451-CE2413 · CANADA $4.95 · U.S. $3.95
POEMS BY
ROBERT FROST
A Boy's Will and North of Boston
INTRODUCTION BY
WILLIAM H. PRITCHARD

Life and Background of Robert Frost

Robert Lee Frost was born in San Francisco, California, in 1874. His father, a graduate of prestigious Harvard University, and a sympathiser with the Southern states named him Robert Lee after the famous General, Robert E. Lee, who led the Southern states during the Civil War.

When Robert was ten years old his father died from tuberculosis. Already, by his life and the way he had faced his illness, the father had passed on to his son a capacity to endure, to fight on and never give up. His mother took a job as a schoolteacher in Lawrence, Massachussetts, and in her class young Robert grew to love language and literature, especially poetry. He eagerly read the classic writers — Dickens, Shakespeare, Milton, Tennyson and others. He began writing his own poems.

Under his grandfather's urgings, Robert enrolled at Dartmouth College, with the rough goal of preparing for a career in business. But the goal had too much of the grandfather and not enough of Robert in it. He soon dropped out and began to travel the countryside taking odd jobs — working at mills, writing for small newspapers, working as a janitor, and doing some occasional teaching. He emerged from this period by marrying a friend from school years, Elinor White, in 1895, and this prompted him to try university once more. From 1897 to 1898 he studied at Harvard but, once again, the academic constraints did not satisfy him. He turned instead, with no background to draw upon, to farming.

The little farm Robert and Elinor settled on was in New Hampshire, one of the states of the New England region in the United States. His family grew while they lived there, and he began to produce a regular flow of poems, although as yet with no real outlet for their publication. After about ten years he, again, took up part-time teaching and moved off the farm. Shortly, the old restlessness manifested itself once more and he and the family moved to England in 1912. Living in rural England, Frost was able to continue writing poetry and also established friendships with a number of poets living there, including Ezra Pound, Wilfred Gibson, Edward Thomas and Rupert Brooke. These writers gave him the recognition his poetry needed and his first two books of poems were published, *A Boy's Will* (1913) and *North of Boston* (1914). *North of Boston* included 'Mending Wall' and 'After Apple-picking'.

In 1915 Frost and his family were forced by the First World War to return to the USA. However, because of the publication of his poems in England, he was now recognised more widely. He was given increasing recognition in the USA and the publication of his many books of poems began there. Over the following years he was given teaching positions at Amherst College, the University of Michigan, and then Amherst College again.

In 1924 he was awarded the Pulitzer Prize for poetry, the first of four such awards. Poems continued to be written, collections were published and honours kept pouring in. In 1961 he lectured at The Hebrew University in Jerusalem, toured Europe, visited friends in England again and lectured in Moscow to an audience of poets and critics.

In January 1963 Robert Frost died at the age of 89. His volumes of poetry, mostly focusing on rural scenes in the New England states, spoke of his great productivity. But how can we assess his quality? By now, years of assessment by critics have firmly established Frost as a major poet, one who wrote with an authentic New England voice.

Features of Robert Frost's Poetry

Simple Language
At a time when modern poetry was becoming increasingly complex and abstract, often requiring the reader to have some knowledge of Latin, French or Greek, Frost's poetry stood out for the simplicity of its subject matter and language. His language is natural, effortless, and simple, characteristic of the people of the New

England area, and able to be enjoyed by people of all ages. The simplicity makes many of his lines easy to remember, and accounts for the wide 'quotability' of Frost.

Nature as Subject

Frost's predominant subject matter is nature. He observes and records woods filling with snow, paths diverging, stacked firewood, stone fences crumbling, birds, animals, trees, fruit, leaves, the myriad aspects of his beloved New England countryside. Aware that nature reveals the deep realities of life, he records and reflects upon its thousand faces.

Subtle Symbolism

Aspects of nature become subtle symbols under Frost's crafting. He observes a crumbling stone fence, and it becomes a symbol of the unnaturalness of divisions between people. He notes two paths diverging in a wood and this becomes a symbol of the unfettered choices we face in life, and the destiny that follows our choosing. The symbolism is never forced and, hence, it can easily be missed. However, once it is appreciated, the richness of the poet's concern opens up powerfully before the reader.

With a long day's labour over, the poet prepares for sleep. He has been picking apples and this task occupies his thoughts.

After Apple-picking

My long two-pointed ladder's sticking through a tree
Toward heaven still,
And there's a barrel that I didn't fill
Beside it, and there may be two or three
Apples I didn't pick upon some bough.
But I am done with apple-picking now.
Essence of winter sleep is on the night,
The scent of apples: I am drowsing off.
I cannot rub the strangeness from my sight
I got from looking through a pane of glass
I skimmed this morning from the drinking trough
And held against the world of hoary grass.
It melted, and I let it fall and break.
But I was well
Upon my way to sleep before it fell,
And I could tell
What form my dreaming was about to take.
Magnified apples appear and disappear.
Stem end and blossom end,
And every fleck of russet showing clear.

My instep arch not only keeps the ache,
It keeps the pressure of a ladder-round.
I feel the ladder sway as the boughs bend.
And I keep hearing from the cellar bin
The rumbling sound
Of load on load of apples coming in.
For I have had too much
Of apple-picking: I am overtired
Of the great harvest I myself desired.
There were ten thousand thousand fruit to touch,
Cherish in hand, lift down, and not let fall.
For all
That struck the earth,
No matter if not bruised or spiked with stubble,
Went surely to the cider-apple heap
As of no worth.
One can see what will trouble
This sleep of mine, whatever sleep it is.
Were he not gone,
The woodchuck could say whether it's like his
Long sleep, as I describe its coming on.
Or just some human sleep.

ROBERT FROST

Examining After Apple-picking

1 Identify two things from the first three lines that indicate the apple-picking has not yet been fully completed.
2 What does the poet identify as 'essence of winter sleep'?
3 What indications are there that winter is coming?
4 What is the main content of the poet's thoughts as he waits for sleep?
5 What two things about his foot remind him of the work he has been doing?
6 What sound does he continue to hear as he drowses?
7 Quote a line from the poem that explains why the poet's mind is restless.
8 'There were ten thousand thousand fruit to touch'. What does the poet achieve by the repetition of the word 'thousand'?
9 'Cherish in hand, lift down, and not let fall'. Which word indicates that the poet treats the apples as precious?
10 What is done with the apples that fall to the ground?
11 'This sleep of mine, whatever sleep it is'. Suggest some kinds of sleep that the poet might be referring to.

12 Why is the woodchuck no longer around to answer the poet's question about his sleep?

13 The poem has a surface meaning as the poet describes the onset of sleep after a hard day picking apples. What deeper issue might he also be writing about?

14 How would you describe the poet's feelings as they are expressed in this poem?

Walking in a frozen swamp area, Frost comes across a cord of wood that has been split some years earlier by an axeman, and then, for no clear reason, left untouched.

The Wood-pile

Out walking in the frozen swamp one grey day,
I paused and said, 'I will turn back from here.
No, I will go on farther—and we shall see.'
The hard snow held me, save where now and then
One foot went through. The view was all in lines
Straight up and down of tall slim trees
Too much alike to mark or name a place by
So as to say for certain I was here
Or somewhere else: I was just far from home.
A small bird flew before me. He was careful
To put a tree between us when he lighted,
And say no word to tell me who he was
Who was so foolish as to think what *he* thought.
He thought that I was after him for a feather—
The white one in his tail; like one who takes
Everything said as personal to himself.
One flight out sideways would have undeceived him.
And then there was a pile of wood for which
I forgot him and let his little fear
Carry him off the way I might have gone,
Without so much as wishing him goodnight.
He went behind it to make his last stand.
It was a cord of maple, cut and split
And piled—and measured, four by four by eight.
And not another like it could I see.
No runner tracks in this year's snow looped near it.
And it was older sure than this year's cutting,
Or even last year's or the year's before.
The wood was grey and the bark warping off it
And the pile somewhat sunken. Clematis
Had wound strings round and round it like a bundle.

What held it though on one side was a tree
Still growing, and on one a stake and prop,
These latter about to fall. I thought that only
Someone who lived in turning to fresh tasks
Could so forget his handiwork on which
He spent himself, the labour of his axe,
And leave it there far from a useful fireplace
To warm the frozen swamp as best it could
With the slow smokeless burning of decay.

ROBERT FROST

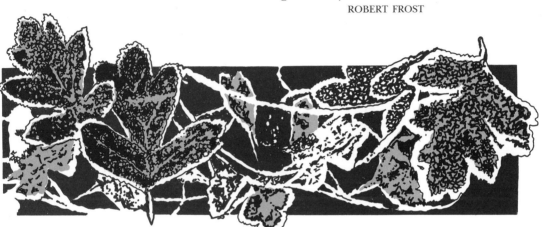

Digging Around in The Wood-pile

1 What was the weather like on this day? What word in the first line captures this picture for us?
2 What choice did the poet have to make?
3 What was his purpose in continuing on?
4 What made it difficult to identify clearly where he was?
5 What evidence is there that the small bird was guarded about this intruder?
6 The poet judges himself to be foolish as far as the bird is concerned. What does he do that seems foolish to himself?
7 What attracts the writer's attention, and allows the bird to fly off unnoticed?
8 What evidence is there that the axeman has been a careful worker?
9 How does the writer deduce that the wood was cut some years earlier?
10 Although the pile is still neatly stacked, there is evidence that it will not remain this way much longer. Why is the stack likely to fall soon?
11 What conclusion about the axeman does the poet arrive at?
12 What mood is evoked by the final picture of the wood-pile, left 'To warm the frozen swamp as best it could/With the slow smokeless burning of decay'?
13 What does the writer reveal about his feelings towards nature in 'The Wood-pile'?
14 Do you think this is more than a descriptive nature poem? Give supporting evidence for your view.

A choice confronts the poet as he walks in the woods. The poem becomes an occasion to reflect on choices in life, and the effects of choosing.

The Road Not Taken

Two roads diverged in a yellow wood,
And sorry I could not travel both
And be one traveller, long I stood
And looked down one as far as I could
To where it bent in the undergrowth;

Then took the other, as just as fair,
And having perhaps the better claim,
Because it was grassy and wanted wear;
Though as for that the passing there
Had worn them really about the same,

And both that morning equally lay
In leaves no step had trodden black.
Oh, I kept the first for another day!
Yet knowing how way leads on to way,
I doubted if I should ever come back.

I shall be telling this with a sigh
Somewhere ages and ages hence:
Two roads diverged in a wood, and I—
I took the one less travelled by,
And that has made all the difference.

ROBERT FROST

Exploring The Road Not Taken

1 What season is suggested by the first line? Give a reason for your answer.
2 What choice confronts the poet in this wood?
3 What word from the first stanza expresses the poet's feelings about not being able to choose both options at once?
4 What action does the poet take to try to assess the quality of each option?
5 What reason does the poet initially give for his choice of path?
6 In what ways does the poet see the two paths as really being about equal?
7 'Oh, I kept the first for another day!' What reassurance does the poet appear to be trying to give himself?
8 What truth does the poet acknowledge to himself in the final lines of the third stanza?
9 Which line in the final stanza returns us to the poem's starting place?

10 What do you think the poet means by the final line: 'And that has made all the difference'?
11 What emotions does the poet seem to feel in this poem? Quote from the poem to support your answer.
12 In your own words, state the poet's theme or message.

In this poem Frost addresses a tree outside his window, drawing out the similarities between himself and the tree. They are, in Frost's musings, very closely related.

Tree at My Window

Tree at my window, window tree,
My sash is lowered when night comes on;
But let there never be curtain drawn
Between you and me.

Vague dream-head lifted out of the ground,
And thing next most diffuse to cloud,
Not all your light tongues talking aloud
Could be profound.

But, tree, I have seen you taken and tossed,
And if you have seen me when I slept,
You have seen me when I was taken and swept
And all but lost.

That day she put our heads together,
Fate had her imagination about her,
Your head so much concerned with outer,
Mine with inner, weather.

ROBERT FROST

The poet stops on his journey to watch snow falling into woods and to reflect on the significance of this moment. It is not surprising for us to know that Jawaharlal Nehru, the first Prime Minister of India after independence was gained in 1947, faced with the enormous task of building a nation, kept the final stanza of this poem on his office desk to remind him that he had 'promises to keep,/And miles to go' before he could rest.

Stopping by Woods on a Snowy Evening

Whose woods these are I think I know.
His house is in the village though;
He will not see me stopping here
To watch his woods fill up with snow.

My little horse must think it queer
To stop without a farmhouse near
Between the woods and frozen lake
The darkest evening of the year.

He gives his harness bells a shake
To ask if there is some mistake.
The only other sound's the sweep
Of easy wind and downy flake.

The woods are lovely, dark and deep,
But I have promises to keep,
And miles to go before I sleep,
And miles to go before I sleep.

ROBERT FROST

Appreciating Stopping by Woods on a Snowy Evening

This beautiful poem has consistently been a favourite among admirers of Robert Frost. The poem is deceptively simple. On the surface it records an unremarkable event, a moment when the poet stops one evening to contemplate the snow and the woods. The poet is alone except for his horse. However, the woods which are the setting for his contemplation are, in some senses, a third 'character'.

The poem's theme, or the deeper meaning, arises out of the poet's musings. The woods, 'lovely, dark and deep', come to symbolise the attractiveness of passivity, withdrawal from life, perhaps even death. Frost feels drawn to this dark beauty. However, he is also drawn to life.

> But I have promises to keep,
> And miles to go before I sleep,
> And miles to go before I sleep.

It is life and personal involvement that he chooses, rather than withdrawal and death. As in other of Frost's poems, such as 'The Road Not Taken', the poet is focusing on the existential choices people make. His moment of choice, or commitment to life, is signalled at the poem's end by the single word 'but' in 'But I have promises to keep'. He is drawn onwards in his journey because of responsibilities. That the way ahead is not easy is emphasised by the repetition of the line, 'And miles to go before I sleep.'

The language of the poem is everyday language, unpretentious, perhaps even humble. It seems to flow, with little to indicate that it has been crafted very carefully. Yet when we look at the rhyme scheme and note the *aaba bbcb ccdc dddd* pattern, we realise that there *is* a very tight structure to the poem. What appears as almost casual, conversational language, has been planned and shaped with great discipline.

We feel an appropriateness in the language. More complex words would somehow not fit the ordinariness of this incident. The poet's 'little horse must think it queer' to stop in this place. The poet could surely contrive more challenging words. But, no, everything is minimal, simple, spare. Frost's language is appropriate to the subject, the setting and the language pattern of New Englanders.

Frost crafts the poem around three separate contrasts. In the first stanza the poet on his journey is contrasted with the owner of the woods, presumably already warm and secure in his village house. We don't really understand why the poet is out journeying in this weather while 'sensible' people are tucked up at home. But his presence on the journey speaks of his commitment to involvement with life, rather than comfortable withdrawal.

The second and third stanzas contrast the poet and his horse: 'My little horse' must think it queer/To stop . . . ' The poet can acknowledge, through his horse, that others might not make much sense of his journey. After all, this is 'the darkest evening of the year', not a very good time for journeying, nor for stopping to meditate on woods filling up with snow. The pony, incapable of understanding the significance of this moment for the poet, ' . . . gives his harness bells a shake/To ask if there is some mistake'. The seductive beauty of passivity and death are not well understood by those who cannot dream and promise.

The final stanza makes another contrast. Here, the woods and their quiet attractiveness are juxtaposed with the clear call to journey on and to fulfil promises. While the woods are full of enchantment for the poet, they also seem to contain certain danger. The word 'lovely' suggests their beauty but the words 'dark and deep' indicate that they could become perilous. For the poet the woods also represent irresponsibility, escapism. While he marvels at their beauty he is able to forget for a time, the goals he has to achieve. Frost is faced with a choice — to stay or to continue on. He responds by choosing responsible involvement in life, and so resumes his journey.

The poem raises two questions: 'Why is the poet making this journey?' and 'Where is he journeying to?' Neither question is answered because neither is important. For the poet to answer these would be to distract us from the larger significance of this moment, and to tie us down excessively with the specifics of this journey. The poem is a metaphor for the Grand Journey — Life.

Nature puts obstructions in the way of people, not so much to try to stop them, but to cause them to think, perhaps even to recognise some of their limitations.

On a Tree Fallen across the Road
(TO HEAR US TALK)

The tree the tempest with a crash of wood
Thrown down in front of us is not to bar
Our passage to our journey's end for good,
But just to ask us who we think we are

Insisting always on our own way so.
She likes to halt us in our runner tracks,
And make us get down in a foot of snow
Debating what to do without an axe.

And yet she knows obstruction is in vain:
We will not be put off the final goal
We have it hidden in us to attain,
Not though we have to seize earth by the pole

And, tired of aimless circling in one place,
Steer straight off after something into space.

ROBERT FROST

Progress sometimes comes at too high a price. In 'The Line-gang', Frost questions the cost of this kind of invasion into the countryside.

The Line-gang

Here come the line-gang pioneering by.
They throw a forest down less cut than broken.
They plant dead trees for living, and the dead
They string together with a living thread.
They string an instrument against the sky
Wherein words, whether beaten out or spoken,
Will run as hushed as when they were a thought.
But in no hush they string it: they go past
With shouts afar to pull the cable taut,
To hold it hard until they make it fast,
To ease away—they have it. With a laugh
And oath of towns that set the wild at naught,
They bring the telephone and the telegraph.

ROBERT FROST

Looking Over The Line-gang

1 What does Frost mean by the phrase 'pioneering by'?
2 'They throw a forest down less cut than broken'. How does the poet appear to feel about the way the line-gang operates?
3 'They plant dead trees'. What are these 'dead trees'?
4 What is the meaning of ' . . . the dead/They string together with a living thread'?
5 What does the poet mean by saying that words 'Will run as hushed as when they were a thought'?
6 How noisy is the line-gang? Support your answer by referring to the poem.
7 What kinds of things do the workers shout about?
8 What evidence is there that these workers do not come from the country?
9 What is the effect of the workers' behaviour on the country? Find a quote to support your answer.
10 What do these men achieve by their labour?
11 How does the poet seem to feel about the line-gang?
12 Do you think the poet wrote 'The Line-gang' from real-life experience? Explain your viewpoint.

'Mending Wall', one of Frost's most famous poems, was recited by the poet to Nikita Kruschev, the leader of Russia, in a visit to the USSR in 1962. This was just the year before Frost's death and he wanted the poem to be a comment at this time on East-West relations.

Mending Wall

Something there is that doesn't love a wall,
That sends the frozen-ground-swell under it,
And spills the upper boulders in the sun;
And makes gaps even two can pass abreast.
The work of hunters is another thing:
I have come after them and made repair
Where they have left not one stone on a stone,
But they would have the rabbit out of hiding,
To please the yelping dogs. The gaps I mean,
No one has seen them made or heard them made,
But at spring mending-time we find them there.
I let my neighbour know beyond the hill;
And on a day we meet to walk the line
And set the wall between us once again.
We keep the wall between us as we go.
To each the boulders that have fallen to each.
And some are loaves and some so nearly balls
We have to use a spell to make them balance:
'Stay where you are until our backs are turned!'
We wear our fingers rough with handling them.
Oh, just another kind of outdoor game,
One on a side. It comes to little more:
There where it is we do not need the wall:
He is all pine and I am apple orchard.
My apple trees will never get across
And eat the cones under his pines, I tell him.
He only says, 'Good fences make good neighbours.'
Spring is the mischief in me, and I wonder
If I could put a notion in his head:
'*Why* do they make good neighbours? Isn't it
Where there are cows? But here there are no cows.
Before I built a wall I'd ask to know
What I was walling in or walling out,
And to whom I was like to give offence.

Something there is that doesn't love a wall,
That wants it down.' I could say 'Elves' to him,
But it's not elves exactly, and I'd rather
He said it for himself. I see him there
Bringing a stone grasped firmly by the top
In each hand, like an old-stone savage armed.
He moves in darkness as it seems to me,
Not of woods only and the shade of trees.
He will not go behind his father's saying,
And he likes having thought of it so well
He says again, 'Good fences make good neighbours.'

ROBERT FROST

Writing on Mending Wall

 1 'Something there is that doesn't love a wall'. What evidence does the poet offer to support his opening statement?
 2 What do hunters do to walls, and why do they do it?
 3 How does Frost seem to feel about hunters?
 4 At what time of the year do they mend the wall?
 5 Where does each man work as they mend the wall?
 6 What determines who picks up each rock or boulder?
 7 What trees does each man's property contain?
 8 Why does Frost not believe that he and his neighbour need this wall?
 9 Why does the neighbour believe the wall is important? Where did he learn this lesson?
10 What supernatural explanation does the poet think of suggesting for the gaps in the wall?
11 ' . . . like an old-stone savage armed'. What impression does this simile give you of the poet's neighbour?
12 'He moves in darkness . . . ' What two meanings are behind this phrase which Frost uses to refer to the neighbour?
13 Why does the neighbour repeat his belief about walls at the poem's end?
14 How would you state the theme of this poem in your own words?
15 What emotions does the poet seem to feel in this poem?
16 What do you see as the strengths of this poem? Illustrate your answer by examples from the poem.

6 Roger McGough

An Imaginary Menagerie

Poems by Roger McGough

Illustrated by Tony Blundell

ROGER McGOUGH

Blazing Fruit

SELECTED POEMS 1967-1987

Life Study of Roger McGough

Roger McGough was born in Liverpool, England, in 1937. He was educated at St Mary's College and the University of Hull.

As a child he was fascinated by all kinds of rhymes, songs and chants. However, his love for poetry did not continue through his schooldays. He complained that the poetry favoured in his classroom was 'heavy, and dusty, old-fashioned and outside my emotional range.' Perhaps this led him to make his well-known comment, 'I am on the side of the ninety-nine per cent of kids who do not come top in English.'

After leaving school, McGough described his need for contact with poetry in this way. 'In my late teens and early twenties I felt a strong need to communicate. I was the outsider, the seer, the shaman, I was a duck who thought he'd invented water. I tried music first, then painting and then I began to listen to the rhythms inside my head and the poetry began.'

McGough began writing verse when he was at the university. These were the 1960s when Liverpool was the Beatles city, a place where freedom of expression was out in the streets. He became one of the group of 'Liverpool poets' whose poems had nothing to do with the romantic subjects of traditional poetry. Instead their inspiration came from the city. Their poems caught the rhythms of the fishmonger, the bus conductor, the school kid and all the other folk who pounded Liverpool's pavements. McGough liked to close his eyes and recite his poems out loud in coffee shop and clubs. Soon he and his fellow poets were reciting to crowds.

His reputation as a popular poet increased when on a train to Liverpool he wrote the words of 'Lily the Pink', the song that became the famous Beatles hit. He also wrote the script of the Beatles film *The Yellow Submarine.*

Roger McGough is concerned with making poetry accessible. He has written poetry for adults and children and has travelled the world reciting his poems.

Subjects and Themes of Roger McGough's Poetry

Roger McGough did not appreciate the 'great chunks of Palgrave's Golden Treasury that were heaved at me and my classmates by teachers — because they were paid to and because the syllabus demanded it.' He failed 'O' level English literature and although this meant he couldn't study English at a higher level he found this was an advantage when he came to create his own poems. He states, 'As a poet I was free to write without the Ghost of Critics Past peering over my shoulder.' The subjects that inspired him were all around him in the city of Liverpool.

The subject of one of his poems is a busconductor:

> My busconductor tells me
> he only has one kidney

In another the poem, the subject is the school bully:

> I'm a nooligan
> don't give a toss
> in our class
> I'm the boss
> (well, one of them)

Roger McGough is not only a poet of the streets. Some of his poetry is concerned with the issues and concerns of modern living. In 'The Commission', the theme is the hypocrisy of those who discuss poverty while dining well:

> In this poem there is a table
> Groaning with food.
> There is also a child
> Groaning for lack of food.

A nuclear war that is started by a combination of accident and madness is the concern of the poem 'Icarus Allsorts'. In these lines the focus is on some of the war victims:

> The poor
> Clutching shattered televisions
> And last week's edition of T.V. Times
> (but the very last)

ROGER McGOUGH **79**

In 'Three Rusty Nails', the poet speculates on the reception Jesus might get if he appeared, like a tramp, begging at the door of a suburban house for some money and a drink of water.

> O.K. I'll give him 5p
> Say that's all we've got today.
> And I'll forget about the water
> I suppose it's a bit unfair
> But honest, he's filthy dirty
> All beard and straggly hair.

Whatever the subject or theme, McGough's poems are always witty and entertaining. This stanza from 'Goodbat Nightman' is typical of the poem:

> They've had a hard day
> helping clean up the town.
> Now they hang from the mantlepiece
> both upside down.

A man who has prepared in every way for a coming nuclear holocaust looks forward to inheriting 'an earth, newly-cleansed'.

Noah's Arc

> In my fallout shelter I have enough food
> For at least three months. Some books,
> Scrabble, and games for the children.
> Calor gas and candles. Comfortable beds
> And a chemical toilet. Under lock and key
> The tools necessary for a life after death.
> I have carried out my instructions to the letter.
>
> Most evenings I'm down here. Checking the stores,
> Our suits, breathing apparatus. Cleaning
> And polishing. My wife, bless her,
> Thinks I'm obsessive—like other men
> About cars or football. But deep down
> She understands. I have no hobbies.
> My sole interest is survival.
>
> Every few weeks we have what I call D.D.,
> Or Disaster Drill. At the sound of the alarm
> We each go about our separate duties:
> Disconnecting services, switching off the mains,
> Filling the casks with fresh water, etc.
> Mine is to oversee everything before finally
> Shooting the dog. (This I mime in private.)

At first, the young ones enjoyed the days
And nights spent below. It was an adventure.
But now they're at a difficult age
And regard extinction as the boring concern
Of grown-ups. Like divorce and accountancy.
But I am firm. Daddy knows best
And one fine day they'll grow to thank me.

Beneath my bunk I keep an Armalite rifle
Loaded and ready to use one fine day
When panicking neighbours and so-called friends
Try to clamber aboard. The ones who scoff,
Who ignore the signs. I have my orders,
There will be no stowaways. No gatecrashers
At my party. A party starting soon.

And the sooner the better. Like a grounded
Astronaut I grow daily more impatient.
Am on tenterhooks. Each night
I ask the Lord to get on with it.
I fear sometimes He has forsaken us.
We His favourite children. Meek, drilled,
And ready to inherit an earth, newly-cleansed.

I scan the headlines, watch the screen.
A doctor thrilling at each fresh tumour:
The latest invasion, a breakdown of talks.
I pray for malignancy. The self-induced
Sickness for which there is only one cure:
Radium treatment. The final absolution.
That part of full circle we have yet to come.

ROGER McGOUGH

Underground Questions

1 What is this poem's setting?
2 What kind of 'a life after death' do you think the speaker in the poem means?
3 ' . . . My wife, bless her,/Thinks I'm obsessive'. Do you agree with her? Why or why not?
4 What does the last line of the third stanza reveal about the speaker's character?
5 How has the attitude of the young ones changed towards the fallout shelter routine?
6 'Loaded and ready to use . . .' What does this reveal about the speaker?
7 What does the speaker mean by 'At my party'?
8 'And the sooner the better'. What does this reveal about the speaker?

9 How is the speaker's real attitude to the nuclear war revealed in his prayer to the Lord?
10 According to the speaker, how will the earth benefit from nuclear war?
11 To whom does the speaker compare himself in the last stanza?
12 What do you think is 'the self-induced sickness'?
13 What is the meaning of 'the final absolution'?
14 Why has the poet called the poem 'Noah's Arc'? What play on words is evident in the title?
15 What is this poem's achievement?
16 What techniques has the poet used to convey his message to the reader?

The busconductor in the poem knows that he is at the end of his life and consequently he savours every aspect of daily living.

My Busconductor

My busconductor tells me
he only has one kidney
and that may soon go on strike
through overwork.
Each busticket
takes on now a different shape
and texture.
He holds a ninepenny single
as if it were a rose
and puts the shilling in his bag
as a child into a gasmeter.
His thin lips
have no quips
for fat factorygirls
and he ignores
the drunk who snores
and the oldman who talks to himself
and gets off at the wrong stop.

He goes gently to the bedroom
of the bus
to collect
and watch familiar shops and pubs passby
(perhaps for the last time?)
The sameold streets look different now
more distinct
as through new glasses.
And the sky
was it ever so blue?
And all the time
deepdown in the deserted busshelter of his mind
he thinks about his journey nearly done.
One day he'll clock on and never clock off
or clock off and never clock on.

ROGER McGOUGH

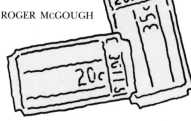

Thinking About My Busconductor

1 When the busconductor speaks of his one kidney going 'on strike', what does he mean is going to happen?
2 Why does each busticket take on 'a different shape and texture' for the busconductor?
3 'As if it were a rose'. What does this comparison reveal about the busconductor's attitude to the busticket?
4 In what manner does the busconductor put the shilling in his bag?
5 What alliteration does the poet use to draw our attention to the factorygirls?
6 What is the busconductor's attitude to the drunk? Why do you think he has this attitude?
7 What do you think is 'the bedroom of the bus'?
8 '(Perhaps for the last time?)' Why do you think the poet has placed brackets around these words?
9 'And the sky/was it ever so blue?' Why does the sky look bluer than ever to the busconductor?
10 What change of mood begins with the words 'And all the time'?
11 Why is it appropriate to compare the busconductor's mind to a 'deserted busshelter'?
12 What is the 'journey' he thinks about all the time?
13 Why do you think the word 'clock' is repeated several times in the poem's last two lines?
14 What is the theme of this poem?

Roger McGough has some fun as he describes Batman and Robin, the famous crime fighters, getting ready for bed.

Goodbat Nightman

God bless all policemen
and fighters of crime,
May thieves go to jail
for a very long time.

They've had a hard day
helping clean up the town.
Now they hang from the mantlepiece
both upside down.

A glass of warm blood
and then straight up the stairs,
Batman and Robin
are saying their prayers.

They've locked all the doors
and they've put out the bat,
Put on their batjamas
(They like doing that)

They've filled their batwater bottles
made their batbeds,
With two springy battresses
for sleepy batheads.

They're closing red eyes
and they're counting black sheep.
Batman and Robin
are falling asleep.

ROGER McGOUGH

This poem is all about pieces. Yet it is held together by the speaker's need to collect all kinds of fragments and join them in a poem.

Smithereens

I spend my days
collecting smithereens.
I find them on buses
in department stores
and on busy pavements.

At restaurant tables
I pick up the leftovers
of polite conversation.
At railway stations
the tearful debris
of parting lovers.

I pocket my eavesdroppings
and store them away.
I make things out of them.
Nice things, sometimes.
Sometimes odd, like this.

ROGER McGOUGH

'The Commission' brings us the contrasting images of those who live in poverty and affluence.

The Commission

In this poem there is a table
Groaning with food.
There is also a child
Groaning for lack of food.
The food is beautifully photographed
The meat more succulent
The fruit as juicy
As you are likely to see.
(The child is sketched in lightly
She is not important.)
The photograph is to be used
In a glossy magazine
As part of a campaign
Advertising after-dinner mints.

This evening the photographer
In receipt of his fee
Celebrates by dining with friends
In a famous West End restaurant.
Doodling on the napkin between courses
The photographer, always creative,
Draws a little Asian girl,
Naked, wide-eyed, pleading
The photographer is pleased.
He has an idea for the next commission,
The one for famine relief.
The tandoori arrives
He puts away his pen
And picks up a fork.

ROGER McGOUGH

Questions About Privilege

1 In what two different senses is the word 'groaning' used?
2 What words does the poet use to describe the taste of the food?
3 Why was the child 'sketched in lightly'?
4 What change of time and place occur in the second stanza?
5 Why does the photographer's celebration seem wrong to us?
6 What contradiction is there between what the photographer is drawing on and what he is drawing?
7 Why is the photographer pleased with his drawing?
8 What is the phrase 'famine relief' contrasted with in the poem's last three lines?
9 Why is the poem's title appropriate?
10 What issue in our society is this poem concerned with?
11 What impression does the poet give us of the photographer?
12 What is your attitude to the photographer?
13 What techniques has the poet used to convey his message to us?
14 What feelings in you has the poet aroused?

In 'Icarus Allsorts' the poet creates a frightening picture of death and destruction.

Icarus Allsorts

'A meteorite is reported to have landed
in New England. No damage is said . . . '

A littlebit of heaven fell
From out the sky one day
It landed in the ocean
Not so very far away
The General at the radar screen
Rubbed his hands with glee
And grinning pressed the button
That started World War Three

From every corner of the earth
Bombs began to fly
There were even missile jams
No traffic lights in the sky
In the time it takes to blow your nose
The people fell, the mushrooms rose

'House!' cried the fatlady
As the bingohall moved to various parts
of the town

'Raus!' cried the German butcher
as his shop came tumbling down

Philip was in the countinghouse
Counting out his money
The Queen was in the parlour
Eating bread and honey
When through the window
Flew a bomb
And made them go all funny

In the time it takes to draw a breath
Or eat a toadstool, instant death.

The rich
Huddled outside the doors of their fallout shelters
Like drunken carolsingers

The poor
Clutching shattered televisions
And last week's edition of T.V. Times
(but the very last)

Civil defence volunteers
With their tin hats in one hand
And their heads in the other

CND supporters
Their ban the bomb badges beginning to rust
Have scrawled 'I told you so' in the dust.

A littlebit of heaven fell
From out the sky one day
It landed in Vermont
North-Eastern U.S.A.
The general at the radar screen
He should have got the sack
But that wouldn't bring
Three thousand million, seven hundred
   and sixty-eight people back.
Would it?

ROGER McGOUGH

Thinking About Catastrophe

1 What comments would you make about the first two lines of the poem?
2 What is the meteorite described as in the second stanza?
3 What impression does the poet give you of the general?
4 What comparison does the poet use to make us aware of the huge numbers of missiles in the sky?
5 ' . . . the mushrooms rose'. What do the mushrooms represent?
6 Why does the poet focus on the disasters experienced by two ordinary individuals?
7 What kind of rhyme does the poet use to tell us how Philip and the Queen met their fate? What does the poet achieve by doing this?
8 What other word used previously in the poem, and suggesting death, does 'toadstool' recall?
9 What impression does the poet give us of the rich and poor?
10 How does the poet shock us when describing the civil defence volunteers ?
11 Icarus, in Greek myth, was the man who made wings of wax and flew out over the sea. He fell into the sea when the sun melted the wax. Why do you think 'Icarus' is used in the title? What other meaning can you hear when you read the title aloud?
12 How does the poet use humour in the poem? Why does he do so?
13 What is the poet's message in this poem?
14 What techniques has the poet used in this poem to make you aware of the horrors of war?

The 'nooligan' is a hooligan who's a tough no-nonsense kid, but honest.

Nooligan

I'm a nooligan
don't give a toss
in our class
I'm the boss
(well, one of them)

I'm a nooligan
got a nard'ead
step out of line
and youre dead
(well, bleedin)

I'm a nooligan
I spray me name
all over town
footballs me game
(well, watchin)

I'm a nooligan
violence is fun
gonna be a nassassin
or a nired gun
(well, a soldier)

ROGER McGOUGH

A boy suffers beatings from his father because it is part of the family tradition.

Beatings

My father beats me up
Just like his father did
And grandad he was beaten
by greatgrandad as a kid

From generation to generation
A poisoned apple passed along
Domestic daily cruelty
No one thinking it was wrong.

And it was:

Not the cursing and the bruising
The frustration and the fear
A normal child can cope with that
It grows easier by the year

But the ignorance, believing
That the child is somehow owned
Property paid for
Violence condoned.

ROGER McGOUGH

In this poem Roger McGough imagines the reception Jesus might get if he arrived
at an ordinary household looking a bit like a tramp.

Three Rusty Nails

Mother, there's a strange man
Waiting at the door
With a familiar sort of face
You feel you've seen before.

Says his name is Jesus
Can we spare a couple of bob
Says he's been made redundant
And now can't find a job.

Yes I think he is a foreigner
Egyptian or a Jew
Oh aye, and that reminds me
He'd like some water too.

Well shall I give him what he wants
Or send him on his way?
O.K. I'll give him 5p
Say that's all we've got today.

And I'll forget about the water
I suppose it's a bit unfair
But honest, he's filthy dirty
All beard and straggly hair.

* * *

Mother, he asked about the water
I said the tank had burst
Anyway I gave him the coppers
That seemed to quench his thirst.

He said it was little things like that
That kept him on the rails
Then he gave me his autographed picture
And these three rusty nails.

ROGER McGOUGH

Caring Questions

1 Who is the speaker in the poem?
2 How does the poet seize our attention at the beginning of the poem?
3 'Says he's been made redundant'. What do you think has made Jesus 'redundant'?
4 What does the speaker say that makes us realise that truth is not valued in the household?
5 What aspects of Jesus' appearance make an unfavourable impression on the child?
6 Why has the poet called the poem 'Three Rusty Nails'?
7 What is the poet's message in this poem?
8 What feelings did you experience while reading this poem?
9 What techniques has the poet used to convey his message?
10 What comments would you make about the child's treatment of Jesus?

Such is the poet's hate of cabbage that he associates it with the worst things in life.

Cabbage

(After *I like that stuff* by Adrian Mitchell)

John Wayne died of it
People are terrified of it
   cancer
  I hate that stuff

Groucho was laid low with it
One in five of us will go with it
   heart attack
  I hate that stuff

Monroe's life turned sour on it
Hancock spent his last half hour on it
sleeping pills
I hate that stuff

Hendrix couldn't wait for it
Chemistshops stay open late for it
heroin
I hate that stuff

Mama Cass choked on it
Blankets get soaked in it
vomit
I hate that stuff

Women learn to live with it
No one can live without it
blood
I hate that stuff

Hospitals are packed with it
Saw my mother racked with it
pain
I hate that stuff ·

Few like to face the truth of it
We're the living proof of it
death
I hate that stuff

Schoolboys are forcefed with it
Cattle are served dead with it
cabbage
I hate that stuff

ROGER McGOUGH

7 Poets and Emotions

Love, hate, wonder, pity, anger, joy, disillusion and sadness are just a few of the emotions that inspire the poet. In turn, the poet aims to awaken our emotions and to make us feel what he or she feels. A good poem has the power to arouse, to excite, to inspire, to soothe. The tools the poets use are words, and with words they are able to work miracles. What could be more moving than Wilfred Owen's cry from the heart in the line 'What passing bells for those who die as cattle?', or Shakespeare's wonderment in 'Shall I compare thee to a summer's day?'

One of the most essential emotions we all experience is happiness. The poet Hugh Clement gives us his own particular recipe for it.

A Recipe for Happiness

An ounce of tv
A slice of disco dancing
Mix up well
With a squeeze of summer sunbaking
Half a cup of raging on Saturday night
And a large tablespoon of tickling the dog
Add a freshly picked ticket to the Grand Final
Stir in a splash of lazing around the pool
Add the mess of records and clothes on my bedroom floor
Bake slowly with a really good late night video
Add a pinch of messing round on lazy afternoons
Sprinkle with a couple of beaut barbecues
Pour in my oldest and most favourite jeans
Serve with a real good helping of family fun.
And there you are—the recipe's done.

HUGH CLEMENT

We cannot fail to be moved by Teresa de Jesús' anger about the suffering caused by poverty.

It Makes Me Furious!

When I come upon a child
sad, dirty, skinny
it makes me furious!

When I see food
tossed into the garbage
and a poor man poking around in case
it isn't rotten yet
it makes me furious!

When a toothless woman
hunched and old tells me
she's 26
it makes me furious!

When a little old man sleeps
by his final corner
it makes me furious!

When the poor wait
for the rich man to finish his business
to ask him
for last week's salary
it makes me furious!

TERESA DE JESÚS

'Milking Before Dawn' evokes the feelings and thoughts of a woman working in the night but experiencing the beauty of the dawn.

Milking Before Dawn

In the drifting rain the cows in the yard are as black
And wet and shiny as rocks in an ebbing tide;
But they smell of the soil, as leaves lying under the trees
Smell of the soil, damp and steaming, warm.
The shed is an island of light and warmth, the night
Was water-cold and starless out in the paddock.

Crouched on the stool hearing only the beat
The monotonous beat and hiss of the smooth machines,
The choking gasp of the cups and rattle of hooves,
How easy to fall asleep again, to think
Of the man in the city asleep; he does not feel
The night encircle him, the grasp of mud.

But now the hills in the east return, are soft.
And grey with mist, the night recedes, and the rain.
The earth as it turns towards the sun is young
Again, renewed, its history wiped away
Like the tears of a child. Can the earth be young again
And not the heart? Let the man in the city sleep.

RUTH DALLAS

Country Questions

1 What simile does the poet use to create in our minds a picture of how the cows in the yard look in the 'drifting rain'? Is it effective? Why?
2 What does the poet compare the smell of the cows to?
3 Why does the poet refer to the shed as 'an island of light and warmth'?
4 What impression of the night in the paddock does the poet evoke with the words 'water-cold and starless'?
5 What sound-words create an atmosphere of activity in the milking shed?
6 What feelings does the poet have as she crouches on the stool in the milking shed?
7 Why does the poet think of 'the man in the city'?
8 What do the words 'the grasp of mud' suggest about country life?
9 What is the meaning of 'But now the hills in the east return . . .'?
10 What does the poet imagine about the earth as it 'turns towards the sun'?
11 ' . . . Can the earth be young again/And not the heart?' What change in attitude seems to have taken place in the poet's mind?
12 Why do you think the poet is now content to 'Let the man in the city sleep'?
13 What was the poet's aim in writing this poem?
14 What has the poet revealed about her own character?

Few readers could fail to be moved by Francis Brett Young's description of the death of the quails flying northward from Africa to the south of Italy, where the peasants put out the eyes of a captured quail so that its cries may attract the flocks of spring migrants into their nets.

The Quails

All through the night
I have heard the stuttering call of a blind quail,
A caged decoy, under a cairn of stones,
Crying for light as the quails cry for love.

Other wanderers,
Northward from Africa winging on numb pinions,
   dazed
With beating winds and the sobbing of the sea,
Hear, in a breach of sweet land-herbage, the call
Of the blind one, their sister . . .
Hearing, their fluttered hearts
Take courage, and they wheel in their dark flight,
Knowing that their toil is over, dreaming to see
The white stubbles of Abruzzi smitten with dawn,
And spilt grain lying in the furrows, the squandered gold
That is the delight of quails in their spring mating.

Land-scents grow keener,
Penetrating the dank and bitter odour of brine
That whitens their feathers;
Far below, the voice of their sister calls them
To plenty, and sweet water, and fulfilment.
Over the pallid margin of dim seas breaking,
Over the thickening in the darkness that is land,
They fly. Their flight is ended. Wings beat no more,
Downward they drift, one by one, like dark petals,
Slowly, listlessly falling
Into the mouth of horror:
The nets . . .
Where men come trampling and crying with bright
   lanterns,
Plucking their weak, entangled claws from the meshes
   of net,
Clutching the soft brown bodies mottled with olive,
Crushing the warm, fluttering flesh, in hands stained
   with blood,
Till their quivering hearts are stilled, and the bright eyes
That are like a polished agate, glaze in death.

But the blind one, in her wicker cage, without ceasing
Haunts this night of spring with her stuttering call,
Knowing nothing of the terror that walks in darkness,
Knowing only that some cruelty has stolen the light
That is life, and that she must cry until she dies.

I, in the darkness,
Heard, and my heart grew sick. But I know that
   to-morrow
A smiling peasant will come with a basket of quails
Wrapped in vine-leaves, prodding them with blood-
   stained fingers,
Saying, 'Signore, you must cook them thus, and thus,
With a sprig of basil inside them.' And I shall thank him,
Carrying the piteous carcases into the kitchen
Without a pang, without shame.

'Why should I be ashamed? Why should I rail
Against the cruelty of men? Why should I pity,
Seeing that there is no cruelty which men can imagine
To match the subtle dooms that are wrought against
   them
By blind spores of pestilence: seeing that each of us,
Lured by dim hopes, flutters in the toils of death
On a cold star that is spinning blindly through space
Into the nets of time?'

So cried I, bitterly thrusting pity aside,
Closing my lids to sleep. But sleep came not,
And pity, with sad eyes,
Crept to my side, and told me
That the life of all creatures is brave and pityful
Whether they be men, with dark thoughts to vex them,
Or birds, wheeling in the swift joys of flight,
Or brittle ephemerids, spinning to death in the haze
Of gold that quivers on dim evening waters;

Nor would she be denied.
The harshness died
Within me, and my heart
Was caught and fluttered like the palpitant heart
Of a brown quail, flying
To the call of her blind sister
And death, in the spring night.

FRANCIS BRETT YOUNG

Feeling Compassion for Quails

1 What situation is the poet describing in the first stanza?
2 What difficulties have been experienced by the quails as they fly from Africa?
3 How do the quails react to the 'call of the blind one'?
4 'Downward they drift, one by one, like dark petals'. Why does the poet compare the quails to dark petals?
5 'Into the mouth of horror'. Explain the effectiveness of the poet's use of personification.
6 What do the words 'trampling', 'plucking', 'clutching' and 'crushing' reveal about the men?
7 What do the words 'soft', 'fluttering' and 'quivering' reveal about the quails?
8 What feelings does the poet arouse in you with his description ' . . . the bright eyes/That are like a polished agate, glaze in death'?
9 ' . . . she must cry until she dies'. What are your feelings towards 'the blind one'?
10 ' . . . my heart grew sick'. What does the poet reveal about himself?
11 ' . . . prodding them with bloodstained fingers'. Why is the poet aware of the peasant's fingers?
12 In what ways, according to the poet, are the lives of men similar to the lives of the quails?
13 What was the poet's purpose in writing this poem?
14 What techniques has the poet used to arouse your emotions?

Dylan Thomas urges his father not to surrender tamely to death.

Do Not Go Gentle into That Good Night

Do not go gentle into that good night,
Old age should burn and rave at close of day;
Rage, rage against the dying of the light.

Though wise men at their end know dark is right,
Because their words have forked no lightning they
Do not go gentle into that good night.

Good men, the last wave by, crying how bright
Their frail deeds might have danced in a green bay,
Rage, rage against the dying of the light.

Wild men who caught and sang the sun in flight,
And learn, too late, they grieved it on its way,
Do not go gentle into that good night.

Grave men, near death, who see with blinding sight
Blind eyes could blaze like meteors and be gay,
Rage, rage against the dying of the light.

And you, my father, there on the sad height,
Curse, bless, me now with your fierce tears, I pray.
Do not go gentle into that good night.
Rage, rage against the dying of the light.

DYLAN THOMAS

Understanding the Rage

1 When the poet uses the words 'that good night', he is referring to death. What is the poet urging his father to do in the first line of the poem?
2 What words in the second line have a similar meaning to 'that good night'?
3 What does the poet mean by 'burn and rave'?
4 What does the poet achieve by repeating the word 'rage'?
5 What do you think the poet means by 'the dying of the light'?
6 What point of view is the poet putting forward in the first stanza?
7 When the poet uses the word 'dark', he is referring to death. What is the meaning of 'Though wise men at their end know dark is right'?
8 Why, according to Dylan Thomas, don't wise men die peacefully?
9 What is the meaning of the metaphor 'the last wave by'?
10 How, according to the poet, do good men die? Why is this so?
11 'Wild men who caught and sang the sun in flight'. What is the poet telling us here about the lives of wild men?

12 How do wild men die?
13 Why do 'grave' (wise in a serious way) men regret the approach of death?
14 In the final stanza, the poet turns again to his ageing father. Why do you think he urges his father to both 'curse' and 'bless' him?
15 Why do you think the poet wants his father to 'rage' against approaching death?
16 What feelings has Dylan Thomas revealed in this poem?

The death of a loved one is always difficult to accept. In 'Until Gran Died', the poet shows us the traumatic effect of a grandmother's death upon a child.

Until Gran Died

The minnows I caught
lived for a few days in a jar
then floated side-up on the surface.
We buried them beneath the hedge.
I didn't cry, but felt sad inside.

I thought
I could deal with funerals,
that is until Gran died.

The goldfish I kept in a bowl
passed away with old age.
Mum wrapped him in newspaper
and we buried him next to a rose bush.
I didn't cry, but felt sad inside.

I thought
I could deal with funerals,
that is until Gran died.

My cat lay stiff in a shoe box
after being hit by a car.
Dad dug a hole and we buried her
under the apple tree.
I didn't cry, but felt *very* sad inside.

I thought
I could deal with funerals,
that is until Gran died.

And when she died
I went to the funeral
with relations dressed in black.
They cried, and so did I.
Salty tears ran down my face. Oh, how I cried.

Yes, I thought
I could deal with funerals,
that is until Gran died.

She was buried in a graveyard
and even the sky wept that day
Rain fell and fell and fell,
and thunder sobbed far away across the town.
I cried and I cried.

I thought
I could deal with funerals,
that is until Gran
died.

KIT WRIGHT

Considering Until Gran Died

1 From whose viewpoint is this poem written?
2 Why does the speaker keep repeating 'I thought/I could deal with funerals,/ that is until Gran died'?
3 How do you know that the cat meant more to the speaker than the minnows and the goldfish?
4 '. . . the sky wept that day'. Explain the effectiveness of the poet's use of personification.
5 'Rain fell and fell and fell'. What does the repetition of 'fell' achieve?
6 '. . . thunder sobbed far away across the town'. What does the poet achieve by making the thunder seem human?
7 The speaker repeats 'I cried'. Why?
8 The poem ends with the word 'died' on a line by itself. Why do you think the poet does this?
9 The language used in this poem is very simple. Why is this so?
10 What emotions are revealed in this poem?
11 What was the poet's purpose in this poem?
12 What techniques has the poet used to achieve his purpose?

The poet has been greatly affected by capturing such a beautiful creature as the trout.

The Trout

Flat on the bank I parted
Rushes to ease my hands
In the water without a ripple
And tilt them slowly downstream
To where he lay, light as a leaf,
In his fluid sensual dream.

Bodiless lord of creation
I hung briefly about him
Savouring my own absence
Senses expanding in the slow
Motion, the photographic calm
That grows before action.

As the curve of my hands
Swung under his body
He surged, with visible pleasure.
I was so preternaturally close
I could count every stipple
But still cast no shadow, until

The two palms crossed in a cage
Under the lightly pulsing gills.
Then (entering my own enlarged
Shape, which rode on the water)
I gripped. To this day I can
Taste his terror on my hands.

JOHN MONTAGUE

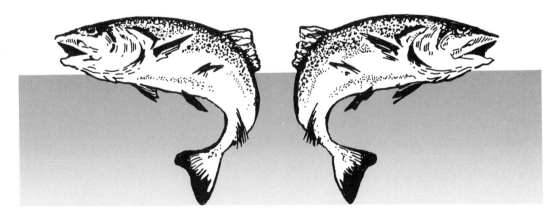

Capturing The Trout

  1 What situation is the poet describing at the beginning of the poem?
  2 How does the poet suggest the weightlessness of the trout in the water?
  3 Why does the poet refer to himself as 'bodiless'?
  4 In what ways is the poet 'lord of creation'?
  5 What does the poet mean by 'Savouring my own absence'?
  6 What feeling did the trout experience when the poet first swung his hands under the trout's body?
  7 How does the poet convince us that he was exceedingly close to the trout?
  8 'But still cast no shadow'. Why was this important for the poet?
  9 'Then (entering my own enlarged/Shape, which rode on water)'. What is happening here?
 10 'I gripped'. What feeling did the trout experience?
 11 What contrast is there between the scene at the beginning of the poem and the final scene?
 12 What are your feelings about the catching of the trout?
 13 Do you think this poem could have been written from personal experience? Why or why not?
 14 What was the poet's purpose in writing this poem?

8 Ted Hughes

Life and Background of Ted Hughes

Ted Hughes was born in 1930 in the small town of Mytholmroyd in Yorkshire on the slopes of the Pennines. It was the same sort of industrial area in the midst of tracts of natural beauty that D. H. Lawrence knew so well.

Ted Hughes went to school at Mexborough Grammar School and was later educated at Cambridge University. Ted, as a boy and young teenager, spent his time capturing and studying animals and birds, and from them came both his inspiration and his need to write poetry. In *Poetry in the Making*, Ted Hughes has given us a clear picture of the influence nature had on his need to write poetry.

> In a way, I suppose, I think of poems as a sort of animal. They have their own life, like animals, by which I mean that they seem quite separate from any person, even from their author, and nothing can be added to them or taken away without maiming and perhaps even killing them. And they have a certain wisdom. They know something special . . . something perhaps which we are very curious to learn . . . It was years before I wrote what you could call an animal poem and several more years before it occurred to me that my writing poems might be partly a continuation of my earlier pursuit. Now I have no doubt. The special kind of excitement, the slightly mesmerised and quite involuntary concentration with which you make out the stirrings of a new poem in your mind, then the outline, the mass and colour and clean final form of it, the unique living reality of it in the midst of the general lifelessness, all that is too familiar to mistake. This is hunting and the poem is a new species of creature, a new specimen of the life outside your own.

For Ted Hughes the conventional side of his life was unsatisfactory. He tried numerous jobs such as gardening and caretaking. However, when the poetry he had been writing with increasing fervour was published in his first book, *The Hawk in the Rain*, his reputation as a poet was ensured. He married the American poet, Sylvia Plath in 1956.

Ted Hughes has written other books of poetry including poems for children in the popular *Meet My Folks*. He has also written talks for the BBC about the origins and creation of poetry.

The critic A. Alvarez has called Hughes 'a poet of the first importance'.

Features of Ted Hughes' Poetry

Themes

Ted Hughes commented about his own poetic inspiration: 'What excites my imagination is the war between vitality and death.' Many of his poems exhibit this 'war' by containing elements of shock and violence expressed in aggressive imagery because, to Hughes, violence was an essential part of the energy of life. The main theme of his poems is power — the kind of power in which violence is a central feature. The poem 'Bayonet Charge' illustrates this:

> Bullets smacking the belly out of the air —
> He lugged a rifle numbed as a smashed arm.

Subjects

The subjects of Hughes' poems are often wild creatures such as the jaguar, the hawk, the fox, the otter, or forces such as the wind that are like animals. These predators are active, defiant and untamed and cannot be conquered by the artificial society that humankind has built around itself. In his poetry, Hughes is sympathetic to the instinctive use of each creature's special life forces. Each animal or bird becomes a symbol of the struggle for life, and each is given a poem to itself so that its most vital qualities can be isolated and subjected to the power of the poet's imagination. The poem 'The Jaguar' shows this:

> His stride is wilderness of freedom:
> The world rolls under the long thrust of his heel.

The human subjects of Hughes' poems often exhibit some pure emotional quality such as courage or endurance. In 'The Retired Colonel', the colonel endures the society in which he is forced to live:

> Wife dead, daughters gone, lived on
> Honouring his own caricature.
> Shot through the heart with whisky wore
> The lurch like ancient courage, would not go down.

Style

Hughes' style of poetry writing is marked by the use of spare, tough words and the constant use of strangely violent phrases and unusual comparisons. There are typical examples of this in 'View of a Pig':

> Pigs must have hot blood, they feel like ovens.
> Their bite is worse than a horse's—
> They chop a half-moon clean out.
> They eat dead cinders, dead cats.

Sound words and phrases that mimic actions and feelings are important elements in Hughes' poetry. In this line from 'The Jaguar', the beat of the syllables makes us hear the pounding of the blood within the enraged jaguar's head:

> By the bang of blood in the brain deaf the ear.

An attribute of Ted Hughes' style that has been called 'verbal belligerence' especially contributes to the uniqueness of his poetry.

Here, Ted Hughes writes about the inspiration for his poem 'Wind'.

> One of the most striking features of weather is the wind. The wind, in all its phases, coming, here, going and gone, might be said to be one of the great subjects of poetry. Almost every poet, when he mentions the wind, touches one of his good moments of poetry. Why poets should be so interested in the wind, or the absence of it, is a bit of a mystery. Perhaps it represents simply inspiration. The Old Testament prophets were often carried off to their visions in a great wind, or heard extraordinary things out of unnatural stillness. A strong wind certainly stirs your mind up, as if it actually could enter your head, and sometimes on such occasions you get the feeling of having lost your bearings, and that something terrible is about to happen, almost as if it were the beginning of an earthquake.
>
> On and off I live in a house on top of a hill in the Pennines, where the wind blows without obstruction across the tops of the moors. I have experienced some gales in that house, and here is a poem I once wrote about one of them. The grass of the fields there is of a particularly brilliant watered green, and the stone walls of the enclosures that cover the hillsides like a great net thrown over whales, look coal black. The poem is called simply: 'Wind'.

Wind

This house has been far out at sea all night,
The woods crashing through darkness, the booming hills,
Winds stampeding the fields under the window
Floundering black astride and blinding wet

Till day rose; then under an orange sky
The hills had new places, and wind wielded
Blade-light, luminous black and emerald,
Flexing like the lens of a mad eye.

At noon I scaled along the house-side as far as
The coal-house door. Once I looked up—
Through the brunt wind that dented the balls of my eyes
The tent of the hills drummed and strained its guyrope,

The fields quivering, the skyline a grimace,
At any second to bang and vanish with a flap:
The wind flung a magpie away and a black-
Back gull bent like an iron bar slowly. The house

Rang like some fine green goblet in the note
That any second would shatter it. Now deep
In chairs, in front of the great fire, we grip
Our hearts and cannot entertain book, thought,

Or each other. We watch the fire blazing,
And feel the roots of the house move, but sit on,
Seeing the windows tremble to come in,
Hearing the stones cry out under the horizons.

TED HUGHES

The retired colonel sees himself as the protector of the British imperial era. However, to some he seems to be only a rare and curious relic.

The Retired Colonel

Who lived at the top end of our street
Was a Mafeking stereotype, ageing.
Came, face pulped scarlet with kept rage,
For air past our gate.
Barked at his dog knout and whipcrack
And cowerings of India: five or six wars
Stiffened in his reddened neck;
Brow bull-down for the stroke.

Wife dead, daughters gone, lived on
Honouring his own caricature.
Shot through the heart with whisky wore
The lurch like ancient courage, would not go down
While posterity's trash stood, held
His habits like a last stand, even
As if he had Victoria rolled
In a Union Jack in that stronghold.

And what if his sort should vanish?
The rabble starlings roar upon
Trafalgar. The man-eating British lion
By a pimply age brought down.
Here's his head mounted, though only in rhymes,
Beside the head of the last English
Wolf (those starved gloomy times!)
And the last sturgeon of Thames.

TED HUGHES

Military Matters

1 Mafeking, a town in South Africa, was the scene of a British victory in the Boer War. What do you think the poet means when he calls the colonel 'a Mafeking stereotype'?
2 What impression does 'face pulped scarlet' give of the colonel's face?
3 What does 'Brow bull-down for the stroke' indicate about the colonel's temperament?
4 'Wife dead, daughters gone'. Why has the poet mentioned this?
5 How did the colonel honour 'his own caricature'?
6 'Shot through the heart with whisky'. What does this reveal about the colonel?
7 Who do you think 'posterity's trash' would be for the colonel?
8 '. . . held/His habits like a last stand'. What does this show about the colonel's character?
9 What symbols does the poet associate with the colonel in the second stanza?
10 What change of mood occurs in the third stanza?
11 Who threatens the imperial symbol, the British lion?
12 How is the poet's idea of the colonel as a relic presented in the second half of the last stanza?
13 Why do you think Ted Hughes was inspired to use the retired colonel as a subject for a poem?
14 What is your attitude to the colonel?
15 What is the theme of this poem?

'Bayonet Charge' is a poem about a few moments of shattering terror experienced by a soldier as he makes a bayonet charge.

Bayonet Charge

Suddenly he awoke and was running—raw
In raw-seamed hot khaki, his sweat heavy,
Stumbling across a field of clods towards a green hedge
That dazzled with rifle fire, hearing
Bullets smacking the belly out of the air—
He lugged a rifle numb as a smashed arm;
The patriotic tear that had brimmed in his eye
Sweating like molten iron from the centre of his chest,—

In bewilderment then he almost stopped—
In what cold clockwork of the stars and the nations
Was he the hand pointing that second? He was running
Like a man who has jumped up in the dark and runs
Listening between his footfalls for the reason
Of his still running, and his foot hung like
Statuary in mid-stride. Then the shot-slashed furrows

Threw up a yellow hare that rolled like a flame
And crawled in a threshing circle, its mouth wide
Open silent, its eyes standing out.
He plunged past with his bayonet toward the green hedge,
King, honour, human dignity, etcetera
Dropped like luxuries in a yelling alarm
To get out of that blue crackling air
His terror's touchy dynamite.

TED HUGHES

Deadly Questions

1 What does the poet achieve by beginning 'Bayonet Charge' with the word 'suddenly'?
2 How is the soldier's discomfort and fear conveyed to us in the poem's first two lines?
3 How does the poet indicate the intensity of the rifle fire from the green hedge?
4 'Bullets smacking the belly out of the air'. How does the poet indicate the noise and force of the bullets?
5 'He lugged a rifle numb as a smashed arm'. What is the poet showing about the rifle?
6 What words show the loss of the soldier's patriotism?
7 What thoughts does the soldier have in the second stanza?
8 What is the meaning of 'shot-slashed furrows'?

9 What impression has the poet given of the hare?
10 'He plunged past'. What does the word 'plunged' convey about the soldier?
11 'King, honour, human dignity, etcetera'. How does the word 'etcetera' affect the importance of the other words in the line?
12 Why were such ideals 'dropped like luxuries' by the soldier?
13 What image of the soldier is presented to us in the poem's last line?
14 What is the poet showing you about war through the experiences of a single soldier?

Ted Hughes describes the conflict between a man and his wife.

Her Husband

Comes home dull with coal-dust deliberately
To grime the sink and foul towels and let her
Learn with scrubbing brush and scrubbing board
The stubborn character of money.

And let her learn through what kind of dust
He has earned his thirst and the right to quench it
And what sweat he has exchanged for his money
And the blood-count of money. He'll humble her

With new light on her obligations.
The fried, woody chips, kept warm two hours in the oven,
Are only part of her answer.
Hearing the rest, he slams them to the fire-back

And is away round the house-end singing
'Come back to Sorrento' in a voice
Of resounding corrugated iron.
Her back has bunched into a hump as an insult . . .

For they will have their rights.
Their jurors are to be assembled
From the little crumbs of soot. Their brief
Goes straight up to heaven and nothing more is heard of it.

TED HUGHES

Quarrelsome Considerations

1 What image of the husband does the poet present in the first line of the poem?
2 What is the husband's attitude towards his wife in the first stanza?
3 What does the poet achieve by the repetition of the word 'scrubbing'?
4 What is the meaning of 'The stubborn character of money'?
5 What idea links the first and second stanzas?
6 What impression does the poet give of the husband in the second stanza?
7 What do you think is meant by 'the blood-count of money'?
8 'He'll humble her'. What does this show about the husband's attitude to his wife?
9 What do 'the fried, woody chips' indicate to the husband about his wife's attitude to him?
10 How does the husband indicate his feelings in the third stanza?
11 ' . . . in a voice/Of resounding corrugated iron'. What does this image tell us about the sound and feeling in the husband's voice?
12 'Her back has bunched into a hump'. What do these words show about the wife?
13 How does the poet tell us that the quarrel between husband and wife is insignificant?
14 What is Hughes' purpose in this poem?

In 'Hawk Roosting', the hawk reveals its desire for ruthless power and violence.

Hawk Roosting

I sit in the top of the wood, my eyes closed.
Inaction, no falsifying dream
Between my hooked head and hooked feet:
Or in sleep rehearse perfect kills and eat.

The convenience of the high trees!
The air's buoyancy and the sun's ray
Are of advantage to me;
And the earth's face upward for my inspection.

My feet are locked upon the rough bark.
It took the whole of Creation
To produce my foot, my each feather:
Now I hold Creation in my foot

Or fly up, and revolve it all slowly—
I kill where I please because it is all mine.
There is no sophistry in my body:
My manners are tearing off heads—

The allotment of death.
For the one path of my flight is direct
Through the bones of the living.
No arguments assert my right:

The sun is behind me.
Nothing has changed since I began.
My eye has permitted no change.
I am going to keep things like this.

TED HUGHES

Appreciating Hawk Roosting

The poem's title, 'Hawk Roosting', prepares us for a still-life study of the bird as opposed to one of the predatory bird in flight. Many of Ted Hughes' poems have as their subjects predatory animals and birds. Hughes was fascinated by the latent feeling of violence and power in untamed creatures. In his poems, animals and birds are not decorative or incidental but central symbols of vitality.

In 'Hawk Roosting' the hawk itself is the speaker in the poem. Its monologue of plain, forceful words matches the arrogant frankness of the speaker.

The first line sets the scene. The hawk is perched in a place that is superior in height to all its surroundings. The hawk's closed eyes suggest sleep, but it is really a dreamless state of mind because dreams would interfere with the ominous function of the 'hooked head and hooked feet' — symbols of the pursuit and death of a prey. The repetition of 'hooked' emphasises the deadly nature of the hawk even in repose.

In the second stanza there is a change in emphasis from the bird itself to its surroundings. The hawk does not take pleasure in 'the high trees', 'the air's buoyancy' or 'the sun's ray'. They are there for the hawk's 'convenience' and 'advantage'. Even the scene spread before the hawk is subjected only to the cold word 'inspection'.

The focus in the third stanza is on the hawk's feet — its killing instruments. The hawk's gloating tone is pronounced in this stanza. Its feet and the feathers have been produced by Creation but instead of showing gratitude, the hawk gloats over its seeming ability to dominate Creation itself. 'Now I hold Creation in my foot'.

In the fourth stanza the hawk arrogantly senses that, in flight, Creation revolves for it 'because it is all mine'. Creation is only a killing ground for the hawk and like the air and sun simply exists as a tool that the hawk will use to fulfil its destiny. The hawk's purpose is single-minded and there is never any need to balance right and wrong. The only argument acceptable to the hawk is catching prey and 'tearing off heads'. The hawk's ruthlessness is paramount. Here is absolute power and violence.

In the fifth stanza the hawk makes its philosophy of life abundantly clear. Other creatures must die in order that it may live. The hawk's violent power is not subject to any check or hesitation. The one path of the hawk's flight is 'through the bones of the living'; it is like an arrow or a bullet that destroys. Might is right and the hawk needs no arguments to justify its actions.

In the poem's last stanza the hawk's arrogance admits no bounds. While it lives it controls. It is at the height of creation and is so sure of its power that nothing will be permitted to challenge it.

The poet depicts an otter as a vital and versatile animal with many skills and a magical affinity with its environment. Unfortunately, its fate is death at the hands of human beings.

An Otter

I

      Underwater eyes, an eel's
Oil of water body, neither fish nor beast is the otter:
   Four-legged yet water-gifted, to outfish fish;
      With webbed feet and long ruddering tail
      And a round head like an old tomcat.

      Brings the legend of himself
From before wars or burials, in spite of hounds and vermin-poles;
   Does not take root like the badger. Wanders, cries;
      Gallops along land he no longer belongs to;
      Re-enters the water by melting.

      Of neither water nor land. Seeking
Some world lost when first he dived, that he cannot come at since,
   Takes his changed body into the holes of lakes;
      As if blind, cleaves the stream's push till he licks
      The pebbles of the source; from sea

      To sea crosses in three nights
Like a king in hiding. Crying to the old shape of the starlit land,
   Over sunken farms where the bats go round,
      Without answer. Till light and birdsong come
      Walloping up roads with the milk wagon.

II

The hunt's lost him. Pads on mud,
Among sedges, nostrils a surface bead,
The otter remains, hours. The air,
Circling the globe, tainted and necessary,

Mingling tobacco-smoke, hounds and parsley,
Comes carefully to the sunk lungs.
So the self under the eye lies,
Attendant and withdrawn. The otter belongs

In double robbery and concealment—
From water that nourishes and drowns, and from land
That gave him his length and the mouth of the hound.
He keeps fat in the limpid integument

Reflections live on. The heart beats thick,
Big trout muscle out of the dead cold;
Blood is the belly of logic; he will lick
The fishbone bare. And can take stolen hold

On a bitch otter in a field full
Of nervous horses, but linger nowhere.
Yanked above hounds, reverts to nothing at all,
To this long pelt over the back of a chair.

TED HUGHES

Reflections on An Otter

1 What does the poet mean by 'water-gifted'?
2 What is the meaning of 'to outfish fish'?
3 What general impression of the otter does the poet give us in the first stanza?
4 How does the poet suggest that the otter has always been a survivor?
5 'Re-enters the water by melting'. What does the poet mean by 'melting'?
6 What words in the fourth stanza indicate the hopelessness of the otter's search for 'some world lost'?
7 'Walloping up roads'. What action does the word 'walloping' describe?
8 How does the poet emphasise the otter's sense of smell?
9 How do water and land contribute to the otter's survival?
10 ' . . . but linger nowhere'. What does this show about the otter?
11 The otter 'reverts to nothing at all'. What does the poet mean?
12 What is the poet's attitude to the otter?

The latent power and violence of the captive jaguar cannot be tamed by crowds or the bars of his cage.

The Jaguar

The apes yawn and adore their fleas in the sun.
The parrots shriek as if they were on fire, or strut
Like cheap tarts to attract the stroller with the nut.
Fatigued with indolence, tiger and lion

Lie still as the sun. The boa-constrictor's coil
Is a fossil. Cage after cage seems empty, or
Stinks of sleepers from the breathing straw.
It might be painted on a nursery wall.

But who runs like the rest past these arrives
At a cage where the crowd stands, stares, mesmerised,
As a child at a dream, at a jaguar hurrying enraged
Through prison darkness after the drills of his eyes

On a short fierce fuse. Not in boredom—
The eye satisfied to be blind in fire,
By the bang of blood in the brain deaf the ear—
He spins from the bars, but there's no cage to him

More than to the visionary his cell:
His stride is wilderness of freedom:
The world rolls under the long thrust of his heel.
Over the cage floor the horizons come.

TED HUGHES

Ted Hughes lays out the hunt for our inspection as it courses through the complex life of the countryside.

Foxhunt

Two days after Xmas, near noon, as I listen
The hounds behind the hill
Are changing ground, a cloud of excitements,
Their voices like rusty, reluctant
Rolling stock being shunted. The hunt
Has tripped over a fox
At the threshold of the village. A crow in the fir
Is inspecting his nesting site, and he expostulates
At the indecent din. A blackbird
Starts up its cat-alarm. The grey-cloud mugginess
Of the year in its pit trying to muster
Enough energy to start opening again
Roars distantly. Everything sodden. The fox
Is flying, taking his first lesson
From the idiot pack-noise, the puppyish whine-yelps
Curling up like hounds' tails, and the gruff military barkers:
A machine with only two products:
Dog-shit and dead foxes. Lorry engines
As usual modulating on the main street hill
Complicate the air, and the fox runs in a suburb
Of indifferent civilised noises. Now the yelpings
Enrich their brocade, thickening closer
In the maze of wind-currents. The orchards
And the hedges stand in coma. The pastures
Have got off so far lightly, are firm, cattle
Still nose hopefully, as if spring might be here
Missing out winter. Big lambs
Are organising their gangs in gateways. The fox
Hangs his silver tongue in the world of noise
Over his spattering paws. Will he run
Till his muscles suddenly turn to iron,
Till blood froths his mouth as his lungs tatter,
Till his feet are raw blood-sticks and his tail
Trails thin as a rat's? Or will he
Make a mistake, jump the wrong way, jump right
Into the hound's mouth? As I write this down
He runs still fresh, with all his chances before him.

TED HUGHES

Ted Hughes views a dead pig and describes his reaction to it.

View of a Pig

The pig lay on a barrow dead.
It weighed, they said, as much as three men.
Its eyes closed, pink white eyelashes.
Its trotters stuck straight out.

Such weight and thick pink bulk
Set in death seemed not just dead.
It was less than lifeless, further off.
It was like a sack of wheat.

I thumped it without feeling remorse.
One feels guilty insulting the dead,
Walking on graves. But this pig
Did not seem able to accuse.

It was too dead. Just so much
A poundage of lard and pork.
Its last dignity had entirely gone.
It was not a figure of fun.

Too dead now to pity.
To remember its life, din, stronghold
Of earthly pleasure as it had been,
Seemed a false effort, and off the point.

Too deadly factual. Its weight
Oppressed me—how could it be moved?
And the trouble of cutting it up!
The gash in its throat was shocking., but not pathetic.

Once I ran at a fair in the noise
To catch a greased piglet
That was faster and nimbler than a cat,
Its squeal was the rending of metal.

Pigs must have hot blood, they feel like ovens.
Their bite is worse than a horse's—
They chop a half-moon clean out.
They eat cinders, dead cats.

> Distinctions and admirations such
> As this one was long finished with.
> I stared at it a long time. They were going to scald it,
> Scald it and scour it like a doorstep.

TED HUGHES

Focus on View of a Pig

1 'Its trotters stuck straight out'. What is the effect of the alliteration of the 's' and 't' letters in this line?
2 Why is 'like a sack of wheat' an effective comparison?
3 Explain the meaning of 'I thumped it without feeling remorse'.
4 Why does the poet keep repeating the word 'dead'?
5 Why do you think Hughes describes his earlier experience with a greased piglet?
6 To what noise does the poet compare the piglet's squeal?
7 What evidence can you find to show that Hughes has closely observed a greased piglet running at a fair?
8 What are the poet's feelings towards the dead pig?
9 What is the effect of the repetition of the word 'scald' at the end of the last stanza?
10 Why do you think the poet has likened the scouring of the pig to that of a doorstep?
11 Do you think the title 'View of a Pig' is suitable for this poem? Why or why not?
12 What words evoke the atmosphere of death throughout the poem?
13 What is Ted Hughes' purpose in this poem?
14 What are your feelings towards the pig?

9 Oodgeroo of the Tribe Noonuccal

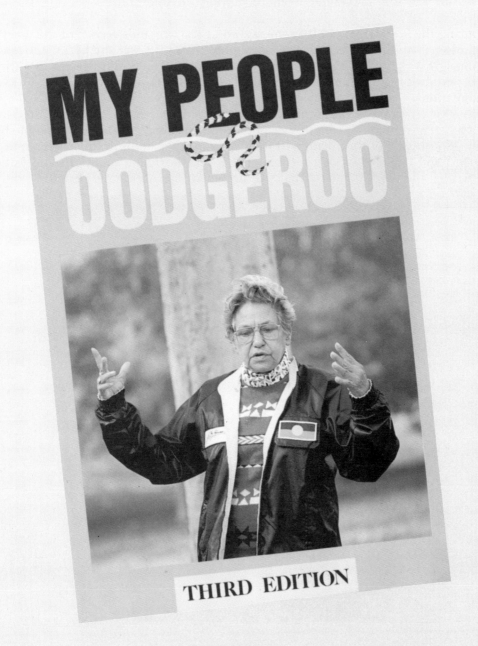

Life Study of Oodgeroo

Oodgeroo (formerly Kath Walker) was born in 1920. She spent her childhood on Stradbroke Island off the Queensland coast near Brisbane. She is of the Noonuccal tribe and her totem is the carpet snake.

Oodgeroo left school at thirteen to help support her family and worked as a domestic servant in Brisbane. Her ambition when she was sixteen was to become a nurse but she was prevented from beginning nursing studies because she was Aboriginal.

During the Second World War she served in the women's service of the army as a telephonist and later became a stenographer. After the war she became involved in Aboriginal rights, working determinedly to correct such injustices to the Aboriginal people as the removal of Aboriginal children from their parents to assist 'assimilation'.

Oodgeroo turned to poetry to gain a wider audience for her work in the black civil rights movement. She wrote her poems to show that, although her people had been dispossessed of their land and their culture, their faith in the earth could be retained and could nourish a rebirth of the old Aboriginal traditions and values. She wrote: 'the earth is the permanent mother of the Aboriginal people'.

Her first volume of poetry, *We Are Going*, was published in 1964. This was the first book of poems by an Aboriginal Australian to be published. Since then she has written many passionate poems attacking the colour bar and the degradation of the Aboriginal way of life.

Since 1974, Oodgeroo has been the inspiration behind 'Moongalba', an educational and cultural centre on Stradbroke Island where Aboriginal, Islander and white children can all experience the natural way of life of the first Australians.

Features of Oodgeroo's Poetry

Oodgeroo has described her poetry as 'civil rightish, plain and simple'. A unifying feature of her poetry is that all her poems possess Aboriginal themes. One of the themes that often appears in her poetry is the nostalgia for lost Aboriginal times. Here are the opening lines from 'Then and Now' in which this theme is well illustrated:

> In my dreams I hear my tribe
> Laughing as they hunt and swim.

Another theme that dominates many of Oodgeroo's poems is anger at white society's cruel attitude to her people. In 'Colour Bar', she expresses this anger in bitter tones:

> The colour bar! It shows the meaner mind
> Of moron kind.

In 'Civilisation', white society's values are questioned:

> But remember, white men, if life is for happiness,
> You, too, surely, have much to change.

The optimism of Oodgeroo's poetry is revealed when her poems express a vision of the future when white and Aboriginal races will live in mutual harmony and respect. Here is an example from 'A Song of Hope':

> To our fathers' fathers
>   The pain, the sorrow;
> To our children's children
>   The glad tomorrow.

Oodgeroo is now respected as a writer who has presented and explained the essence of her Aboriginal heritage in her poetry.

In 'Then and Now', the poet dreams of the old tribal Australia. Her dream is shattered by the harsh sights and sounds of white civilisation.

Then and Now

In my dreams I hear my tribe
Laughing as they hunt and swim,
But dreams are shattered by rushing car,
By grinding tram and hissing train,
And I see no more my tribe of old
As I walk alone in the teeming town.

I have seen corroboree
Where that factory belches smoke;
Here where they have memorial park
One time lubras dug for yams;
One time our dark children played
There where the railway yards are now,
And where I remember the didgeridoo
Calling to us to dance and play,
Offices now, neon lights now,
Bank and shop and advertisement now,
Traffic and trade of the busy town.

No more woomera, no more boomerang,
No more playabout, no more the old ways.
Children of nature we were then,
No clocks hurrying crowds to toil.
Now I am civilised and work in the white way,
Now I have dress, now I have shoes:
'Isn't she lucky to have a good job!'
Better when I had only a dillybag.
Better when I had nothing but happiness.

OODGEROO OF THE TRIBE NOONUCCAL

Appreciating Then and Now

1 What is the poet's mood as the poem begins?
2 How does the mood suddenly change?
3 What words in the first stanza create the harsh-sounding nature of twentieth century living?
4 In the first stanza's last line, what does 'teeming' suggest about the town that the word 'crowded' would not convey?
5 'Where that factory belches smoke'. What visual image does the word 'belches' call up in your mind?

6 What two ways of life are contrasted in the second stanza?
7 What does the poet mean by 'Children of nature we were then'?
8 What is the effect of the repetition of 'no more' in the final stanza?
9 'Isn't she lucky to have a good job!' How does the poet react to these words?
10 'Better when I had nothing but happiness'. Why is this an effective ending to the poem?
11 What feelings does the poet reveal in her poem?
12 What overall impression has the poet given us of white 'civilisation'?
13 Why is 'Then and Now' a suitable title for the poem?
14 What is the poet's aim in this poem?

The poet identifies with the courage of the wild creatures who defy the human beings who hunt them down.

Freedom

For Vivian Charles

Brumby on the wide plain,
All men out to break you.
My warm fellow-feeling
Hopes they never take you!

Dingo on the lone ridge,
Fleeing as you spy them,
Every hand against you,
May you still defy them!

All things wild and tameless,
Hunted down and hated,
Something in my wild heart
With your own is mated.

Dingo, wild bushranger,
Brumby that they ban so,
May you still outmatch them,
May you foil the man-foe!

OODGEROO OF THE TRIBE NOONUCCAL

Civilisation brings change, but it is the purpose of civilisation that is questioned in this poem.

Civilisation

We who came late to civilisation,
Missing a gap of centuries,
When you came we marvelled and admired,
But with foreboding.
We had so little but we had happiness,
Each day a holiday,
For we were people before we were citizens,
Before we were ratepayers,
Tenants, customers, employees, parishioners.
How could we understand
White man's gradings, rigid and unquestioned,
Your sacred totems of Lord and Lady,
Highness and Holiness, Eminence, Majesty.
We could not understand
Your strange cult of uniformity,
This mass obedience to clocks, time-tables.
Puzzled, we wondered why
The importance to you, urgent and essential,
Of ties and gloves, shoe-polish, uniforms.
New to us were jails and orphanages,
Rents and taxes, banks and mortgages.
We who had so few things, the prime things,
We had no policemen, lawyers, middlemen,
Brokers, financiers, millionaires.
So they bewildered us, all the new wonders,
Stocks and shares, real estate,
Compound interest, sales and investments.
Oh, we have benefited, we have been lifted
With new knowledge, a new world opened.
Suddenly caught up in white man ways
Gladly and gratefully we accept,
And this is necessity.
But remember, white man, if life is for happiness,
You too, surely, have much to change.

OODGEROO OF THE TRIBE NOONUCCAL

Questioning Civilisation

1 What is the meaning of 'We who came late to civilisation'?
2 What mixed feelings did the Aboriginal people have towards the coming of white civilisation?
3 'Each day a holiday'. What does this suggest about the Aboriginal way of life?
4 'For we were people before we were citizens'. What does the poet mean?
5 What effect is the poet seeking to achieve by listing the possible social roles of a citizen in a civilised society?
6 Why do you think the tribal people were unable to understand 'This mass obedience to clocks, time-tables'?
7 How did the tribal people react to formal clothing?
8 What does the poet mean by 'the prime things'?
9 Why do you think the poet chose the world of finance to stand for 'all the new wonders'?
10 What is the poet's attitude towards the benefits of civilisation?
11 What warning does the poet give in the last two lines?
12 What do you think was the poet's purpose in writing this poem?
13 Why has the poet called her poem 'Civilisation'?
14 What contrast is there in the poem between the Aboriginal way of life and the white civilisation?
15 What feelings has the poet aroused in you?

The poet describes the violent destruction of the earth that is the inheritance of her people.

Time Is Running Out

The miner rapes
The heart of earth
With his violent spade.
Stealing, bottling her black blood
For the sake of greedy trade.
On his metal throne of destruction,
He labours away with a will,
Piling the mountainous minerals high
With giant tool and iron drill.

In his greedy lust for power,
He destroys old nature's will.
For the sake of the filthy dollar,
He dirties the nest he builds.
Well he knows that violence
Of his destructive kind
Will be violently written
Upon the sands of time.

But time is running out
And time is close at hand,
For the Dreamtime folk are massing
To defend their timeless land.
Come gentle black man
Show your strength;
Time to take a stand.
Make the violent miner feel
Your violent
Love of land.

OODGEROO OF THE TRIBE NOONUCCAL

The Earth — Thinking Deeper

1 What is the poet's attitude towards the miner?
2 How is personification used in the first five lines of the poem to picture the earth's plight?
3 What explanation does the poet give for the mining of the earth?
4 What do you think is the miner's 'metal throne of destruction'?
5 What is the meaning of 'He dirties the nest he builds'?
6 Explain the warning that is contained in the last two lines of the second stanza.
7 What change of mood occurs in the last stanza?
8 What does the poet mean by 'But time is running out/And time is close at hand'?
9 'For the Dreamtime folk are massing'. What meaning does 'massing' suggest that a word such as 'gathering' would not?
10 'Come gentle black man/Show your strength'. What contrast exists in these words?
11 How is the word 'violent' used in two different senses in the last three lines of the poem?
12 What does the poet achieve by the alliteration of the letter 'l' in 'Your violent/Love of land'?
13 What is the significance of the poem's title?
14 What do you think the poet wants you to believe and feel after reading this poem?

The poet thinks of painting as a lonely exploration of the artist's feelings free of the taint of reward and ambition.

Artist Son

My artist son,
Busy with brush, absorbed in more than play,
Untutored yet, striving alone to find
What colour and form can say,
Yours the deep human need,
The old compulsion, ever since man had mind
And learned to dream,
Adventuring, creative, unconfined.
Even in dim beginning days,
Long before written word was known,
Your fathers too fashioned their art
Who had but bark and wood and the cave stone.
Much you must learn from others, yes,
But copy none; follow no fashions, know
Art the adventurer his lone way
Lonely must go.
Paint joy, not pain,
Paint beauty and happiness for men,
Paint the rare insight glimpses that express
What tongue cannot or pen;
Not for reward, acclaim
That wins honour and opens doors,
Not as ambition toils for fame,
But as the lark sings and the eagle soars,
Make us songs in colour and line:
Painting is speech, painter and poet are one.
Paint what you feel more than the thing you see,
My artist son.

OODGEROO OF THE TRIBE NOONUCCAL

Considering the Future Artist

1 'My artist son'. What approach is the poet using in this poem?
2 What does the poet achieve by the alliteration of the letter 'b' in 'busy with brush'?
3 What is 'the old compulsion'?
4 What attitude does the poet have towards the human mind?
5 What does the poet show us about art in the 'dim beginning days'?
6 What advice does the poet give her son about learning from others?
7 How is 'Art' personified?
8 'Paint joy, not pain'. How does this line mark a change of mood in the poem?

9 What is achieved by the repetition of the word 'Paint'?
10 What should the painter strive to achieve?
11 The 'painter and poet are one'. Why is this so?
12 What is achieved in the poem by making the poem's last line the same as its first?
13 Give your opinion of the poet's achievement, pointing out what appeals to you in the poem.
14 What have you learnt about the poet's character and personal values from this poem?
15 What was the poet's aim in writing this poem?

The poet expresses her passionate feelings about the evil of racial prejudice in 'Colour Bar'.

Colour Bar

When vile men jeer because my skin is brown,
This I live down.

But when a taunted child comes home in
tears,
Fierce anger sears.

The colour bar! It shows the meaner mind
Of moron kind.

Men are but medieval yet, as long
As lives this wrong.

Could he but see, the colour-baiting clod
Is blaming God

Who made us all, and all His children He
Loves equally.

As long as brothers banned from brotherhood
You still exclude,

The Christianity you hold so high
Is but a lie,

Justice a cant of hypocrites, content
With precedent.

OODGEROO OF THE TRIBE NOONUCCAL

'Bwalla the Hunter' shows the struggle for survival of a nomadic Aboriginal family.

Bwalla the Hunter

In the hard famine time, in the long drought
Bwalla the hunter on walkabout,
Lubra and children following slow,
All proper hungry long time now.

No more kangaroo out on the plain,
Gone to other country where there was rain.
Couldn't find emu, couldn't find seed,
And the children all time cry for feed.

They saw great eagle come through the sky
To his big stick gunya in a gum near by,
Fine young wallaby carried in his feet:
He bring tucker for his kids to eat.

Big fella eagle circled slow,
Little fella eagles fed below.
'Gwa!' said Bwalla the hunter, 'he
Best fella hunter, better than me.'

He dropped his boomerang. 'Now I climb,
All share tucker in the hungry time.
We got younks too, we got need—
You make fire and we all have feed.'

Then up went Bwalla like a native cat,
All the blackfellows climb like that.
And when he look over big nest rim
Those young ones all sing out at him.

They flapped and spat, they snapped and clawed,
They plenty wild with him, my word,
They shrilled at tucker-thief big and brown,
But Bwalla took wallaby and then climbed down.

OODGEROO OF THE TRIBE NOONUCCAL

Old Willie Mackenzie was the last surviving member of the Darwarbada tribe whose territory was the Caboolture district. His Aboriginal name was Geerbe and the native bee was his tribal totem. He received his name, Willie Mackenzie, from the name of the white boss for whom his family worked.

Last of His Tribe

Change is the law. The new must oust the old.
I look at you and am back in the long ago,
Old pinnaroo lonely and lost here,
Last of your clan.
Left only with your memories, you sit
And think of the gay throng, the happy people,
The voices and the laughter
All gone, all gone,
And you remain alone.

I asked and you let me hear
The soft vowelly tongue to be heard now
No more for ever. For me
You enact old scenes, old ways, you who have used
Boomerang and spear.
You singer of ancient tribal songs,
You leader once in the corroboree,
You twice in fierce tribal fights
With wild enemy blacks from over the river,
All gone, all gone. And I feel
The sudden sting of tears, Willie Mackenzie
In the Salvation Army Home.
Displaced person in your own country,
Lonely in teeming city crowds,
Last of your tribe.

OODGEROO OF THE TRIBE NOONUCCAL

Appreciating Memories

1 'The new must oust the old'. How has Willie been 'ousted'?
2 What thoughts does the poet have when she looks at the old man who is the last of his clan?
3 What contrast is there between Willie's past and his present?
4 What does the poet achieve by the repetition of 'all gone'?
5 'The soft vowelly tongue to be heard now/No more for ever'. What is the poet referring to?
6 What is the effect on the reader of listing all the old man's tribal accomplishments?
7 How does the poet react to the old man's enactment of the old tribal ways?
8 How does the poet emphasise that the old man is a 'displaced person' in his own country?
9 What is the effect of the concluding words, 'Last of your tribe'?

10 Explain how each stanza deals with a different aspect of the old man's existence.
11 What phrase gives a unifying quality to the two stanzas?
12 What do you think was the poet's purpose in writing this poem?

The changes that came to Australia with European 'civilisation' destroyed the Aboriginal way of life.

No More Boomerang

No more boomerang
No more spear;
Now all civilised—
Colour bar and beer.

No more corroboree,
Gay dance and din.
Now we got movies,
And pay to go in.

No more sharing
What the hunter brings.
Now we work for money,
Then pay it back for things.

Now we track bosses
To catch a few bob,
Now we go walkabout
On bus to the job.

Bunyip he finish,
Now got instead
White fella Bunyip,
Call him Red.

Abstract picture now—
What they coming at?
Cripes, in our caves we
Did better than that.

Black hunted wallaby,
White hunt dollar;
White fella witch-doctor
Wear dog-collar.

No more message-stick;
Lubras and lads
Got television now,
Mostly ads.

One time naked,
Who never knew shame;
Now we put clothes on
To hide whatsaname.

No more gunya,
Now bungalow,
Paid by hire purchase
In twenty year or so.

Lay down the stone axe,
Take up the steel,
And work like a nigger
For a white man meal.

No more firesticks
That made the whites scoff.
Now all electric,
And no better off.

Lay down the woomera,
Lay down the waddy.
Now we got atom-bomb,
End *every*body.

OODGEROO OF THE TRIBE NOONUCCAL

In this poem a young Aboriginal girl tells how tribal laws condemned her to be the wife of an old man.

The Child Wife

They gave me to an old man,
Joyless and old,
Life's smile of promise
So soon to frown.
Inside his gunya
My childhood over,
I must sit for ever,
And the tears fall down.

It was love I longed for,
Young love like mine,
It was Dunwa wanted me,
The gay and brown.
Oh, old laws that tether me!
Oh, long years awaiting me!
And the grief comes over me,
And the tears fall down.

Happy the small birds
Mating and nesting,
Shrilling their gladness
No grief may drown.
But an old man's gunya
Is my life for ever,
And I think of Dunwa,
And the tears fall down.

OODGEROO OF THE TRIBE NOONUCCAL

10 Planet Earth

In recent times, more and more concern has been expressed over the pollution of the earth and the destruction of its natural resources, including waterways, forests, plants and animals. Poets, concerned about the fate of planet earth, have begun to add their voices to the general concern, asking that we reassess our concept of progress, and begin giving more consideration to the destruction we are leaving for future generations.

In 'Sonic Boom' the poet marvels a little at progress, as evidenced by the ability to create a sonic boom, and raises a doubt or two over whether or not this progress is really a good thing.

Sonic Boom

I'm sitting in the living room,
When, up above, the Thump of Doom
Resounds. Relax. It's sonic boom.

The ceiling shudders at the clap,
The mirrors tilt, the rafters snap,
And Baby wakens from his nap.

'Hush, babe. Some pilot we equip,
Giving the speed of sound the slip,
Has cracked the air like a penny whip.'

Our world is far from frightening; I
No longer strain to read the sky
Where moving fingers (jet planes) fly.
Our world seems much too tame to die.

And if it does, with one more *pop*,
I shan't look up to see it drop.

JOHN UPDIKE

Checking Out Sonic Boom

1 What picture of the poet's situation and attitude does the first line suggest?
2 What breaks in on the peaceful scene?
3 Why do you think the poet gives capital letters to 'Thump of Doom'?
4 How does the sonic boom affect him at first? What word enables you to conclude this?
5 What are two effects of the sonic boom on the house?
6 Comment on the effect of the rhyming words 'clap', 'snap' and 'nap' in the second stanza.
7 What explanation for the sonic boom does the parent give the baby?

8 'Our world is far from frightening'. Who do you think the poet is reassuring?
Why?
9 What evidence does the poet use to illustrate the fact that he is no longer
worried about anything?
10 'Our world seems much too tame to die'. What does the poet mean by this line?
11 Why does the word 'pop' seem unexpected as a word to describe the ending of
the world?
12 How would you describe the tone of this poem? Why?
13 Comment on the overall effectiveness of the poem. On what features of the
poem do you base your assessment?
14 Did you enjoy reading this poem? Explain your viewpoint.

In this poem the writer focuses on the American pelican as his subject matter. He
feels relatively powerless to do anything to help, and expresses some of his frustration in a mildly satirical finish.

Letter to People About Pelicans

I'd woken early
worried about some
obscure matter

decided to
start a new school of poetry

something to do with temperature

but remembered about the
american pelican

they live on
anacapa island
fifty miles off calif

seemed safe enough

now pollution's
reached them
they lay
funny eggs

only four eggs out of
six hundred
didn't break when laid

and fish are poisoned by the sea
so seals and pelicans who
eat fish
also are poisoned

thinking about my
safe different poems
that help no-one
decided to
try and help the animals

you're killing them
your household
flushing death seawards

it's more to do with
commerce and governments

so i'll not start my
poetry revolution

instead i want a
school of reconstructive chemistry

teach pelicans to
fly to moskba and washington
fly high
drop explosive eggs

MICHAEL DRANSFIELD

Reading Letter to People About Pelicans

1 What explanation does the poet offer for his waking early?
2 What decision does he make in response to waking early?
3 What interrupts his initial plan?
4 Where is the American pelican located?
5 What problem is facing the pelican?
6 What is causing the problem?
7 What contrast does the poet draw between his poetry and the pelicans?
8 What decision does he come to?
9 The poet begins by addressing us with 'you're killing them'. What effect do you think he wants to have?
10 Who does he decide is more to blame than us?
11 What would a 'school of reconstructive chemistry' have to offer for this problem?

12 How do you feel about the poet's final suggestion? Do you think this is what the poet wanted you to feel? Why?
13 What overall response do you have to this poem, and to the poet's subject? Explain your response.
14 What is the poet's purpose in this poem?

The next poet laments the loss of interest in zebras. He humorously puts this down to the coming of colour television, and the loss of interest in things black and white. Sadly, now, our main interest in zebras seems to be in zebra crossings.

Zebra

People have lost interest in the zebra
since the coming of colour television.

At the Serengeti waterhole
he dips his ancient heraldic head,
fills his round belly.

On the dry dust of the plain
he casts a blue shadow.
His heavy eyes watch the acacia trees
for the least sign of movement.
He shakes his mane,
the dark plume of a Roman centurion.

At home we take the zebra for granted,
let him carry us across the road
outside the supermarket.

GILROY FISHER

In 'The Caged Bird in Springtime', the poet imaginatively enters into the world of the caged bird, trying to capture some of the feelings it might have and the confusion it might feel over these feelings.

The Caged Bird in Springtime

What can it be,
This curious anxiety?
It is as if I wanted
To fly away from here.

But how absurd!
I have never flown in my life,
And I do not know
What flying means, though I have heard,
Of course, something about it.

Why do I peck the wires of this little cage?
It is the only nest I have ever known.
But I want to build my own,
High in the secret branches of the air.

I cannot quite remember how
It is done, but I know
That what I want to do
Cannot be done here.

I have all I need—
Seed and water, air and light.
Why, then, do I weep with anguish,
And beat my head and my wings
Against those sharp wires, while the children
Smile at each other, saying: 'Hark how he sings'?

JAMES KIRKUP

'Harvest Hymn' is a parody on the well-known hymn of the Christian church, 'We plough the fields and scatter'. Here the poet is satirising the folly of people in their destructive actions towards the earth.

Harvest Hymn

We plough the fields and scatter
our pesticides again;
our seeds are fed and watered
by gentle acid rain.
We spray the corn in winter
till pests and weeds are dead—
who minds a little poison
inside his daily bread?

All good gifts around us
beneath our ozone layer
are safe, oh Lord,
so thank you Lord
that we know how to care.

JUDITH NICHOLLS

'Prosperity' focuses on the impact of uncontrolled industrialisation, and the pollution of environment and human spirit that it seems to produce.

Prosperity

monday to friday at the plant
concrete yards are busy with
vehicles and movement altho most of what
moves is machinery
now and then a human figure crosses the open
space looking small & helpless
in the sky above the plant not much is blue
behind the buildings in a grey channel something
oozes past seeming to have been a river

on friday night when the machines are silent
& the watchman finishes his rounds
walking away with gun and torch like some
mistaken supplicant then only the dark
finds its way through wire fences
and sometimes due to atmospheric conditions (for which
the management is not responsible) the wind will rise
or in the wasteland hours of industrial sunday
rain might start falling inadvertently as if
still thinking of a plant as some kind of
flower

MICHAEL DRANSFIELD

Soaking Up Our Prosperity

1 How does the phrase 'concrete yards' help to set the mood of the poem?
2 ' . . . altho most of what/moves is machinery'. Why is this statement significant as part of the poem's message?
3 Why does the poet use the expression 'a human figure' rather than, say, 'a person'?
4 Comment on the effect of describing the 'human figure' as 'looking small & helpless'.
5 'In the sky above the plant not much is blue'. Why not?
6 Why is the channel described as 'grey'? Is this a good descriptive word here? Why or why not?
7 What is the effect of including the fact that the plant is surrounded by 'wire fences'?
8 Comment on the phrase 'the wasteland hours of industrial sunday'. What does the poet mean?
9 What effect do you think the wind would have on the scene when it rises? In what way would this seem out of keeping with the whole situation?

10 'Rain might start falling inadvertently'. What is the effect of the word 'inadvertently' here?

11 What two meanings of the word 'plant' does the poet call to mind in the last lines?

12 How would you state the poet's message or theme?

13 One of the poet's techniques is to ignore punctuation in writing this poem. What effect does this have? Do you see it as a useful technique? Why or why not?

14 How successfully has the poet communicated his attitudes in this poem? What has contributed to this?

15 Do you think 'Prosperity' is a suitable title for this poem? Why or why not?

There is great sadness in this poem by an Indian chief, as he recounts what has happened to his people, and the effect of this upon them.

Alabama

My brethren,
among the legends of my people
it is told how a chief,
leading the remnant of his people,
crossed a great river,
and striking his tipi-stake upon the ground,
exclaimed, 'A-la-ba-ma!'
This in our language means
'Here we may rest!'
But he saw not the future.
The white man came:
he and his people could not rest there;
they were driven out,
and in a dark swamp
they were thrust down into the slime
and killed.
The word he so sadly spoke
has given a name to one of the white man's states.
There is no spot under those stars
that now smile upon us,
where the Indian can plant his foot
and sigh 'A-la-ba-ma.'

KHE-THA-A-HI (EAGLE WING)

'Telephone Poles' uses irony in its attempts to justify and see good in the existence of this ubiquitous landscape feature.

Telephone Poles

They have been with us a long time.
They will outlast the elms.
Our eyes, like the eyes of a savage sieving the trees
In his search for game,
Run through them. They blend along small-town streets
Like a race of giants that have faded into mere mythology.
Our eyes, washed clean of belief,
Lift incredulous to their fearsome crowns of bolts, trusses,
    struts, nuts, insulators, and such
Barnacles as compose
These weathered encrustations of electrical debris—
Each a Gorgon's head, which, seized right,
Could stun us to stone.

Yet they are ours. We made them.
See here, where the cleats of linemen
Have roughened a second bark
Onto the bald trunk. And these spikes
Have been driven sideways at intervals handy for human legs.
The Nature of our construction is in every way
A better fit than the Nature it displaces.
What other tree can you climb where the birds' twitter,
Unscrambled, is English? True, their thin shade is negligible,
But then again there is not that tragic autumnal
Casting-off of leaves to outface annually.
These giants are more constant than evergreens
By being never green.

JOHN UPDIKE

Gazing at Telephone Poles

1 What evidence of the endurance of telephone poles does the poet offer at the beginning of the poem?
2 What does the poet mean by 'our eyes . . . run through them'?
3 'They blend along small-town streets'. Why do they 'blend' this way?
4 What is the effect of describing all the bits and pieces that make up the poles?
5 'These weathered encrustations of electrical debris'. Is this a flattering description of the poles or not? Explain your answer.

6 'Could stun us to stone'. What is the poet commenting on?
7 'Yet they are ours'. What is the effect of this short sentence?
8 'The Nature of our construction is in every way/A better fit than the Nature it displaces'. Does the poet really believe this? Justify your answer.
9 What is 'the birds' twitter' referred to in this poem?
10 What deficiency does the poet acknowledge about the poles?
11 What major advantage do the poles have when compared with trees?
12 In what way are these giants 'more constant than evergreens'?
13 What does the poet really feel about the telephone poles? What evidence is there for your view?
14 What impact does this poem have upon you? Explain your answer.

'Chill, Burning Rain' is a brief verse, lamenting the effect of acid rain upon the foliage of the trees.

'Chill, Burning Rain'

Chill, burning rain
Has flayed the trees
And even evergreen
Will never green
To leaf again
JOHN KITCHING

'Big Yellow Taxi' is a song by Joni Mitchell. Its lyrics regret the way humankind doesn't realise what blessings it has, until it's too late.

Big Yellow Taxi

They paved paradise
And put up a parking lot
With a pink hotel, a boutique
And a swinging hot spot
Don't it always seem to go
That you don't know what you've got
Till it's gone
They paved paradise
And put up a parking lot.

They took all the trees
And put them in a tree museum
And they charged all the people
A dollar and a half just to see 'em
Don't it always seem to go
That you don't know what you've got
Till it's gone
They paved paradise
And put up a parking lot.

Hey farmer farmer
Put away that DDT now
Give me spots on my apples
But leave me the birds and the bees
Please!
Don't it always seem to go
That you don't know what you've got
Till it's gone
They paved paradise
And put up a parking lot.

Late last night
I heard the screen door slam
And a big yellow taxi
Took away my old man
Don't it always seem to go
That you don't know what you've got
Till it's gone
They paved paradise
And put up a parking lot.

JONI MITCHELL

11 Kenneth Slessor

Life and Background of Kenneth Slessor

Kenneth Slessor was born at Orange, New South Wales, on 27th of March 1901. He was educated at the Sydney Church of England Grammar School. At the age of fifteen he had one of his poems, 'Goin'', published in the *Bulletin*.

When he left school in 1920, he became a reporter on the Sydney *Sun*. By 1938 he had become editor of the famous *Smith's Weekly*. In the years before he died in June 1971, he was a leader-writer and book reviewer on the Sydney *Daily Telegraph*.

Slessor spent most of his life in Sydney, and its harbour streets and buildings are used as a background and basis for some of his poems. Slessor loved 'the shriek of tram-wheels, the trumpeting of motor-cars, the pounding of machinery, the squawk of gulls, the lugubrious mooing of steamboat whistles, the clamour of bells, the ghostly treble of ten thousand wireless sets and the grumble of flying boats climbing down to their nests in Rose Bay.' Some of the fine descriptive pieces in 'Five Bells' and 'Five Visions of Captain Cook' were inspired by the magnificent view that Slessor had of Sydney Harbour from where he lived. Not only was William Street close to Slessor's home and his place of work at the newspaper, but it was also close to his heart. He writes admiringly of it:

> At night, after a slick of rain has fallen on it, turning the roadway to a long black mirror, William Street comes out like a beautiful adventuress. It is dressed in Neon signs, the blazing arrows and alphabets of light, in mandarin-yellow, tangerine-red, emerald and white, like the witch-fires of the *Ancient Mariner*, 'about, about, in reel and rout'. In the water silvering the pavement, people walk on their reflected heels.

Slessor was a war correspondent with the Australian army from 1940 to 1944. This assignment took him to Greece, Syria, El Alamein and New Guinea. It was during the El Alamein campaign that he wrote his deeply moving poem 'Beach Burial'. Slessor begins his official despatch from El Alamein on 9th of December 1942 with the following description:

> Here at this little speck on the map, between the huddle of stone hut which is El Alamein railway-station and the lonely coast road which they helped to guard so stoutly, they are burying Australia's dead. Patiently and carefully for the past few weeks the soldiers of the A.I.F. who gave their lives in this last and fiercest campaign of the Middle East have been gathered together in a common bivouac.

His poem 'Beach Burial' was not released until 1947 and was among Slessor's last published poems. For the next twenty-three years until his death in 1971, he produced no new poetry for publication.

Kenneth Slessor's Poetry

In 1944 Slessor made a selection of his own poetry from his previously published books, *Thief of the Moon* (1924), *Earth Visitors* (1926), *Cuckooz Contrey* (1932) and *Five Bells* (1939), which he entitled *One Hundred Poems*. In 1957 this was reissued with two additional poems under the new title of *Poems*.

Slessor's poetry writing falls into three periods. In the first period (1919–26), much of Slessor's poetry is concerned with legend, history, fantasy and romance and does not have the modern flavour of his later poetry. During these years, he was strongly influenced by the artist Norman Lindsay and the poet Hugh McCrae.

The next period in Slessor's development as a poet spans the years 1927–32. In this second period Slessor came under the influence of modern poets such as T. S. Eliot and the Sitwells. He abandoned his earlier style and began to adopt modernist techniques. The second phase of his work centres upon things closer to his reader, and particularly upon the theme of the sea. With his 'Five Visions of Captain Cook', Slessor inaugurated a movement towards the writing of 'voyager poetry'.

It is Slessor's third phase that gives him his reputation as a poet. Generally speaking, the poems in this period are poems of impermanence. Themes such as sleep, death, the sea and time are prominent. He manages to fuse sense, sound, image and feeling in much of the poetry of this period. 'Five Bells', 'Sleep' and 'Beach Burial' in particular display his use of contemporary, vivid and sometimes startling imagery and language.

Slessor in 'The Night-ride' describes his experiences as a train traveller in the days of the steam trains.

The Night-ride

Gas flaring on the yellow platform; voices running up and down;
Milk-tins in cold dented silver; half-awake I stare,
Pull up the blind, blink out—all sounds are drugged;
The slow blowing of passengers asleep;
Engines yawning; water in heavy drips;
Black, sinister travellers, lumbering up the station,
One moment in the window, hooked over bags;
Hurrying, unknown faces—boxes with strange labels—
All groping clumsily to mysterious ends,
Out of the gaslight, dragged by private Fates.
Their echoes die. The dark train shakes and plunges;
Bells cry out; the night-ride starts again.
Soon I shall look out into nothing but blackness,
Pale, windy fields. The old roar and knock of the rails
Melts in dull fury. Pull down the blind. Sleep. Sleep.
Nothing but grey, rushing rivers of bush outside.
Gaslight and milk-cans. Of Rapptown I recall nothing else.

KENNETH SLESSOR

Experiencing The Night-ride

1 The poem begins with the train stopped at a station. What picture in the first line does Slessor give you of the railway station in the gaslight?
2 What sounds are heard outside the train? What sounds are heard within the carriage?
3 Slessor creates the feeling of sleepiness. How does he do this?
4 Why does Slessor describe the departing travellers outside the train as 'black' and 'sinister'?
5 Why do you think Slessor refers to the travellers as 'lumbering'?
6 What is the meaning of 'dragged by private Fates'?
7 Why does the poet create the impression that the train is a living creature?
8 'Bells cry out'. What is happening? Comment on the poet's use of personification here.
9 '. . . The old roar and knock of the rails/Melts in dull fury'. What sounds is the poet making you aware of?
10 '. . . Sleep. Sleep'. Why does the poet repeat the word 'sleep'?
11 What is happening when the poet says '. . . grey rushing rivers of bush outside'?
12 What evidence can you find to show that this journey did not take place in a modern train, but happened years ago?

13 Slessor has called this poem 'The Night-ride'. Do you think this is a good title for the poem? Explain your viewpoint. Why do you think Slessor has used the word 'ride' rather than 'journey'?

14 What contrast is there between the scene at the station and the scene when the train is travelling through the countryside?

15 What was the poet's purpose in writing 'The Night-ride'?

Gulliver is a famous character from Jonathan Swift's eighteenth century satirical novel *Gulliver's Travels*. After Gulliver's ship is wrecked in a storm, he is washed up on a strange beach in the land of Lilliput. When he regains consciousness, he finds he cannot move an inch. He describes his helplessness: 'My arms and legs were now tied down to the ground and even my hair, which was long and thick had been tied down with string so that I could not move my head to see what had happened to me.' Kenneth Slessor sees himself as a modern-day Gulliver bound down by seemingly insoluble human problems.

Gulliver

I'll kick your walls to bits, I'll die scratching a tunnel,
If you'll give me a wall, if you'll give me simple stone,
If you'll do me the honour of a dungeon—
Anything but this tyranny of sinews.
Lashed with a hundred ropes of nerve and bone
I lie, poor helpless Gulliver,
In a twopenny dock for the want of a penny,
Tied up with stuff too cheap, and strings too many.
One chain is usually sufficient for a cur.

Hair over hair, I pick my cables loose,
But still the ridiculous manacles confine me.
I snap them, swollen with sobbing. What's the use?
One hair I break, ten thousand hairs entwine me.
Love, hunger, drunkenness, neuralgia, debt,
Cold weather, hot weather, sleep and age—
If I could only unloose their spongy fingers,
I'd have a chance yet, slip through the cage.
But who ever heard of a cage of hairs?
You can't scrape tunnels in a net.

If you'd give me a chain, if you'd give me honest iron,
If you'd graciously give me a turnkey,
I could break my teeth on a chain, I could bite through metal,
But what can you do with hairs?
For God's sake, call the hangman.

KENNETH SLESSOR

Analysing Gulliver

1 What is the poet's mood at the beginning of the poem?
2 'Sinews' are tendons. What does the poet mean by 'tyranny of sinews'?
3 'Lashed with a hundred ropes of nerve and bone'. How is the poet like the original Gulliver?
4 What is the poet complaining about in the first stanza?
5 What point is Slessor making when he says 'One chain is usually sufficient for a cur'?
6 In the second stanza, Slessor uses a number of words that suggest being bound or tied up. Jot them down. What impression do they create?
7 What evidence can you find to show that the poet is trying to solve his problems?
8 'What's the use?' What do these words suggest about the poet's state of mind?
9 Why does the poet believe his problems are beyond him?
10 Why are the bonds described as 'spongy fingers'?
11 What point is the poet making about his problems when he says 'You can't scrape tunnels in a net'?
12 In the third stanza, what imagery does the poet use to try to prove that his problems are not able to be overcome?
13 'For God's sake, call the hangman'. What is the poet's mood?
14 In what ways is the poet like the Gulliver of the novel?
15 What has the poet revealed about his attitude to life?
16 What was the poet's purpose in writing 'Gulliver'?

Kenneth Slessor comments on 'William Street'

'William Street' is a sort of flashlight photograph of the swarming city channel that runs up the hill of King's Cross, taken on a rainy night when the surface of the road is coated with a slick of reds and greens and whites reflected from the neon sky-signs (the 'red globes' and 'pulsing arrows').

William Street

The red globes of light, the liquor-green,
The pulsing arrows and the running fire
Split on the stones, go deeper than a stream;
You find this ugly, I find it lovely.

Ghosts' trousers, like the dangle of hung men,
In pawnshop-windows, bumping knee by knee,
But none inside to suffer or condemn;
You find this ugly, I find it lovely.

Smells rich and rasping, smoke and fat and fish
And puffs of paraffin that crimp the nose,
Or grease that blesses onions with a hiss;
You find it ugly, I find it lovely.

The dips and molls, with flip and shiny gaze
(Death at their elbows, hunger at their heels)
Ranging the pavements of their pasturage;
You find it ugly, I find it lovely.

KENNETH SLESSOR

Kenneth Slessor comments on 'Beach Burial'

'Beach Burial' comes from the period when Australian soldiers were fighting in the Western Desert of Egypt near Alamein, where the German advance had been halted in 1942. Many of their camps were on the Mediterranean coast, and in the morning it was not uncommon to find the bodies of drowned men washed up on the beaches. They were buried in the sandhills under improvised crosses, identification usually being impossible. Most of them were sailors, some British, some German or Italian, some of them 'neutrals'.

Beach Burial

Softly and humbly to the Gulf of Arabs
The convoys of dead sailors come;
At night they sway and wander in the waters far under,
But morning rolls them in the foam.

Between the sob and clubbing of the gunfire
Someone, it seems, has time for this,
To pluck them from the shallows and bury them in
    burrows
And tread the sand upon their nakedness.

And each cross, the driven stake of tide-wood,
Bears the last signature of man,
Written with such perplexity, with such bewildered
    pity,
The words choke as they begin.

'*Unknown seaman*'—the ghostly pencil
Wavers and fades, the purple drips,
The breath of the wet season has washed their
    inscription
As blue as drowned men's lips.

Dead seamen, gone in search of the same landfall,
Whether as enemies they fought,
Or fought with us, or neither; the sand joins them
    together,
Enlisted on the other front.

KENNETH SLESSOR

Sleep is the speaker of the poem. She takes on the human qualities of a mother and the sleeper becomes a child within her womb.

Sleep

Do you give yourself to me utterly,
    Body and no-body, flesh and no-flesh,
Not as a fugitive, blindly or bitterly,
    But as a child might, with no other wish?
Yes, utterly.

Then I shall bear you down my estuary,
Carry you and ferry you to burial mysteriously,
Take you and receive you,
Consume you, engulf you,
In the huge cave, my belly, lave you
With huger waves continually.

And you shall cling and clamber there
And slumber there, in that dumb chamber,
Beat with my blood's beat, hear my heart move
Blindly in bones that ride above you,
Delve in my flesh, dissolved and bedded,
Through viewless valves embodied so—

Till daylight, the expulsion and awakening,
    The riving and the driving forth,
Life with remorseless forceps beckoning—
    Pangs and betrayal of harsh birth.

KENNETH SLESSOR

Examining Sleep

1 Sleep is personified as a mother. What is her relationship in the first stanza with the poet, who is falling asleep?
2 What question does Sleep ask the poet?
3 What does Sleep mean by 'body and no-body, flesh and no-flesh'?

4 How do you know that the poet is prepared to completely surrender himself to Sleep?

5 What comments would you make about the rhythm of the second stanza?

6 What words in the second stanza suggest that the poet is falling into a deep sleep?

7 What image in the second stanza suggests that the sleeper is within Sleep's womb?

8 In the third stanza, what words suggest that the sleeper is nourished and protected by Sleep?

9 What is 'the expulsion'?

10 'The riving and the driving forth'. What does the poet achieve by the alliteration of the 'r' and the 'v'?

11 'Life with remorseless forceps beckoning'. Life is personified here. Why would life have 'forceps'? What is going to happen to the sleeper?

12 What techniques has Slessor used to suggest that waking up is a painful process?

13 What contrast is there between the mood of the last stanza and the other stanzas of the poem?

14 Do you think Slessor's personification of Sleep has been successful? Why or why not?

15 What was Slessor's purpose in this poem?

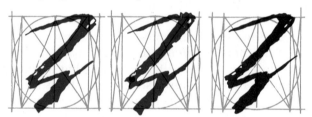

Here Slessor presents his observations and feelings about Australian country towns before the motor-car arrived in force.

Country Towns

Country towns, with your willows and squares,
And farmers bouncing on barrel mares
To public-houses of yellow wood
With '1860' over their doors,
And that mysterious race of Hogans
Which always keeps General Stores. . . .

At the School of Arts, a broadsheet lies
Sprayed with the sarcasm of flies:
'The Great Golightly Family
Of Entertainers Here To-night'
Dated a year and a half ago,
But left there, less from carelessness
Than from a wish to seem polite.

Verandas baked with musky sleep,
Mulberry faces dozing deep,
And dogs that lick the sunlight up
Like paste of gold—or, roused in vain
By far, mysterious buggy-wheels,
Lower their ears, and drowse again. . . .

Country towns with your schooner bees,
And locusts burnt in the pepper-trees,
Drown me with syrups, arch your boughs,
Find me a bench, and let me snore,
Till, charged with ale and unconcern,
I'll think it's noon at half-past four!

KENNETH SLESSOR

Evaluating Country Towns

In 'Country Towns', the images come one on top of the other, and the total effect is a wide spectrum of places, people and happenings of typical country towns in bygone days. Slessor begins by addressing the towns as though they are living entities. He does this so that he may talk directly about the life within them. After mention of 'willows and squares', he rapidly moves to the light-hearted and rather humorous picture of 'farmers bouncing on barrel mares'. The alliteration of the letter 'b' conveys an impression of the farmers bobbing up and down as they ride their horses to the public houses. Slessor surprises with his use of the word 'barrel' to describe the farmers' mares, but it certainly serves to emphasise the contours of the mares in relationship to the farmers bouncing on their backs.

While Slessor is primarily concerned to present us with his immediate impressions and feelings about life in country towns, he is also conscious of the past. He is aware that the 'yellow wood' of the public houses has weathered time and is impressed by their age, denoted by the '1860' over their doors.

Slessor next takes us to the School of Arts, an important part of life in every country town. Whereas the first stanza gives us a wide range of images, this stanza concentrates entirely on a solitary broadsheet left at the School of Arts. The tone changes abruptly. The mood of the first stanza is gay and lively. Now, as the present merges with the past, Slessor becomes more philosophical as he concentrates on the passing of time. The Great Golightly Family of Entertainers has been and gone. All that remains as a reminder of their visit is a broadsheet 'sprayed with the sarcasm of flies'. Slessor says of these lines, 'I did see, printed on a brown and peeling poster, the news that The Great Golightly Family of Entertainers had been there in the past. As I remember it, their principal entertainment was playing the musical glasses.'

The tone of the third stanza changes once again. It is full of tired, sluggish feelings. Words such as 'dozing deep' and 'drowse again' convey an atmosphere of tiredness and apathy. The sense of heat and tiredness is evoked in 'Verandas baked with musky sleep'. The alliteration of the letter 's' here is used to convey the sleepiness and tranquillity that pervade the towns. The exaggerated image of the dogs licking up the sunlight strengthens the picture of inertia that Slessor is conveying. This stanza is rich in colourful imagery; phrases such as 'mulberry faces' and 'paste of gold' intensify the sense of the heat.

It is in the last stanza that Slessor directly declares his love for the country. The bees themselves symbolise the richness of life. Slessor describes them as 'schooner bees', bees with large wings that look like sailing ships. Life is pleasurable and for the poet, who is 'charged with ale and unconcern', time passes quickly: 'I'll think it's noon at half-past four!' The poet is physically and spiritually intoxicated with life as he concludes his tribute to country towns.

As the poet comes upon an old orchard, the sight of wild grapes remind him of a girl called Isabella who once lived there.

Wild Grapes

The old orchard, full of smoking air,
Full of sour marsh and broken boughs, is there,
But kept no more by vanished Mulligans,
Or Hartigans, long drowned in earth themselves,
Who gave this bitter fruit their care.

Here's where the cherries grew that birds forgot,
And apples bright as dogstars; now there is not
An apple or a cherry; only grapes,
But wild ones, Isabella grapes they're called,
Small, pointed, black, like boughs of musket-shot.

Eating their flesh, half-savage with black fur,
Acid and gipsy-sweet, I thought of her,
Isabella, the dead girl, who has lingered on
Defiantly when all have gone away,
In an old orchard where swallows never stir.

Isabella grapes, outlaws of a strange bough,
That in their harsh sweetness remind me somehow
Of dark hair swinging and silver pins,
A girl half-fierce, half-melting, as these grapes,
Kissed here—or killed here—but who remembers now?

KENNETH SLESSOR

Reviewing Wild Grapes

1 What words suggest the decay of the orchard?
2 In the first stanza, how does the poet evoke the passing of time?

3 What quality of the apples is Slessor emphasising in the phrase 'apples bright as dogstars'?
4 What does Slessor mean by 'Isabella, the dead girl, who has lingered on/ Defiantly'?
5 'Acid and gipsy-sweet, I thought of her'. Why do you think the grapes reminded the poet of Isabella?
6 Why does the poet refer to the grapes as 'outlaws'?
7 'A girl half-fierce, half-melting, as these grapes'. In what ways, according to this description, is Isabella similar to the grapes?
8 What does the poet suggest could have happened to Isabella?
9 ' . . . but who remembers now?' Is this an effective conclusion to the poem? Explain your viewpoint.
10 How has the poet created a sense of sadness in this poem?
11 In this poem Slessor has blended the past with the present. Explain how he has achieved this.
12 What was Slessor's purpose in writing this poem?

The Reverend Samuel Marsden was an important public figure in the penal colony of New South Wales. When he was appointed a magistrate, he acquired the nickname of the 'Flogging Parson' because of the severity of the punishments he imposed on the convicts.

Vesper-song of the Reverend Samuel Marsden

My cure of souls, my cage of brutes,
Go lick and learn at these my boots!
When tainted highways tear a hole,
I bid my cobbler welt the sole,
O, ye that wear the boots of Hell,
Shall I not welt a soul as well?
   O, souls that leak with holes of sin,
   Shall I not let God's leather in,
   Or hit with sacramental knout
   Your twice-convicted vileness out?

Lord, I have sung with ceaseless lips
A tinker's litany of whips,
Have graved another Testament
On backs bowed down and bodies bent.
My stripes of jewelled blood repeat
A scarlet Grace for holy meat.
   Not mine, the Hand that writes the weal
   On this, my vellum of puffed veal,
   Not mine, the glory that endures,
   But Yours, dear God, entirely Yours.

Are there not Saints in holier skies
Who have been scourged to Paradise?
O, Lord, when I have come to that,
Grant there may be a Heavenly Cat
With twice as many tails as here—
    And make me, God, Your Overseer.
    But if the veins of Saints be dead,
    Grant me a whip in Hell instead,
    Where blood is not so hard to fetch.

But I, Lord, am Your humble wretch.

KENNETH SLESSOR

Examining the Vesper-song

1 A vesper song is an evening prayer. What evidence can you find to show that Samuel Marsden is praying?
2 'My cage of brutes'. What does Marsden's use of the word 'brutes' suggest about his attitude to the convicts?
3 'Go lick and learn at these my boots!' What do these words reveal about Marsden's character?
4 Marsden believes he has been entrusted by God to convert the sinful convicts to Christianity. What is Marsden's method for removing the convict's sin?
5 'When tainted highways tear a hole,/I bid my cobbler welt the sole'. These words are part of an extended metaphor. Explain Slessor's use of 'sole' and 'soul'. Who is Marsden's 'cobbler'?
6 What violent words can you find in the first stanza?
7 Marsden considers the convicts have been 'twice convicted'. How is this so?
8 In stanza two, what examples of his cruelty does Marsden reveal?
9 'On backs bowed down and bodies bent'. What is the effect of the alliteration of the letter 'b'?
10 'Have graved another Testament'. What are the meanings of 'graved'?
11 Explain the metaphor 'my vellum of puffed veal'. How do you react to it?
12 Explain the meaning of 'scourged to Paradise'.
13 What examples of Marsden's brutality can you find in the third stanza?
14 Why is the fourth stanza only one line?
15 Why do you think Marsden completes his prayer with the words 'But I, Lord, am Your humble wretch'?
16 What is Slessor's purpose in this poem?
17 Comment on Slessor's use of biblical imagery in the poem.
18 Do you think that having Marsden speak personally was a good technique? Why or why not?

12 Wilfred Owen

The Poems of
WILFRED OWEN
Edited by Jon Stallworthy

CHATTO
POETRY

Wilfred Owen's Life and Background

Wilfred Owen was only twenty-five years of age when he died in action on November 4th, 1918, one week before the end of the First World War. He was killed by machine-gun fire while encouraging his men who were trying to construct a makeshift bridge across the Sambre Canal. He had already earned the Military Cross a month earlier, on the 4th of October, when he and a young lance-corporal had captured several German machine guns and had taken many prisoners. Unfortunately, before his death, he had only seen five of his poems in print.

Wilfred Owen was born in Oswestry, Shropshire in 1893. He was the eldest of four children. Owen was educated at the Birkenhead Institute, Liverpool and at London University. In 1913, he left England for France because of poor health and became a tutor at Bordeaux. In 1915, he returned home and enlisted in the Artists' Rifles. In January 1917, he went as an officer to join the Second Battalion of the Manchester Regiment on the Somme. Here he experienced the horrors of war, which he vividly recounted in his poems and his letters. In a letter to his mother on the 16th of January, he described the appalling conditions of the battlefront:

> The ground was not mud, not sloppy mud, but an octopus of sucking clay, 3, 4 and 5 feet deep relieved only by craters full of water. Men have been known to drown in them. Many stuck in the mud and only got on by leaving their waders, equipment and in some cases their clothes. High explosives were dropping all around, and machine guns spluttered every few minutes.

Because of shell-shock Owen was invalided back to Craiglockhart War Hospital in Scotland. Here he had the good fortune to meet Siegfried Sassoon, a decorated veteran and well-known anti-war poet. Owen greatly admired Sassoon's poetry and his pacifist stand against the war. Sassoon's encouragement and advice led to Owen's completion of 'Anthem for Doomed Youth', 'The Next War', 'Disabled', 'Dulce et Decorum Est' and other poems.

By the end of August, 1918, Owen returned to duty in France. His letters at the time showed that he had a premonition of death. His final words to his mother were a quotation from Tagore's 'Gitanjali': 'When I go from hence let this be my parting word, that what I have seen is unsurpassable.'

Wilfred Owen's Poetry

A few months before his death, Owen started to prepare a collection of his poems for publication under the title *Disabled and Other Poems*. He had hastily jotted down a draft preface stating his purpose:

> This book is not about heroes. English Poetry is not yet fit to speak of them. Nor is it about deeds, or lands, nor anything about glory, honour, might, majesty, dominion, or power, except War. Above all I am not concerned with Poetry. My subject is War, and the pity of War. The Poetry is in the pity. Yet these elegies are to this generation in no sense consolatory. They may be to the next. All a poet can do today is warn. That is why the true Poets must be truthful.

As a result of sharing the horrifying experiences in the trenches with his fellow soldiers, Owen, through his poetry, was able to become a speaker for all of them.

In all of his poems, Owen focuses on 'the pity of war'. He explores different aspects of this pity in a wide variety of scenes and themes: bombardment ('The Sentry'), the harshness of nature ('Exposure'), chemical warfare ('Dulce et Decorum Est'), hospitalisation ('Conscious'), the waste of human life ('Anthem for Doomed Youth'), maimed ('Disabled'), departure for war ('The Send-off'), the self-destruction of war ('Strange Meeting'), derangement of the mind ('Mental Cases').

As a young man, Owen greatly admired the poetry of Keats. In his earlier poems he excessively imitated Keats' style. It was Siegfried Sassoon who advised Owen to become more direct and forceful. Sassoon wrote: 'I was sometimes a little severe on what he showed me, censuring the over-luscious writing in his immature pieces.' The result of Sassoon's advice was borne out in poems, such as 'Exposure', in which Owen was sensuously able to evoke the cold and agony of trench warfare.

Owen was very much aware of the effect of the sound of words. He frequently used onomatopoeia and assonance to suggest the action of the battlefield. Here is an example from 'Anthem For Doomed Youth':

> Only the stuttering rifles' rapid rattle
> Can patter out their hasty orisons.

He also experimented with a new type of rhyme, later called para-rhyme, which helped him to better evoke his emotional response to the purposeless slaughter of young men. In poems such as 'Strange Meeting', the para-rhymes help to give the poem a melancholy effect (groined/groaned; teeth/death; years/yours), thus creating a sense of futility and failure.

Owen came to use poetry as a most powerful weapon. His passionate protest cannot help but move us all. 'The Poetry is in the pity.'

Owen makes a passionate protest against the senseless waste of young lives on the battlefield in 'Anthem For Doomed Youth'.

Anthem for Doomed Youth

What passing-bells for these who die as cattle?
—Only the monstrous anger of the guns.
Only the stuttering rifles' rapid rattle
Can patter out their hasty orisons.
No mockeries now for them; no prayers nor bells;
Nor any voice of mourning save the choirs,—
The shrill, demented choirs of wailing shells;
And bugles calling for them from sad shires.

What candles may be held to speed them all?
Not in the hands of boys, but in their eyes
Shall shine the holy glimmers of good-byes.
The pallor of girls' brows shall be their pall;
Their flowers the tenderness of patient minds,
And each slow dusk a drawing-down of blinds.

WILFRED OWEN

Thinking About Anthem for Doomed Youth

1 ' . . . for these who die as cattle'. What does Owen achieve by comparing the death of the young men to that of cattle?
2 Instead of the sound of bells, what sound will be heard for those who die on the battlefield?
3 The word 'orisons' means prayers. What will replace the prayers of the funeral ceremony?
4 'Only the stuttering rifles' rapid rattle.' What does Owen achieve by the alliteration (repetition) of the letters 'r' and 't'?
5 'Stuttering' and 'rattle' are onomatopoeic words. Why are they suitable here?
6 The battlefield dead will not be able to have a church choir to farewell them. What kind of choir will they have?
7 What words suggest the sound of the shells in flight?

8 'Demented' means insane. Do you think 'demented' is a suitable word to describe the shells? Why or why not?
9 In peacetime at a funeral, candles might be held by choirboys. What will the dead youth have instead of candles?
10 A pall is a cloth used to cover a coffin. What will the doomed youth have instead of a pall?
11 'Their flowers the tenderness of patient minds'. What will there be for them instead of flowers?
12 It was the custom to draw down the blinds of a house as a mark of respect for someone's death. How could 'each slow dusk' be 'a drawing-down of blinds'? What does the poet achieve here by this metaphor?
13 An anthem is a song of praise. Do you think 'Anthem for Doomed Youth' is a suitable title for the poem? Explain your viewpoint.
14 What is the poet's message in the poem?

'The Sentry' is a study in realism, showing the horror of war from a personal viewpoint. In a letter to his mother, Owen wrote: 'I kept my own sentries half way down the stairs during the more terrific bombardment. In spite of this one lad was blown down and, I am afraid, blinded.'

The Sentry

We'd found an old Boche dug-out, and he knew,
And gave us hell, for shell on frantic shell
Hammered on top, but never quite burst through.
Rain, guttering down in waterfalls of slime
Kept slush waist-high that, rising hour by hour,
Choked up the steps too thick with clay to climb.
What murk of air remained stank old, and sour
With fumes of whizz-bangs, and the smell of men
Who'd lived there years, and left their curse in the den,
If not their corpses. . . .
         There we herded from the blast
Of whizz-bangs, but one found our door at last,—
Buffeting eyes and breath, snuffing the candles.
And thud! flump! thud! down the steep steps came thumping
And splashing in the flood, deluging muck—
The sentry's body; then, his rifle, handles
Of old Boche bombs, and mud in ruck on ruck.
We dredged him up, for killed, until he whined
'O sir, my eyes—I'm blind—I'm blind, I'm blind!'
Coaxing, I held a flame against his lids
And said if he could see the least blurred light
He was not blind; in time he'd get all right.

'I can't,' he sobbed. Eyeballs, huge-bulged like squids',
Watch my dreams still; but I forgot him there
In posting next for duty, and sending a scout
To beg a stretcher somewhere, and floundering about
To other posts under the shrieking air.

Those other wretches, how they bled and spewed,
And one who would have drowned himself for good,—
I try not to remember these things now.
Let dread hark back for one word only: how
Half listening to that sentry's moans and jumps,
And the wild chattering of his broken teeth,
Renewed most horribly whenever crumps
Pummelled the roof and slogged the air beneath—
Through the dense din, I say, we heard him shout
'I see your lights!' But ours had long died out.

WILFRED OWEN

Appraising The Sentry

1 How do the Germans react to the British sheltering in the flooded dug-out?
2 What words does Owen use to emphasise the horror of the water in the trenches?
3 Why are the smells of the dug-out repulsive?
4 How does the poet indicate the falling of the sentry down the steps?
5 'I'm blind — I'm blind, I'm blind!' What are your feelings towards the sentry?
6 How does Owen emphasise the swelling of the sentry's eyeballs?
7 ' . . . I forgot him there'. What caused Owen to forget the blinded sentry?
8 Why does the poet describe the air as 'shrieking'?
9 'And one who would have drowned himself for good'. Why would a soldier think of drowning himself in this situation?
10 'I try not to remember these things now'. Why?
11 What sound-words does the poet use to convey the intensity of the shelling?
12 Why are the sentry's words 'I see your lights' especially sad?
13 What does the poet mean at the end of the poem when he says 'ours had long died out'?
14 Do you think this poem was written from first-hand experience? Why?
15 What did you learn about the poet himself from your reading of the poem?
16 What is the poet's message to the reader in 'The Sentry'?

Here, Owen proves beyond any doubt that it is not sweet and glorious to lay down one's life for one's country.

Dulce et Decorum Est

Bent double, like old beggars under sacks,
Knock-kneed, coughing like hags, we cursed through sludge,
Till on the haunting flares we turned our backs
And towards our distant rest began to trudge.
Men marched asleep. Many had lost their boots
But limped on, blood-shod. All went lame; all blind;
Drunk with fatigue; deaf even to the hoots
Of tired, outstripped Five-Nines that dropped behind.

Gas! GAS! Quick, boys!—An ecstasy of fumbling,
Fitting the clumsy helmets just in time;
But someone still was yelling out and stumbling,
And flound'ring like a man in fire or lime . . .
Dim, through the misty panes and thick green light,
As under a green sea, I saw him drowning.

In all my dreams, before my helpless sight,
He plunges at me, guttering, choking, drowning.

If in some smothering dreams you too could pace
Behind the wagon that we flung him in,
And watch the white eyes writhing in his face,
His hanging face, like a devil's sick of sin;
If you could hear, at every jolt, the blood
Come gargling from the froth-corrupted lungs,
Obscene as cancer, bitter as the cud
Of vile, incurable sores on innocent tongues,—
My friend, you would not tell with such high zest
To children ardent for some desperate glory,
The old Lie: Dulce et decorum est
Pro patria mori.

WILFRED OWEN

Evaluating Dulce et Decorum Est

The title and last lines of this poem are taken from one of the Odes of the Roman poet Horace. These Latin words may be translated as 'It is sweet and honourable to die for one's country'. This same belief of the Romans was held by the English people two thousand years later during the First World War. Owen, by presenting us with horror of the battlefield, mockingly condemns the 'old Lie' that it is sweet and honourable to die for one's country.

Owen's graphic description of the suffering and anguish of the soldiers in 'Dulce et Decorum Est' shocks the reader. At the beginning of the poem, Owen confronts us with the utter exhaustion of the soldiers. The simile 'like old beggars under sacks' not only evokes the difficulty of the soldiers' movements through the sludge but it also shows the degradation that war brings. The soldiers have no glory. The simile 'like hags' following closely upon the previous one further arouses our pity for the men.

Owen's vivid visual images following quickly one upon the other give us the sense of sharing the men's weariness and hardship. We feel compassion for the soldiers who are so exhausted that they 'marched asleep'. We cannot help but pity the physical suffering of those who 'limped on, blood-shod'. By the alliteration of the 'l' in 'limped on, blood-shod. All went lame; all blind', Owen conveys the sluggish and anguished movement of the soldiers struggling to return to their base. They are so 'drunk with fatigue' that they are unaware of the gas shells dropping softly behind them.

The second stanza begins with a dramatic and abrupt end to the soldiers' weariness. The sudden appearance of gas brings with it the fear of death. This fear is clearly seen in the 'ecstasy of fumbling' as the weary soldiers suddenly become alert and agitated as they struggle to save themselves from the horrifying death by gas. The alliteration of the letters 'f' and 'm' in the words 'An ecstasy of fumbling,/ Fitting the clumsy helmets just in time' creates a sense of frenzied and distraught movement as the soldiers hasten to put on their gas masks.

The poem then focuses on the plight of the unfortunate soldier who has no gas mask. The scene quickly assumes nightmarish qualities. Owen likens the gas to a green sea enveloping the soldier who seems to be 'floundering' as would a drowning swimmer. Owen emphasises the consuming and destructive qualities of the gas through his use of the simile 'like a man in fire or lime'. The harsh sounds of 'guttering' and 'choking' emphasise the anguish of the gassed soldier. Experiencing this scene so deeply affected Owen that it continued to haunt him in his dreams.

In the final stanza of the poem, Owen makes a blatant attack on those who glorify war. It is here, when Owen focuses on the horrifying effects of the gas on the soldier in the wagon, that we experience our greatest compassion. Owen's words 'And watch the white eyes writhing in his face' both shock us and cause us to have pity for the soldier. The alliteration of the 'w' and the assonance of the 'i' intensify the horrifying picture of the destruction of the soldier's eyes. Owen not only confronts us with the sight of the dying soldier, but also the sounds made by his 'froth-corrupted lungs'. The onomatopoeic word 'gargling' shocks us with the sounds of the soldier's terrible suffering.

Now that his readers' senses have been touched by those same horrors that he himself has endured on the battlefield, Owen passionately endeavours to convince them to refrain from preaching 'The old Lie: Dulce et decorum est/Pro patria mori' to the innocent young.

'The Send-off' describes soldiers who, after completing their training in camp, leave by train for the front. These soldiers are 'sent off' with flowers and patriotic words by the women of the district.

The Send-off

Down the close, darkening lanes they sang their way
To the siding-shed,
And lined the train with faces grimly gay.

Their breasts were stuck all white with wreath and spray
As men's are, dead.

Dull porters watched them, and a casual tramp
Stood staring hard,
Sorry to miss them from the upland camp.
Then, unmoved, signals nodded, and a lamp
Winked to the guard.

So secretly, like wrongs hushed-up, they went.
They were not ours:
We never heard to which front these were sent.

Nor there if they yet mock what women meant
Who gave them flowers.

Shall they return to beatings of great bells
In wild train-loads?
A few, a few, too few for drums and yells,
May creep back, silent, to village wells
Up half-known roads.

WILFRED OWEN

Thinking About The Send-off

1 Why are the soldiers faces 'grimly gay'?
2 What is the significance of the word 'wreath'?
3 How did the observers react to the departure of the soldiers?
4 Explain the poet's use of personification in 'signals nodded and a lamp/Winked to the guard'.
5 'So secretly, like wrongs hushed-up, they went'. How did the soldiers depart for the front?
6 Why would the soldiers have reason later to 'mock what women meant/Who gave them flowers'?
7 How does Owen arouse our pity for the departing soldiers?
8 Why do you think Owen asks the question 'Shall they return to beatings of great bells/In wild trainloads?'
9 Why does Owen keep repeating the word 'few'?
10 'May creep back, silent . . .' Why are the survivors likely to be silent?
11 Why do you think Owen wrote 'The Send-off'?
12 Do you think 'The Send-off' is a good anti-war poem?

In 'Futility', the speaker, in a desperate but unavailing attempt to restore life to his dead friend, orders that the body be moved into the sun.

Futility

Move him into the sun—
Gently its touch awoke him once,
At home, whispering of fields unsown.
Always it woke him, even in France,
Until this morning and this snow.
If anything might rouse him now
The kind old sun will know.

Think how it wakes the seeds,—
Woke, once, the clays of a cold star.
Are limbs, so dear-achieved, are sides,
Full-nerved,—still warm,—too hard to stir?
Was it for this the clay grew tall?
—O what made fatuous sunbeams toil
To break earth's sleep at all?

WILFRED OWEN

This famous poem is a powerful condemnation of war. The narrator describes meeting in Hell a sleeper who has views about life and war that are identical to his own. When the sleeper finally reveals his identity and the cause of his death, the reader is shocked by the savagery of war.

Strange Meeting

It seemed that out of battle I escaped
Down some profound dull tunnel, long since scooped
Through granites which titanic wars had groined.

Yet also there encumbered sleepers groaned,
Too fast in thought or death to be bestirred.
Then, as I probed them, one sprang up, and stared
With piteous recognition in fixed eyes,
Lifting distressful hands, as if to bless.
And by his smile, I knew that sullen hall,—
By his dead smile I knew we stood in Hell.

With a thousand pains that vision's face was grained;
Yet no blood reached there from the upper ground,
And no guns thumped, or down the flues made moan.
'Strange friend,' I said, 'here is no cause to mourn.'
'None,' said that other, 'save the undone years,
The hopelessness. Whatever hope is yours,
Was my life also; I went hunting wild
After the wildest beauty in the world,
Which lies not calm in eyes, or braided hair,
But mocks the steady running of the hour,
And if it grieves, grieves richlier than here.
For by my glee might many men have laughed,
And of my weeping something had been left,
Which must die now. I mean the truth untold,
The pity of war, the pity war distilled.
Now men will go content with what we spoiled,
Or, discontent, boil bloody, and be spilled.
They will be swift with swiftness of the tigress.
None will break ranks, though nations trek from progress.

Courage was mine, and I had mystery,
Wisdom was mine, and I had mastery:
To miss the march of this retreating world
Into vain citadels that are not walled.
Then, when much blood had clogged their chariot-wheels,
I would go up and wash them from sweet wells,
Even with truths that lie too deep for taint.
I would have poured my spirit without stint
But not through wounds; not on the cess of war.
Foreheads of men have bled where no wounds were.

I am the enemy you killed, my friend.
I knew you in this dark: for so you frowned
Yesterday through me as you jabbed and killed.
I parried; but my hands were loath and cold.
Let us sleep now. . . .'

WILFRED OWEN

Examining Strange Meeting

 1 How was the narrator able to escape from the battle?
 2 What has the poet achieved by his use of alliteration and assonance in, 'down some profound dull tunnel'?
 3 What was unusual about the sleepers?
 4 What evidence can you find to show that one of the sleepers seemed to recognise the narrator?
 5 'I knew we stood in Hell'. How did the narrator know this?
 6 What evidence is there to show that the sleeper had suffered greatly?
 7 Which lines suggest that their meeting place is cut off from the war?
 8 'And no guns thumped'. Why is 'thumped' a forceful word?
 9 What 'cause to mourn' did the 'strange friend' have?
10 What beauty did the 'strange friend' seek beyond that of physical beauty or love?
11 What do you understand by the words 'steady running of the hour'?
12 What 'truth' must now remain 'untold'?
13 How does the 'strange friend' see the dangers of the future?
14 What words show that he would give all his energy to cleanse the world of war, but not to fight in war?
15 'I am the enemy you killed, my friend'. What horrifying deed has the narrator committed.
16 'I knew you in this dark'. What evidence to support this can you find in the second stanza?
17 ' . . . as you jabbed and killed'. Why is 'jabbed' a forceful word?
18 'Let us sleep now . . .' How do these words convey the feeling that there is no hope for mankind?
19 What similarities do the narrator and the 'strange friend' possess?
20 Why is the poem title 'Strange Meeting'?
21 How does this poem stress the futility of war?

In 'Conscious', Owen describes the confusion of a soldier awakening in a hospital ward.

Conscious

His fingers wake, and flutter; up the bed.
His eyes come open with a pull of will,
Helped by the yellow may-flowers by his head.
The blind-cord drawls across the window-sill . . .
What a smooth floor the ward has! What a rug!
Who is that talking somewhere out of sight?
Why are they laughing? What's inside that jug?
'Nurse! Doctor!'—'Yes; all right, all right.'

But sudden evening muddles all the air—
There seems no time to want a drink of water,
Nurse looks so far away. And here and there
Music and roses burst through crimson slaughter.
He can't remember where he saw blue sky.
More blankets. Cold. He's cold. And yet so hot.
And there's no light to see the voices by;
There is no time to ask—he knows not what.

WILFRED OWEN

In 'The Chances', Owen recreates the language and attitude to war of the common soldier, and again he is concerned to show 'the pity of war'.

The Chances

I mind as 'ow the night afore that show
Us five got talkin',—we was in the know.
'Over the top to-morrer; boys, we're for it.
First wave we are, first ruddy wave; that's tore it!'
'Ah well,' says Jimmy,—an' 'e's seen some scrappin'—
'There ain't no more nor five things as can 'appen:
Ye get knocked out; the wounded—bad or cushy;
Scuppered; or nowt except yer feelin' mushy.'

One of us got the knock-out, blown to chops.
T'other was 'urt, like, losin' both 'is props.
An' one, to use the word of 'ypocrites,
'Ad the misfortoon to be took be Fritz.
Now me, I wasn't scratched, praise God Amighty,
(Though next time please I'll thank 'im for a blighty).
But poor young Jim, 'e's livin' an' 'e's not;
'E reckoned 'e'd five chances, an' 'e 'ad;
'E's wounded, killed, and pris'ner, all the lot,
The bloody lot all rolled in one. Jim's mad.

WILFRED OWEN

In 'Spring Offensive', the beauty and life-giving force of spring is quickly transformed into death and destruction by the fury of war.

Spring Offensive

Halted against the shade of a last hill,
They fed, and lying easy, were at ease
And, finding comfortable chests and knees,
Carelessly slept. But many there stood still
To face the stark blank sky beyond the ridge,
Knowing their feet had come to the end of the world.

Marvelling they stood, and watched the long grass swirled
By the May breeze, murmurous with wasp and midge,
For though the summer oozed into their veins
Like an injected drug for their bodies' pains,
Sharp on their souls hung the imminent line of grass,
Fearfully flashed the sky's mysterious glass.

Hour after hour they ponder the warm field,—
And the far valley behind, where the buttercup
Had blessed with gold their slow boots coming up,
Where even the little brambles would not yield
But clutched and clung to them like sorrowing hands.
They breathe like trees unstirred.

Till like a cold gust thrills the little word
At which each body and its soul begird
And tighten them for battle. No alarms
Of bugles, no high flags, no clamorous haste,—
Only a lift and flare of eyes that faced.
The sun, like a friend with whom their love is done.
O larger shone that smile against the sun,—
Mightier than his whose bounty these have spurned.

So, soon they topped the hill, and raced together
Over an open stretch of herb and heather
Exposed. And instantly the whole sky burned
With fury against them; earth set sudden cups
In thousands for their blood; and the green slope
Chasmed and steepened sheer to infinite space.

Of them who running on that last high place
Leapt to swift unseen bullets, or went up
On the hot blast and fury of hell's upsurge,
Or plunged and fell away past this world's verge,
Some say God caught them even before they fell.

But what say such as from existence' brink
Ventured but drave too swift to sink,
The few who rushed in the body to enter hell,
And there out-fiending all its fiends and flames
With superhuman inhumanities,
Long-famous glories, immemorial shames—
And crawling slowly back, have by degrees
Regained cool peaceful air in wonder—
Why speak not they of comrades that went under?

WILFRED OWEN

Analysing Spring Offensive

 1 What impression is given of the soldiers' life at the beginning of the poem?
 2 What indication does the poet give in the first stanza that this pleasant situation would come to an end?
 3 'Marvelling they stood'. Why were they 'marvelling'?
 4 Why is the word 'murmurous' especially suitable here?
 5 ' . . . the summer oozed into their veins'. What is happening?
 6 'Like an injected drug for their bodies' pains'. Explain the comparison that the poet is making.
 7 'Sharp on their souls hung the imminent line of grass'. What do you think the soldiers were worrying about?
 8 In the third stanza, how does the poet evoke the beauty of the sunlight and spring?
 9 In the fourth stanza, how does the poet suggest the change of mood that comes to the soldiers when they have to prepare for battle?
10 Why is 'exposed' a forceful word to describe the soldiers' new situation?
11 ' . . . And instantly the whole sky burned/With fury against them'. What is happening? What contrast is there between their new situation and their previous one?
12 What is the meaning of ' . . . earth set sudden cups/In thousands for their blood'?
13 In what ways did the soldiers die?

14 In the last stanza, Owen describes the experiences of the few who survived the battle. How does he bring out the horror of their experiences?

15 'Regained cool peaceful air in wonder'. Why do you think the survivors were 'in wonder'?

16 What contrast is there between the soldier's experiences in the first three stanzas of the poem and the last three stanzas?

17 Why is 'Spring Offensive' a good title for this poem?

18 What was Owen's purpose in writing this poem?

'Mental Cases' presents us with an alarming description of those soldiers who have suffered a complete mental breakdown as a result of enduring the horrors of trench warfare.

Mental Cases

Who are these? Why sit they here in twilight?
Wherefore rock they, purgatorial shadows,
Drooping tongues from jaws that slob their relish,
Baring teeth that leer like skulls' teeth wicked?
Stroke on stroke of pain,—but what slow panic,
Gouged these chasms round their fretted sockets?
Ever from their hair and through their hands' palms
Misery swelters. Surely we have perished
Sleeping, and walk hell; but who these hellish?

—These are men whose minds the Dead have ravished.
Memory fingers in their hair of murders,
Multitudinous murders they once witnessed.
Wading sloughs of flesh these helpless wander,
Treading blood from lungs that had loved laughter.
Always they must see these things and hear them,
Batter of guns and shatter of flying muscles,
Carnage incomparable, and human squander
Rucked too thick for these men's extrication.

Therefore still their eyeballs shrink tormented
Back into their brains, because on their sense
Sunlight seems a blood-smear; night comes blood-black;
Dawn breaks open like a wound that bleeds afresh.
—Thus their heads wear this hilarious, hideous,
Awful falseness of set-smiling corpses.
—Thus their hands are plucking at each other;
Picking at the rope-knouts of their scourging;
Snatching after us who smote them, brother,
Pawing us who dealt them war and madness.

WILFRED OWEN

13 Poets Around the World

Every country in the world has its own rich store of poems that describe its people, landscape and character. Poets the world over have a common bond in the way they respond with their emotions and ideas wherever they are.

The Vietnamese poet Te Hahn views the sampan with admiration in the poem 'In My Village'.

> Restless and ardent the sampan as a racehorse,
> Swift are the oars, down the tide bravely.

In his poem 'The Drifters' the Aboriginal poet Jack Davis sadly laments the loss of the Aboriginal way of life.

> No more the chant of the hunting song:
> The laughing face and the laughing eyes.

The American poet Robert Lowell appreciates the quiet of the night in 'Skunk Hour':

> I stand on top
> of our back steps and breathe the rich air.

Australia

DAVID CAMPBELL

David Campbell was born in 1916 in the Australian bush. A number of his poems were inspired by the time he spent with Harry Pearce, the bullock driver, and the drovers of 'Ellerslie', a cattle station near Adelong.

He was educated at The Kings School, Parramatta, and at Cambridge University, England. In the Second World War, David Campbell was a pilot in the RAAF. He mostly served in New Guinea where the poem 'Harry Pearce' was written in 1942. David Campbell died in Canberra in 1979.

Harry Pearce

> I sat beside the red stock route
> And chewed a blade of bitter grass
> And saw in mirage on the plain
> A bullock wagon pass.
> Old Harry Pearce was with his team
> 'The flies are bad,' I said to him.
>
> The leaders felt his whip. It did
> Me good to hear old Harry swear,
> And in the heat of noon it seemed
> His bullocks walked on air.
> Suspended in the amber sky
> They hauled the wood to Gundagai.

He walked in Time across the plain,
An old man walking in the air;
For years he wandered in my brain,
And now he lodges here.
And he may drive his cattle still
When Time with us has had his will.

DAVID CAMPBELL

Time for Questions

1 What is this poem's setting?
2 'And chewed a blade of bitter grass'. Why do you think the poet uses the alliteration of hard 'b' sounds in this line?
3 How do we know that the mirage seemed real to the poet?
4 What evidence can you find to show the poet liked Harry?
5 What impression does the poet give of the bullocks in the second stanza?
6 What does the poem show about the life of a bullock driver?
7 What is the meaning of 'For years he wandered in my brain'?
8 'And may he drive his cattle still'. Why does the poet say this?
9 What is the meaning of 'When Time with us has had his will'?
10 What are your feelings about Harry?
11 What evidence can you find to show that this is an Australian poem?
12 What do you think was the poet's purpose in writing this poem?

JACK DAVIS

The Aboriginal poet Jack Davis was born in Perth in 1917. His poems describe the racism and injustice suffered by the Aboriginal people in white Australia.

Jack Davis led a hard life working as an engine driver, a drover and a factory hand. He was able to see at first hand the suffering forced on his people.

His first book of poetry was published in 1970. It was called *The First Born*, the title being taken from the line 'Where are my first born, said the brown land, sighing'.

The Drifters

We are the drifters, the faceless ones.
Turn your heads as we walk by.
We are the lost, forgotten sons,
Bereft in a land of plenty.

Where is the spear of the days gone by?
No more the chant of the hunting song:
The laughing face and the laughing eyes,
So sad in a land of plenty.

We have lost the peal of the Mission bell,
Drowned out by the sounds of the city streets.
We have lots to say and none to tell
Of hell in a land of plenty.

Oh, this earth! This sun! This sky I see
Is part of my heart, my heritage!
Oh God, I cry. Cry God for me.
For a place in a land of plenty.

JACK DAVIS

Russia

YEVGENY YEVTUSHENKO

This famous Soviet poet was born in 1933 and achieved his popularity shortly after the death of Stalin in 1953. His poems appealed to young people because they probed issues that had long been hidden or on which discussion was forbidden. In the more liberal era after Stalin, Yevtushenko travelled in the West and gave poetry readings.

Picture of Childhood

Elbowing our way, we run.
Someone is being beaten up in the market.
You wouldn't want to miss it!
We put on speed, racing to the uproar,
scooping up water in our felt-boots
and forgetting to wipe our sniffles.

And stood stock-still . . . In our little hearts something tightened,

when we saw how the ring of sheepskin coats,
fur-coats, hooded coats, was contracting,
how he stood up near the green vegetable stall
with his head pulled into his shoulders from the hail
of jabs, kicks, spitting, slaps in the face.

Suddenly someone from the left bashed his forehead with a
    chunk of ice.

Blood appeared—and then they started in, in earnest.
All piled up in a heap they began to scream together,
pounding with sticks, reins,
and iron pins out of wheels.

In vain he wheezed to them: 'Mates, you're my mates—
what's the matter?'

The mob wanted to make a job of it.
The mob were quite deaf. They were raging.
The mob grumbled at those who weren't putting the boots in,
and they trampled something that looked like a body
into the spring snow that was turning into mud.

They beat him up with relish. With ingenuity. Juicy.
I saw how skilfully and precisely
one man kept putting the boots in,
boots with greasy tags on them,
right under the belt of the man who was down,
smothered in mud and *dungy* water.

Their owner, a bloke with an honest enough mug,
very proud of his high principles,
was saying with each kick: 'We won't let you get away with it!'
booting him deliberately, with the utmost conviction,
and, sweat pouring, with a red face, he jovially called to me:
'Come on youngster, be in it!'
I can't remember—how many there were, making a din, beating
    him up.

It may have been a hundred, it may have been more,
but I, just a boy, wept for shame.
And if a hundred are beating somebody up,
howling in a frenzy,—even if for a good cause,
I will never make a hundred and one!

YEVGENY YEVTUSHENKO

  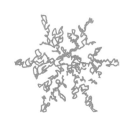

Condemning Cruelty

1 What is the setting at the beginning of the poem?
2 How does the poet create the impression of speed and excitement expressed in the first stanza?
3 'And stood stock still . . . ' What effect does the poet want to achieve by the use of this single line?
4 What impression of the crowd does the poet want to create by repeating 'coats'?
5 What words in the third stanza emphasise the violence that was occurring?
6 Why is the attack with the chunk of ice in a separate stanza?
7 'Blood appeared'. How did the crowd react to the sight of the blood?
8 What attitude did the victim have towards the crowd?
9 In the seventh stanza, what effect is achieved by the repetition of 'The mob'?
10 How did they feel towards their victim?
11 What details of the beating did the poet remember?
12 Why do you think the word '*dungy*' is placed in italics?
13 What contrast exists between the 'high principles' of the owner of the boots and his behaviour?
14 What attitude did he display towards the poet?
15 How did the poet feel towards the beating?
16 What promise did he make to himself?
17 Why is it likely that this was a real-life experience for the poet?
18 What is the poet's purpose in this poem?

Czechoslovakia

MIROSLAV HOLUB

Holub was born in Czechoslovakia in 1923. In his writing he combines poetry and scientific journalism so that sometimes the themes of his poems are intertwined with medical or scientific concepts.

Often his verse sets out to comment on everyday life. It provided an escape from the totalitarian oppression that pervaded the Czech way of life in the recent past.

A Boy's Head

In it there is a space-ship
and a project
for doing away with piano lessons.

And there is
Noah's ark,
which shall be first.

And there is
an entirely new bird,
an entirely new hare,
an entirely new bumble-bee.

There is a river
that flows upwards.

There is a multiplication table.

There is anti-matter.

And it just cannot be trimmed.

I believe
that only what cannot be trimmed
is a head.

There is much promise
in the circumstance
that so many people have heads.

MIROSLAV HOLUB
(*Translated from the Czech by Ian Milner*)

England

WILLIAM SHAKESPEARE

This great English dramatist and poet was born at Stratford-on-Avon in 1564 and survived the plague that was raging violently in Stratford that year. His time at school was short because of his family's financial troubles. At the age of thirteen he became an apprentice butcher. When he was eighteen years old he married Anne Hathaway.

Most of Shakespeare's plays and poems were written between his twenty-seventh and his forty-seventh year. Both Queen Elizabeth and King James I recognised the greatness of his work. In his later life he was a famous and wealthy man. He died in 1616 at the age of fifty-two. The following extract is from *King Richard II* (Act II, scene i).

This England

This royal throne of kings, this scepter'd isle,
This earth of majesty, this seat of Mars,
This other Eden, demi-paradise;
This fortress built by Nature for herself
Against infection and the hand of war;

This happy breed of men, this little world;
This precious stone set in the silver sea,
Which serves it in the office of a wall,
Or as a moat defensive to a house,
Against the envy of less happier lands,
This blessed plot, this earth, this realm, this England.

WILLIAM SHAKESPEARE

RUDYARD KIPLING

Rudyard Kipling was born in Bombay, India, in 1907. Kipling became the first English writer to receive the Nobel Prize for Literature. Because much of his poetry dealt with the responsibilities and duties of the English in Imperial India, Kipling became known as 'the poet of the Empire'.

If

If you can keep your head when all about you
    Are losing theirs and blaming it on you,
If you can trust yourself when all men doubt you,
    But make allowance for their doubting too;
If you can wait and not be tired by waiting,
    Or being lied about, don't deal in lies,
Or being hated don't give way to hating,
    And yet don't look too good, nor talk too wise:

If you can dream—and not make dreams your master—
    If you can think—and not make thoughts your aim:
If you can meet with Triumph and Disaster
    And treat those two imposters just the same;
If you can bear to hear the truth you've spoken
    Twisted by knaves to make a trap for fools,
Or watch the things you gave your life to, broken,
    And stoop and build 'em up with worn-out tools:

If you can make one heap of all your winnings
    And risk it on one turn of pitch-and-toss,
And lose, and start again at your beginnings
    And never breathe a word about your loss;
If you can force your heart and nerve and sinew
    To serve your turn long after they are gone,
And so hold on when there is nothing in you
    Except the Will which says to them: 'Hold on!'

If you can talk with crowds and keep your virtue.
  Or walk with Kings—nor lose the common touch,
If neither foes nor loving friends can hurt you,
  If all men count with you, but none too much;
If you can fill the unforgiving minute
  With sixty seconds' worth of distance run.
Yours is the Earth and everything that's in it,
  And—which is more—you'll be a Man, my son!

RUDYARD KIPLING

United States of America

ROBERT LOWELL

Robert Lowell was born in Boston in 1917 and grew up as a member of one of Boston's famous families. However, he rejected his family's influence and became a conscientious objector for which he was jailed during the Second World War. Lowell received the Pulitzer Prize for poetry in 1947. He died in 1977.

Skunk Hour
(For Elizabeth Bishop)

Nautilus Island's hermit
heiress still lives through winter in her Spartan cottage;
her sheep still graze above the sea.
Her son's a bishop. Her farmer
is first selectman in our village,
she's in her dotage.

Thirsting for
the hierarchic privacy
of Queen Victoria's century,
she buys up all
the eyesores facing her shore,
and lets them fall.

The season's ill—
we've lost our summer millionaire,
who seemed to leap from an L. L. Bean
catalogue. His nine-knot yawl
was auctioned off to lobstermen.
A red fox stain covers Blue Hill.

And now our fairy
decorator brightens his shop for fall,
his fishnet's filled with orange cork,
orange, his cobbler's bench and awl,
there is no money in his work,
he'd rather marry.

One dark night,
my Tudor Ford climbed the hill's skull,
I watched for love-cars. Lights turned down,
they lay together, hull to hull,
where the graveyard shelves on the town . . .
My mind's not right.

A car radio bleats,
'Love, O careless Love . . . ' I hear
my ill-spirit sob in each blood cell,
as if my hand were at its throat . . .
I myself am hell,
nobody's here—

only skunks, that search
in the moonlight for a bite to eat.
They march on their soles up Main Street:
white stripes, moonstruck eyes' red fire
under the chalk-dry and spar spire
of the Trinitarian Church.

I stand on top
of our back steps and breathe the rich air—
a mother skunk with her column of kittens swills the garbage pail.
She jabs her wedge-head in a cup
of sour cream, drops her ostrich tail
and will not scare.

ROBERT LOWELL

Appreciating Skunk Hour

'Skunk Hour' is drawn from Robert Lowell's personal experience. Robert Lowell
explains the title: 'Skunk hour is the hour in the quiet of the night, about two say,
when the garbage is out in the garbage pails and the skunks are out for the garbage.'

The poet spent some of his summer vacations in the quiet New England village
of Castine, Maine. During the summers it was a holiday resort, but during the severe
winters the guest houses closed, leaving only a few permanent inhabitants in residence. Robert Lowell himself watched skunks foraging in the deserted Main Street
of the village and in them he found the stimulus and inspiration for the poem.

The village is the poem's physical setting and the time, as the poem begins, is the end of the holiday season. The poem's opening lines are slow in pace and wandering in thought as if the poet, as an observer of the scene, is producing random items of gossip to interest us. This slow, wandering pace continues throughout the poem's first four stanzas, maintained by the loose rhyme scheme that is in striking contrast to the tight rhyme that is suddenly introduced in the important fifth stanza.

Robert Lowell describes his purpose for the first half of the poem in this way: 'The first four stanzas are meant to give a dawdling more or less amiable picture of a declining Maine sea town.'

There are always a few eccentric residents left behind after the holiday resorts have closed. One such is the ancient heiress who lives in solitude in her comfortless cottage on Nautilus Island. The loneliness and madness surrounding the heiress set a scene and create a mood in the poem that is sad, regretful and vaguely ominous. We are given some apparently random facts about her life — where her sheep graze, who her son is, and the fact that her farmer has an official position in the village. The heiress is a senile woman from another century and her aristocratic privacy is so precious to her that she buys up the decaying houses facing her property in order to let them fall down.

The opening line of the third stanza, 'The season's ill —', describes the sense of reduced activity of the scene following the end of the summer vacation. On another level, the words suggest that the poet is projecting his feeling of despair onto the landscape around him.

After the first line, the third stanza continues the collection of details about the end of the holiday season. The millionaire who was there for the summer and who looked like the stereotype of a millionaire out of a mail-order catalogue has sold his pleasure yacht to the local lobstermen and has left. There is a humorous touch in this description but the sense of regret persists.

The third stanza's last line is vivid, mysterious and seems menacing. 'The red fox stain' evolved from the poet's combination of the reddish colours of autumn and the sight of foxes he had seen playing on a road one night. 'Blue Hill' was a hill with blueberry patches near the village. These images merged in Lowell's mind to produce the vivid and sinister sense of an omen — 'A red fox stain covers Blue Hill'.

The final eccentric character, depicted in the fourth stanza, is the homosexual decorator who brightens his shop for autumn using an ornamental fishnet 'filled with orange cork'. However, his business is so financially unrewarding that he'd rather marry for money. At the end of this stanza we are left with another impression of sadness and defeat.

In the fifth stanza the mood changes sharply to one of anguish. Now the observer becomes the observed as the poet looks into himself in this stanza the rhyme scheme becomes tauter and gives a relentless effect to the mood of the stanza. The tense has also changed from present to past suggesting loss or death. The atmosphere of death is openly evoked by the use of the words 'dark', 'skull' and 'graveyard'. His car, the Tudor Ford, seems to take the poet to the hilltop as if it has a will of its own. He sees cars lying together but the lovers in them are hidden. The stanza ends with the chilling statement, 'My mind's not right'. In stanza six, a familiar song 'bleats' from the car radio. This strange verb has a lonely sound that is linked with the sheep in the first stanza. The song brings no comfort to the poet.

It makes him aware of his need of love and adds to his extreme feeling of despairing loneliness. The hand at the throat is an image both of suicide and disintegration. The poet's feelings of desolation, emptiness and aloneness have created his own 'hell'.

There is a shift in time and place in the seventh stanza which introduces the skunks. The setting for the two last stanzas is no longer the dark night on the hill but moonlight on Main Street. Lowell is watching skunks marching along the street full of energy, life and hope as they search for food in the garbage bins. They replace Lowell's despair with hope because their presence is an antidote to his loneliness. The skunks' 'white stripes' and the 'red fire' of their eyes represent life and indomitability.

In the last stanza, the poet, invigorated by contact with the skunks, is able to 'breathe the rich air', a sign of his return to the enjoyment of life. His mind is no longer sick. In a word full of grotesque images the skunks are natural and fully affirm life and living. A sense of strength is conveyed by the poet's use of short decisive action words such as 'swills', 'jabs', 'drops'. They prepare us for the confidence of the last line, 'and will not scare'. The poem ends with feelings of affirmation. The skunks will not scare and neither will the poet.

Vietnam

TÉ HANH

Té Hanh was born in South Vietnam in 1921. During the Vietnam War he fought against the French and the Americans and their allies.

In this poem Té Hanh shows how fishing is a way of life for the Vietnamese villagers living on the coast.

In My Village

My village is one where nets are cast
Where fishing is the life.
Water surrounds it to the distant sea.
Fair weather when the wind is light
First blue of morning out together
The young men go to search the seas.

Restless and ardent the sampan as a racehorse,
Swift are the oars, down the tide bravely,
Strong, wide-open, like the heart of our village
The winged mainsail spreads out
Stretching its white curve, scooping the wind.

Next day to shore our sampan comes home
Toilers in triumph bearing the sea's harvest.
All our village is there to welcome the boat
'Thanks to Heaven the sea was good, our nets are full'

Shining like pearl the heaped wet fish,
Brown limbs training, dark-bronzed by the sun.
And tired the boat rests now, hauled close to shore,
As brine bites the fibres of her timber, deck and gear.

This day from very far my heart remembers well
The shimmer of blue water, silvery fish, the lime-washed sails
Memory of a sampan breasting the waves out to the main.
I dream the smells, rough, salty, keen . . .

                                        TÉ HANH

Netting Answers

1 What is this poem's setting?
2 What impression does the poet give of fishing in the first stanza?
3 Why is the comparison of a fast boat with a racehorse a good one?
4 What kind of action is suggested in 'scooping the wind'?
5 What shift of time occurs in the third stanza?
6 What is the meaning of 'the sea's harvest'?
7 What feelings dominate the third stanza?
8 Why does the poet compare the fish to 'pearl'?
9 What impression does the poet give of the fishermen in the fourth stanza?
10 Why does the poet describe the boat as 'tired'?
11 'As brine bites the fibres of her timber'. Comment on the poet's use of personification.
12 What change of mood occurs in the last stanza?
13 What impression does the poet give of the lives of the Vietnamese fishermen?
14 Which image did you enjoy most? Explain your viewpoint.

14 Bruce Dawe

Life and Background of Bruce Dawe

Bruce Dawe, who was once described as 'an ordinary bloke with a difference', was born in 1930 in Geelong. He has two elder sisters and an elder brother, all at least twenty years his senior. He has been married for over thirty years and has two sons and two daughters.

Throughout Dawe's childhood, his family was always shifting from place to place, moving from Geelong to Melbourne to Carlton and on to Fitzroy. He later wrote about a similar situation in his poem 'The Drifters'. He was not close to either his mother or father. However, despite such a childhood, he remained content with his life, as is shown by these lines from the collection *No Fixed Address*.

> When I was six I used to play
> In salt-bush flats day after day
> Gathering prehistoric shells
> From early morning to the bells
> Of sunset jangled in the trees
> — I was as happy as you please.

At high school, Dawe was placed in the Commercial Schooling stream and gained his Intermediate Certificate. His literary talent was first noticed by a teacher during his final year of schooling. He wrote so well in an examination that the teacher accused him of memorising a magazine article! He had already been writing plays from the age of twelve, and poetry from the age of thirteen.

Six months after completing his Intermediate Certificate, Dawe left school. His first job was as a legal clerk. He had become increasingly restless and more unhappy as his adolescence progressed. Perhaps, as a result, his jobs did not last long. Dawe often became dissatisfied and left of his own volition. He worked as a newspaper copy-boy, labourer, insurance salesman and writer of advertising copy. He often overcame boredom and monotony at work by composing songs.

In 1953, Dawe completed Adult Matriculation with honours in English literature and gained entrance to Melbourne University. However, on failing to pass his exams, he became a postman. In 1959 he joined the Royal Australian Air Force and served in the Education section for nine years. He finally completed his Bachelor of Arts degree by correspondence in 1969. He has since obtained a Bachelor of Letters, Master of Arts and a Doctor of Philosophy and now teaches at the Darling Downs Institute of Advanced Education.

Bruce Dawe's Poetry

It is obvious that Bruce Dawe's background has contributed to his success as a poet. Bruce Dawe writes about ordinary people in the suburbs confronting their everyday problems. He says of his poetry:

> The themes I deal with are the common ones of modern civilisation: loneliness, old age, death, dictatorship and love. I like the dramatic monologue form and use it in free, blank and rhymed verse-forms, attempting at the same time to capture something of the evanescence of contemporary idioms which is far richer and more allusive than the stereotyped stone-the-crows popular concept of Australian speech would have people believe.

Dawe sympathises with the 'underdog'. He observes and records the sorrows and hardships of ordinary people struggling to survive. His poems such as 'The Drifters', 'The Family Man' and 'The Victims' show Dawe's compassion for their suffering and tragedy.

Dawe is concerned to point out injustices and those aspects of society that need to be changed. He often uses humour, irony or ridicule to achieve this. Consequently, many of his readers consider him to be a satirical poet. However, Dawe himself is unhappy with this designation. He says, 'I wouldn't like to think that I thought of myself exclusively as a satirical poet.'

Dawe believes poets should be 'at the barricades, fighting alongside those others who feel it part of their responsibility as citizens to resist those who would turn Australia into a quarry-hole surrounded by an oil-slick.' In 'Search and Destroy', 'In the New Landscape' and other poems he condemns the ever-increasing destruction of the environment. He makes us aware of the moral decay in society in poems such as 'Planning a Time Capsule' and 'Enter without So Much as Knocking'.

Nor is he afraid to criticise governments and politicians who cause destruction and the senseless waste of lives. Poems such as 'Homecoming' and 'Vietnam Postscript, 1975' attest to this. He feels that writers 'have a responsibility to be attuned to the suffering of those who cannot speak for themselves, the migrant peoples, the old-age pensioners, the mentally-ill, the prisoners.'

Bruce Dawe could well be called a poet of the people. His collections of poems, such as *Condolences of the Season* and *Sometimes Gladness* have sold tens of thousands of copies. Because he writes about the problems of life in a language that everyone can understand, he has the ability to interest those who do not normally care for poetry.

God expelled Adam and Eve from the Garden of Eden because they had eaten of the fruit of the tree of knowledge. Bruce Dawe likens the experiences of young people at school to those of the original Adam and Eve cast out into a hostile world.

Genesis

School began again this week . . .
　　Mincing in their brand-new tunics,
　　Cocky in their blue and grey,
　　Shouldering their cardboard school-bags,
　　Getting in each other's way,
　　Entering their different class-rooms
　　(Like old 'lags' to whom all's one!),
　　Stabbing first flies with new biros,
　　Watching, corner-eyed, the sun
　　No longer at their beck and calling
　　Answering, like them, the bell,
　　Carefully printing names on note-books
　　In a script too soon pell-mell,
　　Opening with sinking spirits
　　Text-books whose right answers loom
　　Like jet 'planes so far above them,
　　Waiting for the sonic boom
　　Of comprehension, eating lunches,
　　Or part thereof: tooth-rotting cakes,
　　Mind-destroying Fizzi-Cola,
　　Dumping wholesome snacks Mum makes
　　In the school incinerator—
　　Ah, what ink-stained webs we weave
　　When first from Eden's garden sending
　　Little Adam, little Eve!

BRUCE DAWE

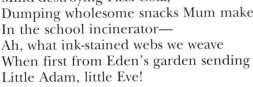

Experiencing School Days

1 The word 'genesis' means a beginning. Why is the poem called 'Genesis'?
2 What scene is the poet describing in the first three lines of the poem?
3 A 'lag' was the name given to a convict in the early days of Australia's history. What is the meaning of 'Like old "lags" to whom all's one!'
4 'Stabbing first flies with new biros'. What does this show about the students' attitude to school?
5 Why are the students watching the sun 'corner-eyed'?
6 Why is the sun 'No longer at their beck and calling'?
7 'In a script too soon pell-mell'. What happens to the students' writing as time passes?
8 Why do you think the students open their text-books 'with sinking spirits'?
9 Why does the poet compare the 'right answers' to 'jet planes'?
10 What impression does the poet give of the students' food and drink?
11 What is the meaning of 'ink-stained webs we weave'?
12 What is 'Eden's garden'?
13 Who are 'little Adam' and 'little Eve'?
14 What is the poet's attitude to school?
15 Do you think Bruce Dawe gives a true-life picture of school? Explain your viewpoint.

Bruce Dawe is concerned to show how our environment is being destroyed by twentieth century living.

Search and Destroy   *A Bi-Centenary Poem*

Fear no more the heat o' the sun
—its rays are filtered, every one.

The fumes from car-exhausts and fires
from dumps and furnaces aspires

to poison heaven where the bird
sings on a diminished third

or totters from the well-sprayed tree
replete with years and DDT.

Now nature grinds her basic gears,
the big-end knocks, the junk-yard nears . . .

Now fish float belly-up downstream caught
by chemicals too vague to be fought,

the forests sigh and fall, the hills
blink baldly as the new wind chills,

the grasslands waver and are gone,
the concrete Nothing blunders on,

black gold fountains to the sky,
the sands are mined, the sea-coasts die,

the land runs ruin to our pride!
Lord, give us, for our patricide,

two hundred more years like the last
and what shall then withstand the blast?

BRUCE DAWE

Understanding Search and Destroy

1 Why has the poet called this poem 'Search and Destroy'?
2 Why does the poet describe the sun's rays as 'filtered'?
3 How is the bird life being destroyed?
4 What does the poet compare nature to in the fifth stanza?
5 What words does he use to suggest that nature is breaking down?
6 How does Dawe create a sense of hopelessness in the sixth stanza?
7 'The forests sigh and fall'. What does Dawe achieve by his personification of the forests?
8 What is the meaning of 'the hills blink baldly'? What does the poet achieve by his repetition of the letter 'b'?
9 What is the meaning of 'the concrete Nothing blunders on'? Why is 'blunders' an effective word?
10 'Black gold fountains to the sky'. What is happening?
11 What does the poet mean by 'the land runs ruin to our pride'?
12 What warning is the poet giving us at the end of the poem?
13 What is the poet's purpose in this poem?
14 What techniques has he used to achieve his purpose?
15 What concerns about the environment have you experienced while reading this poem?
16 To what extent do you feel Bruce Dawe's criticisms are justified?

In 'Homecoming', Bruce Dawe makes us aware of the senseless waste of human lives during the Vietnam War.

Homecoming

All day, day after day, they're bringing them home,
they're picking them up, those they can find, and bringing them home,
they're bringing them in, piled on the hulls of Grants, in trucks, in convoys,
they're zipping them up in green plastic bags,
they're tagging them now in Saigon, in the mortuary coolness
they're giving them names, they're rolling them out of
the deep-freeze lockers—on the tarmac of Tan Son Nhut
the noble jets are whining like hounds,
they are bringing them home
—curly-heads, kinky-hairs, crew-cuts, balding non-coms
—they're high, now, high and higher, over the land, the steaming *chow mein*,
their shadows are tracing the blue curve of the Pacific
with sorrowful quick fingers, heading south, heading east,
home, home, home—and the coasts swing upward, the old ridiculous
                                            curvatures
of earth, the knuckled hills, the mangrove-swamps, the desert emptiness . . .
in their sterile housing they tilt towards these like skiers
—taxiing in, on the long runways, the howl of their homecoming rises
surrounding them like their last moments (the mash, the splendour)
then fading at length as they move
on to small towns where dogs in the frozen sunset
raise muzzles in mute salute,
and on to cities in whose wide web of suburbs
telegrams tremble like leaves from a wintering tree
and the spider grief swings in his bitter geometry
—they're bringing them home, now, too late, too early.

BRUCE DAWE

Questioning Vietnam

1 What does the poet achieve by the repetition of the word 'day' in 'All day, day after day'?
2 Why is the poem called 'Homecoming'?
3 'Those they can find.' What point is the poet making?
4 How does the poet create the impression that many soldiers have been killed?
5 How does the poet show that the dead men have lost their individuality?
6, Why does the poet mention 'the deep-freeze lockers'?
7 'The noble jets are whining like hounds'. What is the poet making us aware of in this scene?
8 What effect does the poet create by describing the different hairstyles of the dead soldiers?

9 Why do you think the poet compares the Mekong Delta in Vietnam to a 'steaming *chow mein*'?
10 '. . . heading south, heading east'. Where are the planes going?
11 What impression does the poet give of the Australian landscape?
12 What do the words 'the mash, the splendour' suggest about the last moments of the soldiers in battle?
13 How do the dogs in the small towns react to the arrival of the bodies of the dead soldiers?
14 How is grief brought to those living in the cities?
15 Do you think the poet's 'spider grief' metaphor is effective? Why or why not?
16 'They're bringing them home, now, too late, too early'. Why 'too late'? Why 'too early'?
17 What techniques has Bruce Dawe used to make us aware of the horrors of war?
18 After reading this poem, what are your feelings about the dead soldiers?

In 'Planning a Time-capsule', Bruce Dawe, by his choice of special objects, makes us aware of the many problems of modern society.

Planning a Time-capsule

As typical of these times I would include:
a dirty needle and a rip-top can,
pebbled glass from a windscreen, some spent cartridges,
a singlet noose fresh from a prisoner's neck,
a pamphlet proving
pornography is love, a flask of tears
from battered women (laced with children's blood),
a cassette-tape of cries from bitter tenants
faced with rent-hikes, a food-voucher
for the many hidden hungry, a door key
to signify the homeless, and a colour-shot
of a billion-dollar Parliament House, a press release
from the Bureau of Statistics showing
things are getting better all the time
—and for their rarity I would include:
a bottle of sand
from an undeveloped foreshore, a whole spadeful
of earth that's still Australian, a fern-frond
from the last rain-forest, and a feather
from a free-range hen, a breath
of uncontaminated ozone, and a drop (a single drop)
of water as pure as grief . . .

BRUCE DAWE

Bruce Dawe has described this poem as 'a statement about the rat-race: the pressures of modern living'.

Enter without So Much as Knocking

Memento, homo, quia pulvis es, et in pulverem reverteris . . .

Blink, blink, HOSPITAL, SILENCE.
Ten days old, carried in the front door in his
mother's arms, first thing he heard was
Bobby Dazzler on Channel 7:
Hello, hello, hello all you lucky people and he
really was lucky because it didn't mean a thing
to him then . . .

      A year or two to settle in and
get acquainted with the set-up; like every other
well-equipped smoothly-run household, his included
one economy-size Mum, one Anthony Squires-
Coolstream-Summerweight Dad, along with two other kids
straight off the Junior Department rack.

      When Mum won the
Luck's-A-Fortch Tricky-Tune Quiz she took him shopping
in the good-as-new station-wagon (£495 dep. at Reno's).
Beep, beep. WALK. DON'T WALK. TURN
LEFT. NO PARKING. WAIT HERE. NO
SMOKING. KEEP CLEAR/OUT/OFF GRASS. NO
BREATHING EXCEPT BY ORDER. BEWARE OF
THIS. WATCH OUT FOR THAT. My God (beep)
the congestion here just gets (beep)
worse every day, now what the (beep beep) does
that idiot think he's doing (beep beep and BEEP).

However, what he enjoyed most of all was when they
went to the late show at the local drive-in, on a clear night
and he could see (beyond the fifty-foot screen where
giant faces forever snarled screamed or made
incomprehensible and monstrous love) a pure
unadulterated fringe of sky, littered with stars
no-one had got around to fixing up yet; he'd watch them
circling about in luminous groups like kids at the circus
who never go quite close enough to the elephant to get kicked.

Anyway, pretty soon he was old enough to be
realistic like every other godless
money-hungry back-stabbing miserable
so-and-so, and then it was goodbye stars and the soft
cry in the corner when no-one was looking because
I'm telling you straight, Jim, it's Number One every time
for this chicken, hit wherever you see a head and
kick whoever's down, well thanks for a lovely
evening Clare, it's good to get away from it all
once in a while, I mean it's a real battle all the way
and a man can't help but feel a little soiled, himself,
at times, you know what I mean?

                Now take it easy
on those curves, Alice, for God's sake,
I've had enough for one night, with that Clare Jessup,
hey, ease up, will you, watch it—

                Probity & Sons, Morticians,
did a really first-class job on his face
(everyone was very pleased) even adding a
healthy tan he'd never had, living, gave him back for keeps
the old automatic smile with nothing behind it,
winding the whole show up with a
nice ride out to the underground metropolis:
permanent residentials, no parking tickets, no taximeters
ticking, no Bobby Dazzlers here, no down payments,
nobody grieving over halitosis
flat feet shrinking gums falling hair.

Six feet down nobody interested.

Blink, blink, CEMETERY. Silence.

                          BRUCE DAWE

Understanding Enter without So Much as Knocking

1 The Latin epigraph of the poem, *Memento, homo, quia pulvis es, et in pulverem reverteris . . .*, means 'Remember, man, thou art dust, and unto dust thou shalt return'. What does this epigraph show about life?
2 Dawe says of the poem, 'It starts with the neon signs outside a hospital and ends with a neon sign.' What does Dawe show about life between the neon signs?
3 What is the poet's attitude to television and Bobby Dazzler?
4 What does the poet reveal about the family the child has been born into?
5 'WALK. DON'T WALK. TURN LEFT. NO PARKING . . .' What do the many signs show about modern living?

6 What effect does the poet achieve by the repetition of 'beep' in the third stanza?
7 What impression does the poet give of the drive-in?
8 What does the main character in the poem discover about nature when he is at the drive-in?
9 ' . . . he was old enough to be/realistic'. What did being 'realistic' involve?
10 'The old automatic smile with nothing behind it'. What criticism is the poet making about the main character in the poem?
11 What does the poet mean by 'Six feet down nobody interested'?
12 Do you think Dawe's view of modern living is too depressing and pessimistic in this poem? Explain your viewpoint.
13 Bruce Dawe has said, 'So life is a rush through a spurious [not genuine] existence lived between the brackets of neon signs.' How has Bruce Dawe created the impression of life being 'a rush'?
14 Do you think the ending of the poem is effective? Why or why not?

Bruce Dawe warns us about the kind of life we can expect in the new world of the future.

In the New Landscape

In the new landscape there will be only cars
and drivers of cars and signs saying
FREE SWAP CARDS HERE
and exhaust-fumes drifting over the countryside
and sounds of acceleration instead of birdsong

In the new landscape there will be no more streets
begging for hopscotch squares, only roads
the full width between buildings and a packed mob
of hoods surging between stop-lights
—so dense a sheep-dog with asbestos pads
could safely trot across
(Streets will be underground and pedestrians pale.
Motorists on the other hand will be tanned.)

In the new landscape there will be no trees
unless as exotica for parking-lots
—and weeds,
weeds, too, will be no more

And we will construct in keeping with these times
a concrete god with streamlined attributes
not likely to go soft at the sight or sound of
little children under the front wheels
or lovers who have wilfully forgotten
to keep their eyes on the road,
while by a ceremonial honking of motor-horns
we'll raise a daily anthem of praise
to him in whose stone lap are laid
the morning sacrifices, freshly-garlanded, death's rictus carved
on each face with the sharp obsidian blade
of fortuitousness (steam-hoses will be used
to cleanse the altar . . .)

And in the new landscape after a century or so
of costly research it will be found
that even the irreplaceable parts
will be replaceable, after which
there will be only cars

BRUCE DAWE

Experiencing the New Landscape

1 How does the poet gain your attention at the beginning of the poem?
2 '. . . sounds of acceleration instead of birdsong'. What point is the poet making here?
3 What impression does the poet give you of the roads in the new landscape?
4 Why do you think the pedestrians would be 'pale'?
5 'Weeds, too, will be no more'. What point is the poet making?
6 'A concrete god with streamlined attributes'. What is the poet referring to here?
7 How does the poet suggest the concrete god will be worshipped?
8 What does the poet mean by 'the morning sacrifices'?
9 Why do you think the poet repeats 'in the new landscape' throughout the poem?
10 'There will only be cars'. Do you think this is an effective ending to the poem? Why or why not?
11 What is Bruce Dawe's purpose in this poem?
12 What techniques has he used to achieve this purpose?
13 Has the poet succeeded in making you concerned about the future? Why or why not?
14 Do you think Bruce Dawe would be a conservationist? Explain your viewpoint.

In this poem Bruce Dawe gives us a true-life picture of one aspect of life in the suburbs.

Homo Suburbiensis *for Craig McGregor*

One constant in a world of variables
—a man alone in the evening in his patch of vegetables,
and all the things he takes down with him there

Where the easement runs along the back fence and the air
smells of tomato-vines, and the hoarse rasping tendrils
of pumpkin flourish clumsy whips and their foliage sprawls

Over the compost-box, poising rampant upon
the palings . . .
 He stands there, lost in a green
confusion, smelling the smoke of somebody's rubbish

Burning, hearing vaguely the clatter of a dish
in a sink that could be his, hearing a dog, a kid,
a far whisper of traffic, and offering up instead

Not much but as much as any man can offer
—time, pain, love, hate, age, war, death, laughter, fever,

 BRUCE DAWE

Bruce Dawe has described this poem as 'something like a religious love poem'. He strongly denies it is an attack on Australian Rules Football.

Life-cycle *for Big Jim Phelan*

When children are born in Victoria
they are wrapped in the club-colours, laid in beribboned cots,
having already begun a lifetime's barracking.

Carn, they cry, Carn . . . feebly at first
while parents playfully tussle with them
for possession of a rusk: Ah, he's a little Tiger! (And they are . . .)

Hoisted shoulder-high at their first League game
they are like innocent monsters who have been years swimming
towards the daylight's roaring empyrean

Until, now, hearts shrapnelled with rapture,
they break surface and are forever lost,
their minds rippling out like streamers

In the pure flood of sound, they are scarfed with light, a voice
like the voice of God booms from the stands
Ooohh you bludger and the covenant is sealed.

Hot pies and potato-crisps they will eat,
they will forswear the Demons, cling to the Saints
and behold their team going up the ladder into Heaven,

And the tides of life will be the tides of the home-team's fortunes
—the reckless proposal after the one-point win,
the wedding and honeymoon after the grand-final . . .

They will not grow old as those from more northern States grow old,
for them it will always be three-quarter-time
with the scores level and the wind advantage in the final term,

That passion persisting, like a race-memory, through the welter of seasons,
enabling old-timers by boundary-fences to dream of resurgent lions
and centaur-figures from the past to replenish continually the present,

So that mythology may be perpetually renewed
and Chicken Smallhorn return like the maize-god
in a thousand shapes, the dancers changing

But the dance forever the same—the elderly still
loyally crying Carn . . . Carn . . . (if feebly) unto the very end,
having seen in the six-foot recruit from Eaglehawk their hope of salvation.

BRUCE DAWE

15 Sylvia Plath

Sylvia Plath's Life and Background

Sylvia Plath was born in 1932 in Boston, Massachusetts, USA. Both her mother and father were teachers. During her childhood Sylvia soon showed that she was full of curiosity about nature and about the people and objects around her. Her first poem was published when she was only eight years old.

During the years of her high school and college education she was a prize-winning student who was also very popular socially with a full program of boyfriends and parties. However, the ruthless efficiency which she made the basis of her life caused her to have a nervous breakdown when she was nineteen. In her early twenties, her intellectual brilliance gained her a scholarship to Cambridge University, England. About this time the poet Christopher Levenson who edited *Delta*, a literary magazine, wrote about Sylvia Plath with something like awe: 'She was almost a golden girl, gifted and poised, energetic, serious and intent. My main impression remains one of the combination of intensity and sophistication. For me at least she came across as a strong, confident, experienced young woman.'

In 1955 she met Ted Hughes, later to become a famous poet. She wrote about their relationship: 'In the last two months I have fallen terribly in love, which can only lead to great hurt. I met the strongest man in the world, ex-Cambridge, brilliant poet whose work I loved before I met him, a large, hulking healthy Adam with a voice like the thunder of God — a singer, story-teller, lion . . .'

They were married in 1956 and went to America where Sylvia taught, but in 1959 they returned to England where they lived for the rest of Sylvia's life. Most of her best poetry is full of the emotions that the crises of her life inspired. *The Colossus*, her first book of poetry, was published in 1960. In the same year her first child Frieda was born. Sylvia, however, had profound and self-destructive depths of feeling that few others realised. She wrote of these feelings: 'Life is loneliness . . . yes there is joy, fulfilment and companionship but the loneliness of the soul in its appalling self-consciousness is horrible and overpowering.'

Sylvia Plath suicided in London in February 1963. Nearly twenty years later her *Collected Poems* won the Pulitzer Prize for Poetry.

Features of Sylvia Plath's Poetry

Starting Points

Sylvia Plath wrote many of her poems about the places, experiences, objects, ideas and people in the ordinary world around her, and many of her images evoke the beauty and wonder of the commonplace. Yet in her creative vision the commonplace subjects of her poems equally hint at nightmarish possibilities. Here is her own comment about the sources of her inspiration:

> I think my poems come immediately out of the sensuous and emotional experiences I have . . . I believe that one should be able to control and manipulate experiences, even the most terrifying.

Titles

The titles of her poems are often a single word explanation of the poem's subject. Examples are 'Mushrooms', 'Insomniac', 'Blackberrying' and 'Cut'. Sometimes such a title summarises the subject of the poem without being present anywhere in the poem itself. For example, 'Cut' summarises the subject of the poem but the word is not mentioned in the poem.

Style

Sylvia Plath's writing style has been called terse, disciplined and witty. Most of her poems are lyrical in the sense of being intensely concerned with the poet's thoughts, emotions and moods. Such intense concern occurs in the first lines of 'Cut':

> What a thrill —
> My thumb instead of an onion.
> The top quite gone
> Except for a sort of hinge.

Unity is often achieved in her poems by developing meaning through the thoughtful use of image and metaphor. Impact is achieved by the massing of vivid, often surprising images. For example, from 'Insomniac':

> Under the eyes of the stars and the moon's rictus
> He suffers his desert pillow, sleeplessness
> Stretching its fine, irritating sand in all directions.

Sylvia Plath's poetry is characterised by a flexible range of vocabulary in which the apt word or phrase seems to occur naturally — even though the word or phrase may be startling as in these lines from 'The Arrival of the Bee Box':

> It is dark, dark,
> With the swarmy feeling of African hands.

In this poem the humble mushrooms explain their view of life.

Mushrooms

Overnight, very
Whitely, discreetly,
Very quietly

Our toes, our noses
Take hold on the loam,
Acquire the air.

Nobody sees us,
Stops us, betrays us;
The small grains make room

Soft fists insist on
Heaving the needles,
The leafy bedding,

Even the paving,
Our hammers, our rams,
Earless and eyeless,

Perfectly voiceless,
Widen the crannies,
Shoulder through holes. We

Diet on water,
On crumbs of shadow,
Bland-mannered, asking

Little or nothing.
So many of us!
So many of us!

We are shelves, we are
Tables, we are meek,
We are edible,

Nudgers and shovers
In spite of ourselves.
Our kind multiplies:

We shall by morning
Inherit the earth.
Our foot's in the door.

SYLVIA PLATH

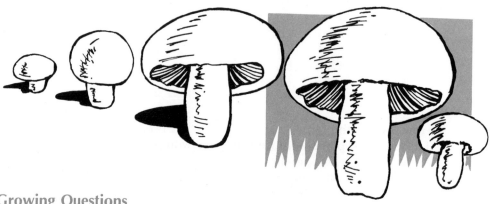

Growing Questions

1 From whose point of view is the poem written?
2 'Whitely, discreetly/Very quietly'. What does this reveal about the mushrooms?
3 How is the mushrooms' grip on the soil personified by the poet?
4 How could the mushrooms be betrayed?
5 What are the mushrooms' 'soft fists'?
6 What contrast exists between the 'soft fists' and the images in the next stanza?
7 What has the poet achieved by the assonance of the 'a' and the alliteration of the 'm' in 'Our hammers, our rams'?
8 What human qualities are not possessed by the mushrooms?
9 What words of the poet suggest an insignificant amount of nourishment?
10 What is the impact of the repeated line 'So many of us'?
11 What does the poet compare the mushrooms' characteristic shape to in the ninth stanza?
12 'The meek shall inherit the earth'. How does the poet apply this saying from the Bible to the mushrooms?
13 'Our foot's in the door'. What do the mushrooms mean?
14 What human qualities has the poet shown the mushrooms to possess?

In the following poem Sylvia Plath probes the destructive aspects of insomnia or sleeplessness. She does so in a flow of imagery that focuses on a man whose mind cannot rest and for whom daylight is 'his white disease'.

Insomniac

The night sky is only a sort of carbon paper,
Blueblack, with the much-poked periods of stars
Letting in the light, peephole after peephole—
A bonewhite light, like death, behind all things.
Under the eyes of the stars and the moon's rictus
He suffers his desert pillow, sleeplessness
Stretching its fine, irritating sand in all directions.

Over and over the old, granular movie
Exposes embarrassments—the mizzling days
Of childhood and adolescence, sticky with dreams,
Parental faces on tall stalks, alternately stern and tearful,
A garden of buggy roses that made him cry.
His forehead is bumpy as a sack of rocks.
Memories jostle each other for face-room like obsolete
       film stars.

He is immune to pills; red, purple, blue—
How they lit the tedium of the protracted evening!
Those sugary planets whose influence won for him
A life baptized in a no-life for a while,
And the sweet, drugged waking of a forgetful baby.
Now the pills are wornout and silly, like classical gods.
Their poppy-sleepy colours do him no good.

His head is a little interior of grey mirrors.
Each gesture flees immediately down an alley
Of diminishing perspectives, and its significance
Drains like water out the hole at the far end.
He lives without privacy in a lidless room,
The bald slots of his eyes stiffened wide-open
On the incessant heat-lightning flicker of situations.

Nightlong, in the granite yard, invisible cats
Have been howling like women, or damaged instruments.
Already he can feel daylight, his white disease,
Creeping up with her hatful of trivial repetitions.
The city is a map of cheerful twitters now,
And everywhere people, eyes mica-silver and blank,
Are riding to work in rows, as if recently brainwashed.

SYLVIA PLATH

Sleepless Considerations

1 What similarities does the poet see between the night sky and carbon paper?
2 What simile does the poet use to make 'the bonewhite light' a threatening quality for the insomniac?
3 'Under the eyes of the stars and the moon's rictus'. The word 'rictus' means a grin. How has the poet made the stars and moon seem human?
4 Why does the poet compare sleeplessness to 'irritating sand'?
5 What does the poet mean by 'Over and over the old, granular movie'?
6 'Mizzling' means raining lightly. Why are the days of the poet's childhood and adolescence 'mizzling'?
7 What memory does the insomniac have of his parents?
8 'His forehead is bumpy as a sack of rocks'. Why is the insomniac having difficulty sleeping?
9 How are taste and shape emphasised in the poet's description of the sleeping pills as 'sugary planets'?
10 Why doesn't the insomniac take sleeping pills?
11 What is happening in the insomniac's mind?
12 Why is daylight the insomniac's 'white disease'?
13 What outside sounds are heard by the insomniac in the last stanza?
14 What impression does the poet give you of the people going to work?
15 The pattern of the poem depends on a series of images. Which of our senses is mainly engaged by them?
16 What was the poet's purpose in writing 'Insomniac'?

The poet sees the balloons as 'soul-animals' that delight the heart. Their ideal relationship with humans is destroyed when the small boy in the poem imagines a balloon might be something good to eat.

Balloons

Since Christmas they have lived with us,
Guileless and clear,
Oval soul-animals,
Taking up half the space,
Moving and rubbing on the silk

Invisible air drifts,
Giving a shriek and pop
When attacked, then scooting to rest, barely trembling.
Yellow cathead, blue fish—
Such queer moons we live with

Instead of dead furniture!
Straw mats, white walls
And these travelling
Globes of thin air, red, green,
Delighting

The heart like wishes or free
Peacocks blessing
Old ground with a feather
Beaten in starry metals.
Your small

Brother is making
His balloon squeak like a cat.
Seeming to see
A funny pink world he might eat on the other side of it,
He bites,

    Then sits
    Back, fat jug
    Contemplating a world clear as water.
    A red
    Shred in his little fist.

SYLVIA PLATH

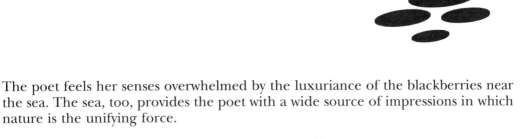

The poet feels her senses overwhelmed by the luxuriance of the blackberries near
the sea. The sea, too, provides the poet with a wide source of impressions in which
nature is the unifying force.

Blackberrying

Nobody in the lane, and nothing, nothing but blackberries,
Blackberries on either side, though on the right mainly,
A blackberry alley, going down in hooks, and a sea
Somewhere at the end of it, heaving. Blackberries
Big as the ball of my thumb, and dumb as eyes
Ebon in the hedges, fat
With blue-red juices. These they squander on my fingers.
I had not asked for such a blood sisterhood; they must love me.
They accommodate themselves to my milkbottle, flattening their sides.

Overhead go the choughs in black, cacophonous flocks—
Bits of burnt paper wheeling in a blown sky.
Theirs is the only voice, protesting, protesting.
I do not think the sea will appear at all.
The high, green meadows are glowing, as if lit from within.
I come to one bush of berries so ripe it is a bush of flies,
Hanging their bluegreen bellies and their wing panes in a Chinese
screen.
The honey-feast of the berries has stunned them; they believe in
heaven.
One more hook, and the berries and bushes end.

The only thing to come now is the sea.
From between two hills a sudden wind funnels at me,
Slapping its phantom laundry in my face.
These hills are too green and sweet to have tasted salt.
I follow the sheep path between them. A last hook brings me
To the hills' northern face, and the face is orange rock
That looks out on nothing, nothing but a great space
Of white and pewter lights, and a din like silversmiths
Beating and beating at an intractable metal.

SYLVIA PLATH

Picking Answers

1 How does the poet use repetition to suggest the overwhelming presence of the blackberries?
2 What do you think the poet wants you to see and imagine as you read the words 'A blackberry alley, going down in hooks'?
3 How does the poet suggest the large size of the blackberries?
4 ' . . . fat/With blue-red juices'. What quality of the blackberries is the poet emphasising?
5 ' . . . These they squander on my fingers'. What is happening here?
6 'Choughs' are dark-coloured birds of the crow family. How do we know they are noisy?
7 Which line pictures the way the choughs in flight look to the poet?
8 When the poet comes to the 'bush of flies' she attempts to create in our minds an image of the bush that is both rich and strange. What words and phrases does she use that help her to achieve her aim?
9 Identify the poet's use of personification to show the force of the wind as it comes at her 'from between two hills'.
10 ' . . . a great space/Of white and pewter lights'. What sea scene confronts the poet?
11 What does the poet compare the sounds of the sea to?
12 What do you think Sylvia Plath's purpose is in writing 'Blackberrying'?

A minor accident becomes an intense and imaginative experience in 'Cut'.

Cut

What a thrill—
My thumb instead of an onion.
The top quite gone
Except for a sort of a hinge

Of skin,
A flap like a hat,
Dead white.
Then that red plush.

Little pilgrim,
The Indian's axed your scalp.
Your turkey wattle
Carpet rolls

Straight from the heart.
I step on it,
Clutching my bottle
Of pink fizz.

A celebration, that is.
Out of a gap
A million soldiers run,
Redcoats, every one.

Whose side are they on?
O my
Homunculus, I am ill.
I have taken a pill to kill

The thin
Papery feeling.
Saboteur,
Kamikaze man—

The stain on your
Gauze Ku Klux Klan
Babushka
Darkens and tarnishes and when

The balled
Pulp of your heart
Confronts its small
Mill of silence

How you jump—
Trepanned veteran,
Dirty girl,
Thumb stump.

SYLVIA PLATH

Painful Questions

1 What situation is the poet describing in the first stanza?
2 How does the poet initially react to the accident?
3 What simile does the poet employ to describe her cut finger?
4 Explain and comment on the poet's use of personification in the third stanza.
5 What change of mood occurs in the third stanza?
6 What metaphor conveys the poet's image of her thumb in the fourth stanza?
7 'A million soldiers run'. What makes this an effective description?
8 Comment on the poet's use of the word 'Redcoats'.
9 'Homunculus' means a little man. How does the poet develop the idea of 'a little man' through her use of personification?
10 'Babushka' is the head scarf worn by Russian peasant women. Why is this a suitable word to describe the poet's thumb?
11 What is the meaning of 'The balled/Pulp of your heart'?
12 How is the poem's last stanza linked to its first?
13 Did you find the poet's approach to her subject unusual? Why?
14 Is the tone of this poem lighthearted or serious? Explain your viewpoint.
15 Why do you think Sylvia Plath wrote this poem?

'The Arrival of the Bee Box' provides an intriguing experience for the poet. Her feelings about the creatures living in the box dominate the poem.

The Arrival of the Bee Box

I ordered this, this clean wood box
Square as a chair and almost too heavy to lift.
I would say it was the coffin of a midget
Or a square baby
Were there not such a din in it.

The box is locked, it is dangerous.
I have to live with it overnight
And I can't keep away from it.
There are no windows, so I can't see what is in there.
There is only a little grid, no exit.

I put my eye to the grid.
It is dark, dark,
With the swarmy feeling of African hands
Minute and shrunk for export,
Black on black, angrily clambering.

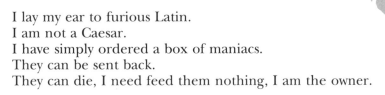

How can I let them out?
It is the noise that appals me most of all,
The unintelligible syllables.
It is like a Roman mob,
Small, taken one by one, but my god, together!

I lay my ear to furious Latin.
I am not a Caesar.
I have simply ordered a box of maniacs.
They can be sent back.
They can die, I need feed them nothing, I am the owner.

I wonder how hungry they are.
I wonder if they would forget me
If I just undid the locks and stood back and turned into a tree.
There is the laburnum, its blond colonnades,
And the petticoats of the cherry.

They might ignore me immediately
In my moon suit and funeral veil.
I am no source of honey
So why should they turn on me?
Tomorrow I will be sweet God, I will set them free.

The box is only temporary.

SYLVIA PLATH

Boxed Questions

1 What comparison does the poet use in the first stanza that shocks the reader?
2 In what way is the word 'din' more forceful than 'noise'?
3 'And I can't keep away from it'. Why does the poet find the box irresistible?
4 What words does the poet use to stress the intensity of the darkness in the box?
5 What, in reality, are the minute black hands that the poet sees through the grid?
6 Explain the meaning of 'Black on black, angrily clambering'.
7 What word in the fourth stanza tells us how strongly the poet felt about the noise?
8 What does the poet compare the noise of the bees to?
9 'I have simply ordered a box of maniacs'. Why does the poet refer to the bees as 'maniacs'?
10 In the fifth stanza, what words of the poet show her power over the bees?
11 Explain the shift of mood that occurs in the sixth stanza.
12 Why does the poet refer to herself as 'sweet God'?
13 Why do you think the last line of the poem is separated from the rest?
14 What have you learned about the character of the poet herself from your reading of the poem?
15 What was the poet's purpose in writing this poem?

16 Douglas Stewart

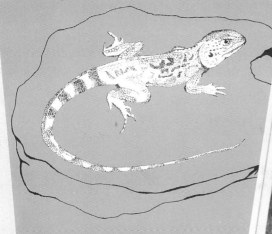

Life and Background of Douglas Stewart

Douglas Stewart, son of a New Zealand lawyer, was born in Eltham, Taranaki Province, New Zealand, in 1913. He attended primary school in his home town, and a high school thirty miles away, before studying at the University of Wellington. He began studying law there, but soon changed courses to major in writing and journalism.

As a young boy, Stewart fell in love with the New Zealand countryside. He roamed its valleys, rivers and mountains, often camping out and frequently indulging his love of fishing. This appreciation of the wonders of nature was to last throughout his lifetime, so that in 1938, when he moved to Australia, it was understandable that he would begin a rest-of-life appreciation of the Australian bush in all its uniqueness. This he sought to capture in his poetry.

Stewart wrote his first poetry at fourteen years of age, while he still lived in New Zealand. He began initially because of the need to produce a poem for his school magazine, but his love for reading and writing poetry developed rapidly. He read widely, including Shakespeare, Wordsworth, Milton and Coleridge, enjoying their ability to compact powerful description into language, and to convey emotion through sound, rhythm and word selection. As he read he worked on his own writing. His father was a subscriber to *The Bulletin* from Australia and the young Stewart regularly sent poems to that magazine, the vast majority of which were rejected. However, he had the thrill of seeing some of his poems published in a companion magazine, *The Australian Women's Mirror*, as well as newspapers and magazines in New Zealand. This encouraged him to continue.

After his university studies, Stewart worked as a journalist in New Zealand in the early 1930s. In 1936, he published his first volume of poems, *Green Lions*, before moving permanently to Australia in 1938 to become Assistant Literary Editor of *The Bulletin*. Two years later he was appointed Literary Editor and he retained this position for the next twenty years.

The years working for *The Bulletin* were immensely productive years, both on a personal level and because of his contribution to the Australian literary and artistic movement. His contemporaries included a number of young poets such as Judith Wright and James McAuley. *The Bulletin*, *Meanjin* and *Southerly* were significant magazines for promoting the poetic achievement of these writers and for establishing a cultural milieu in which a younger breed of poets like Rosemary Dobson, William Hart-Smith and David Campbell could refine their skills.

Stewart is recognised as a major Australian poet, but more than a poet. He stands out as one who has made a significant contribution through his poetry, his verse-plays for radio ('Fire on the Snow' and 'Ned Kelly' being the best known), his short stories and his critical essays. Geoffrey Serle, literary critic, has described Stewart as 'the greatest all-rounder of modern Australian literature'.

During his editorship with *The Bulletin*, Stewart published six volumes of his own poems and co-edited two books of Australian poetry, as well as produced a number of verse-plays and a volume of short stories. He received a number of awards in recognition of his achievements, the most significant being the Order of the British Empire (OBE) in 1960. From 1960 onwards he took a position as a Literary Editor with Angus and Robertson, continuing to write, edit and critique particularly in the area of poetry. He died in 1985, one of Australia's best-known and widely recognised poets.

Stewart has written about his approach to writing poetry:

> When I was younger I used to have these 'given' poems. I'd have the inspiration and down it would go. My artistry was pretty rough, but it didn't worry me. But that changes as you get older. It's very complex. I don't think anyone really understands how poems happen. You've half got an idea and you have to find out what you really want to say. Then it's a matter of saying it in lines that you can accept yourself. I feel that the whole thing is there — a complete poem exists somewhere — and you've got to fight your way through it. It's a matter of chopping away — throwing away the bad lines, lines where you're going in the wrong direction.

Features of Douglas Stewart's Poetry

Variety and Richness of Themes

While Stewart certainly emerges as perhaps Australia's best known nature poet, he has contributed significant numbers of poems to other theme areas as well. These include meditative poems often drawn from specific, historical incidents, love poems, ballads and light verse. While most of the poems in our selection are drawn from his nature poems, 'Leopard Skin' serves as an example of light verse, because of its tongue-in-cheek humorous quality.

Detailed Description and Rich Images

Stewart is noted for the richness of his description of aspects of nature. He seems able to focus, and stay focused, on his subject, detailing through rich images, first this aspect, then that. Thus, in 'Wombat', the unusual bush creature is described as 'old pig, old bear', 'poor lump of movable clay', and 'old tree-root's companion', each phrase capturing a specific aspect of the wombat's being. He tries to capture the essence of what he describes. Some writers have seen Stewart's description as clinically observant, rather than emotional, though this appears to vary from poem to poem.

Powerful, Clear Language

Across the range of poems he has written, Stewart has shown himself to be a poet skilled in using powerful, lyrical phrases. For example:

> Thin stone is in this chill wind from the south . . .
> Like the lean soul of steel, like spinster's lips.

and

> It has an acid taste, unhumanised.

His words tend not to be complex; at times they are colloquial. For example:

> Waddle away with a wounded air, the blue-tongued lizard said.

He shows a certain fascination with colour words in his descriptive poetry. Indeed his first volume of poems was called *Green Lions* and his second, *The White Cry*.

In 'Wombat', Douglas Stewart explores some of the many aspects of this strange creature that make it distinctive.

Wombat

> Ha there! old pig, old bear, old bristly and gingery
> Wombat out of the red earth peering gingerly
> Was there some thud of foot in the mist and the silence
> That stiffens whisker and ear in sound's fierce absence,
> Some smell means man?
> I see the dewdrop trembling upon the rushes,
> All else is the mist's now, river and rocks and ridges.
> Poor lump of movable clay, snuffling and blinking,
> Too thick in the head to know what thumps in your thinking,
> Rears in the rain—
> Be easy, old tree-root's companion; down there where your burrow
> Dips in its yellow shadow, deep in the hollow,
> We have one mother, good brother; it is Her laughter
> That sends you now snorting and plunging like red flood-water
> To earth again.

> DOUGLAS STEWART

Checking Out Wombat

1 'Ha there!' What does this particular start to the poem suggest about the circumstances in which the poet sees the wombat?

2 ' . . . old pig, old bear, old bristly and gingery'. Why do you think the poet repeats the word 'old' three times? What suggests oldness so strongly to him?

3 How does the wombat look around when it surfaces?

4 What sound does the poet think may have brought the wombat up to look around?

5 What other aspect of the poet's presence does this poem suggest may have stirred the wombat to surface?

6 'In sound's fierce absence'. Explain what the poet means.

7 What sort of a morning is it as the poet watches the wombat? Quote from the poem in support of your answer.

8 'Poor lump of movable clay'. What aspect of the wombat does this image identify?

9 How does the poet want the wombat to feel? Refer to the poem for evidence.

10 Who is the 'one mother' that the wombat and the poet share?

11 What does the poet imagine causes the wombat to plunge back into its hole?

12 Identify two examples of alliteration from the poem. What effect do they have?

13 How does the poet feel about the wombat? Find evidence from the poem.

14 How well do you think the poet has captured this moment of discovery — the moment when he sees the wombat in the bush? Give reasons for your answer.

In the bush you can run across a snake anywhere. This poem records an encounter between the poet and a brown snake, and the impact it had on the poet.

The Brown Snake

I walked to the green gum-tree
Because the day was hot;
A snake could be anywhere
But that time I forgot.

The Duckmaloi lazed through the valley
In amber pools like tea
From some old fossicker's billy,
And I walked under the tree.

Blue summer smoked on Bindo,
It lapped me warm in its waves,
And when that snake hissed up
Under the shower of leaves

Huge, high as my waist,
Rearing with lightning's tongue,
So brown with heat like the fallen
Dry sticks it hid among,

I thought the earth itself
Under the green gum-tree,
All in the sweet of summer
Reached out to strike at me.

DOUGLAS STEWART

Keeping an Eye on The Brown Snake

1 Why did the poet walk to the gum-tree?
2 What lesson of the bush did the poet momentarily forget?
3 What do you think the Duckmaloi was?
4 What colour was the Duckmaloi, and why was it this colour?
5 What did the colour of the Duckmaloi remind the writer of?
6 Why does the poet describe summer as 'blue'?
7 What do you think Bindo was?
8 What sounds marked the snake's attack?
9 Why does the poet describe the snake's tongue as 'lightning's tongue'?
10 Why did the poet not see the snake under the tree?
11 What did the poet think had happened?
12 How do you think the poet felt, judging from the description of what he thought had happened?
13 In each stanza the poet uses a colour. Identify these and comment on the effect of colour in the poem.
14 The poem is a very simple one. Is this a strength or a weakness? Why?

In 'The Lizards', Stewart is observing two lizards and the fight that ensues between them. In imagination he enters into the experience of the blue-tongued lizard, describing what might have gone through that lizard's mind.

The Lizards

My wife is a lovely leathery green, the blue-tongued lizard said;
Her eyes are as red as bulldog ants, lurking in holes in her head;
Her body is made of the speckled grass, a violet grows on her
    tongue,
And I could watch her for fifty years if nobody blundered along.

The broken ridge like a bullock's ribs lies crumbling under the
    blue,
But the granite skull will last my time, and there's room for my
    truelove, too;
If I were a lizard half my size and out for a girl or a walk,
I think I'd be taking another track, and I wouldn't stop to talk.

Down in the valley the river shines, the willows waver and gleam,
And maybe it's you the plovers mean when they open their beaks
    and scream.
If I were as young and green as you, I'd take no risks, my boy—
Why not go off and drown yourself in the glimmering Duckmaloi?

Over the valley the gum-trees grow, the vast blue ranges loom,
The world is crowded with wives to steal and the world is full of
    room.
If I had hissed and glared like you I'd feel that I'd done enough—
Why don't you climb Mount Bindo there and see if you can't fall
    off?

If I opened my jaws myself like that, the blue-tongued lizard said,
And then if they closed again like this they'd just about fit your
    head;
There's a certain pain in having to fight but there's also a certain
    joy,
And the more you bite my belly or leg the more you'll pay, my boy.

I lay on my rock with the sun on my back and nothing but love
    in my soul,
But if I am forced to gasp and claw and roll and fight in a hole,
If I am forced to fight in the dirt under the blue of the sky
—The black snake lives in the briar-bush and he will be kinder
    than I.

Waddle away with a wounded air, the blue-tongued lizard said,
The ant and the crow will nurse you well and tuck you safely in
    bed.
We were at peace, my wife and I, before you blundered along,
And now she will soothe my scaly side with her beautiful purple
    tongue.

DOUGLAS STEWART

Levelling with The Lizards

1. How does the blue-tongued lizard feel about his wife? What evidence is there?
2. What is the blue-tongued lizard doing at the start of the poem?
3. In the second stanza we are given some description of the other lizard. What facts are we given about it?
4. In the third stanza the blue-tongued lizard begins 'warning off' its opponent. Why does it suggest the other lizard should not take any risks?
5. What two humorous, alternative actions to fighting does the blue-tongued lizard suggest to its opponent in this poem?
6. What are the preliminary warlike actions of the smaller lizard?
7. 'If I opened my jaws myself like that . . . ' What action has the smaller lizard just taken? What action will the blue-tongued lizard take?
8. What threat does the blue-tongued lizard make if its opponent bites its belly or leg?
9. What two aspects of the blue-tongued lizard's nature are depicted in the second-last stanza?
10. Who would be an easier opponent than the blue-tongued lizard?
11. 'Waddle away with a wounded air'. What has taken place?
12. What does the word 'blundered' suggest about the way the blue-tongued lizard feels about the intruder?
13. What consolation does the blue-tongued lizard look forward to at the end of the poem?
14. How would you describe the tone of this poem? What gives it this tone?
15. What do you think was the poet's purpose in writing this poem?

The poet observes an old lady who daily comes to feed the alley-cats that live around
the Domain in Sydney. He sees a certain grandness in her humble actions and the
response of the cats.

Lady Feeding the Cats

I

Shuffling along in her broken shoes from the slums,
A blue-eyed lady showing the weather's stain,
Her long dress green and black like a pine in the rain,
Her bonnet much bedraggled, daily she comes
Uphill past the Moreton Bays and the smoky gums
With a sack of bones on her back and a song in her brain
To feed those outlaws prowling about the Domain,
Those furtive she-cats and those villainous toms.

Proudly they step to meet her, they march together
With an arching of backs and a waving of plumy tails
And smiles that swear they never would harm a feather.
They rub at her legs for the bounty that never fails,
    They think she is a princess out of a tower,
    And so she is, she is trembling with love and power.

2

Meat, it is true, is meat, and demands attention
But this is the sweetest moment that they know
Whose courtship even is a hiss, a howl and a blow.
At so much kindness passing their comprehension
—Beggars and rogues who never deserved this pension—
Some recollection of old punctilio
Dawns in their eyes, and as she moves to go
They turn their battered heads in condescension.

She smiles and walks back lightly to the slums.
If she has fed their bodies, they have fed
More than the body in her; they purr like drums,
Their tails are banners and fountains inside her head.
    The times are hard for exiled aristocrats,
    But gracious and sweet it is to be queen of the cats.

DOUGLAS STEWART

'Leopard Skin', like 'The Lizards', has a touch of light, tongue-in-cheek humour to it. The poet uses the sight of leopard-skin underpants to write about adolescence and its mystical passage into adulthood.

Leopard Skin

Seven pairs of leopard-skin underpants
Flying on the rotary clothes-line! Oh, look, look, virgins,
How with the shirts and pyjamas they whirl and dance.
And think no more, trembling in your own emergence
Like butterflies into the light, that tall soft boy
Who nightly over his radio crooned and capered
Alone in his room in weird adolescent joy
Is mother's boy, softy: has he not slain a leopard?

But more than that: does he not wear its skin,
Secretly, daily, superbly? Oh, girls, adore him,
For dreaming on velvet feet to slay and to sin
He prowls the suburb, the wild things flee before him,
He miaous at the leopardesses, and they stop:
He *is* a leopard—he bought himself in a shop.

DOUGLAS STEWART

Lifting the Lid on Leopard Skin

1 Where does the poet see the seven pairs of leopard-skin underpants?
2 What other articles of clothing are with them?
3 Who does the poet address, asking them to see the underpants?
4 The poet suggests that young girls, too, move very timidly into adulthood. What simile does he use to describe their emergence into adult life?
5 What activities of the 'tall soft boy' does the poet depict as taking place 'nightly'?
6 How does the poet ask the young girls to readjust their thinking about this boy?
7 What humorous evidence does the poet offer to prove that the boy has become a man?
8 How does the boy feel when he is wearing the leopard-skin underpants? What evidence is there in the poem?
9 How does the poet invite the girls to respond to this mighty creature? Quote from the poem to support your answer.
10 'He prowls the suburb'. Why is 'prowls' an appropriate word to use here?
11 'He miaous at the leopardesses'. What word is deliberately used to poke fun here?
12 What is the effect of the last line of the poem?
13 How would you classify this poem? Explain your answer.
14 How would you describe the achievement of 'Leopard Skin'? Why?

The poet is fascinated to find a crab hanging onto a cicada. He has a warning for the crab.

Crab and Cicada

Some flying-fish then? Some green fantastic lobster?
But never in wave or crevice was seen such a monster.
Why then, old claw of the ocean, blood-red and purple,
Gripping so rare a banquet of splendour and peril
Where, warily, tip of your nipper to wing's fine shoulder,
You crouch on the sunny rock with the big cicada
Who fell down dazed and singing from the shining air—
That's the green earth you clutch: and ages and ages
Ago it climbed the cliff where no wave reaches
And towered with the powers that strike from the air, old pirate.
See, even this green innocent, beating and desperate,
Stares with its eyes like suns to burn and startle;
'Chir! Chir!' it says with its hard rocky rattle
And dine you may, but you may well beware.

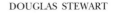

DOUGLAS STEWART

On the Brindabella Mountains the poet is caught up in a moment of mystery. He imagines he hears the mountain speaking, and sees the effect of its words on nature. A magpie makes a distinct response.

Brindabella

Once on a silver and green day, rich to remember,
When thick over sky and gully rolled winter's grey wave
And one lost magpie was straying on Brindabella
I heard the mountain talking in a tall green cave
Between the pillars of the trees and the moss below:
It made no sound but talked to itself in snow.

All the white words were falling through the timber
Down from the old grey thought to the flesh of rock
And some were of silence and patience, and spring after winter,
Tidings for leaves to catch and roots to soak,
And most were of being the earth and floating in space
Alone with its weather through all the time there is.

Then it was, struck with wonder at this soliloquy,
The magpie lifting his beak by the frozen fern
Sent out one ray of a carol, softened and silvery,
Strange through the trees as sunlight's pale return,
Then cocked his black head and listened, hunched from the cold,
Watching that white whisper fill his green world.

DOUGLAS STEWART

The poet observes a wasp, trapped inside a car, trying to find a way out through the windscreen. Once again his keen powers of observation and his word-craft enable him to recreate for us his experience as he watches the wasp.

Wasp

Well wasp what's
To do about you
Battering at the windscreen
You can't get through?

World's all wrong,
Air itself in treason
Turns a sudden solid
And shuts you in prison.

And still through the wall wasp
The long green paddocks sweeten
With trigger-flower and daisy
And gold billy-button;

But up wasp down wasp
Climb wasp and fall,
Can't beat your way
Through the clear strange wall.

Out and away then
When the car stops;
World's come right again
And happy goes wasp.

DOUGLAS STEWART

17 Poets and People

Poets have been writing about people for thousands of years. Sometimes the poets are just observers, sometimes they are wondrous admirers and at other times they are bitter critics. The poems of Roman poets such as Catullus, Horace, Juvenal, Martial and others seem as vital today as they were when they were first written some two thousand years ago.

As the centuries have passed, famous poets such as Pope, Browning, Tennyson, Wordsworth, Coleridge, Yeats, Eliot, Frost, Owen, Hughes, Heaney and many others have created a wonderful heritage of people poems. Here is an enjoyable sample of these poems from countries around the world.

Geoffrey Chaucer, who is considered by many as the father of English poetry, is famous for *The Canterbury Tales*. Written in the fourteenth century, *The Canterbury Tales* is a collection of stories in verse about a party of pilgrims going from London to the shrine of St Thomas à Becket at Canterbury. A mediaeval pilgrimage brought all kinds of people together. Chaucer's characters include such people as a knight, a squire, a miller, a cook, a nun, a monk, a physician, a wife and a pardoner. Each pilgrim tells a story more or less in keeping with his or her character and personality. The following sketch of a squire is from Chaucer's 'General Prologue', which introduces the tales. For your interest, a translation of Chaucer's fourteenth century English has been included.

The Squire

With hym ther was his sone, a yong squier,
A lovyere, and a lusty bacheler,
With lokkes crulle, as they were leyd in presse.
Of twenty yeer of age he was, I gesse.
Of his stature he was of evene lengthe,
And wonderly deliver, and of greet strengthe;
And he had been somtyme in chivachye,
In Flandres, in Artoys and Picardye,
And born him weel, as of so litel space,
In hope to stonden in his lady grace.
Embrouded was he, as it were a meede
Al ful of fresshe floures, whyte and reede;
Singynge he was, or floytinge, al the day.
He was as fressh as is the month of May.
Short was his gowne, with sleves longe and wyde;
Wel koude he sitte on hors and faire ryde; . . .
He koude songes make and wel endyte,
Juste and eek daunce, and weel purtreye and write.
So hoote he lovede that by nyghtertale
He sleep namoore than dooth a nyghtingale.
Curteis he was, lowly and servisable,
And carfbiforn his fader at the table.

GEOFFREY CHAUCER

Translation of **The Squire**

He had his son with him, a fine young Squire,
A lover and cadet, a lad of fire
With locks as curly as if they had been pressed.
He was some twenty years of age, I guessed.
In stature he was of a moderate length,
With wonderful agility and strength.
He'd seen some service with the cavalry
In Flanders and Artois and Picardy
And had done valiantly in little space
Of time, in hope to win his lady's grace.
He was embroidered like a meadow bright
And full of freshest flowers, red and white.
Singing he was, or fluting all the day;
He was as fresh as is the month of May.
Short was his gown, the sleeves were long and wide;
He knew the way to sit a horse and ride.
He could make songs and poems and recite,
Knew how to joust and dance, to draw and write.
He loved so hotly that till dawn grew pale
He slept as little as a nightingale.
Courteous he was, lowly and serviceable,
And carved to serve his father at the table.

GEOFFREY CHAUCER
(*Translated by Nevil Coghill*)

Meeting Chaucer's Squire

1 What impression do the words 'a lad of fire' ('a lusty bacheler') give of the squire?
2 What does Chaucer tell us about the squire's hair?
3 What war service had the squire completed. What does the poet achieve by mentioning the names of the places where the squire fought?
4 By what means had the squire hoped 'to win his lady's grace'?
5 'He was embroidered like a meadow bright/And full of freshest flowers, red and white'. What is this description suggesting about the squire's clothing? Comment on the effectiveness of the simile.
6 Do you think a twentieth century poet would use a simile such as this? Why or why not?
7 What does Chaucer achieve by the alliteration of the letters 'f' and 'l' in 'full of freshest flowers'?
8 'Singing he was, or fluting all the day'. What does this suggest about the squire's temperament?
9 'He was as fresh as is the month of May'. What qualities of the squire is this simile emphasising? (In England the month of May is part of spring.)

10 What do the last two lines of the description reveal about the squire's relationship with his father?
11 The squire is a young man of the fourteenth century. What details about him belong to his period of history?
12 In what ways does he resemble a modern teenager?
13 In what ways does he differ from a modern teenager?
14 From your reading of this description of the squire, suggest why Chaucer's *Canterbury Tales* is still enjoyed by readers today.

The speaker in the poem is a young woman who, in her silhouette heels, is able for a while to escape from the problems of real life and become a princess.

Silhouette Heels

I have me a place which is all me own
When me old man dags me
   and me mother—she can't stop her moan
I put on me silhouette heels and go
   clicking down the stairs.

At the bus stop I pay me fare—one and six
And I go find me a seat at the top
Where the wind changes me from a dumb sheila
   with good legs to *someone.*
My mind is free to think and dream;
I become a princess, Sophia Loren, the Queen;
   —not myself.

Suddenly the bus stops—I get off and walk through
   the town
And I can't help myself from wiggling and noticing
   all the eyes on me
And if there's a 'nicee' I might give him a 'come-on.'
I drop in at the pub and have me a few
But soon it's time for me, again, to get home.

Again I pay me one and six and sit in the top—my
   special place
where I can wish, dream, I was someone.

I get off at my stop
And go clicking up the stairs in my silhouette heels
Me old man will dag me
   and me mother won't stop her moan;
And maybe again I'll go to me special place—
   to dream, to wish . . .

IRENE KOLTUNIEWICZ

Putting Yourself in Someone Else's Shoes

1 In the first stanza, the speaker uses the word 'me', often incorrectly, six times. What is its effect?
2 What problems does the speaker face at home?
3 How does she solve them for the time being?
4 'Clicking down the stairs' Why is 'clicking' a better word than 'walking'?
5 What effect does the wind have on her attitude to life?
6 '. . . a dumb sheila/with good legs'. What is the speaker's opinion of herself? Why do you think she comments on her 'good legs'?
7 'And I can't help myself from wiggling and noticing/all the eyes on me'. What does this reveal about the speaker?
8 How do the words 'nicee' and 'come-on' help to make the poem true to life?
9 Why does she refer to the top of the bus as her 'special place'?
10 'I can wish, dream, I was someone'. Why does she need to do this?
11 'And go clicking up the stairs in my silhouette heels'. This is the second time she mentions her silhouette heels. Why are they so important to her?
12 'To dream, to wish . . .' Do you think this is a good ending to the poem? Why or why not?
13 In this poem we learn about the young woman's innermost feelings and thoughts. How has the poet been able to do this?
14 What are your feelings towards the young woman?

A clown brings happiness to others, but what about the clown himself? The poet Phoebe Hesketh sets out to answer this question.

Clown

He was safe
behind the whitened face
and red nose of his trade,
vocation more certain
than doctor's or priest's
to cheer and heal.
Hidden away from himself
he could always make us laugh
turning troubles like jackets
inside out, wearing
our rents and patches.
Tripping up in trousers too long
he made us feel tall;
and when we watched him
cutting himself down,
missing the ball,
we knew we could cope.

What we never knew
was the tightrope he walked
when the laughter had died.
Nowhere to hide in the empty night,
no one to catch his fall.

PHOEBE HESKETH

The poet Roy Campbell provides us with a true-life study of a Zulu girl and her baby.

The Zulu Girl

When in the sun the hot red acres smoulder,
Down where the sweating gang its labour plies,
A girl flings down her hoe, and from her shoulder
Unslings her child tormented by the flies.

She takes him to a ring of shadow pooled
By thorn-trees: purples with the blood of ticks,
While her sharp nails, in slow caresses ruled,
Prowl through his hair with sharp electric clicks.

His sleepy mouth plugged by the heavy nipple,
Tugs like a puppy, grunting as he feeds:
Through his frail nerves her own deep languors ripple
Like a broad river sighing through its reeds.

Yet in that drowsy stream his flesh imbibes
An old unquenched unsmotherable heat—
The curbed ferocity of beaten tribes,
The sullen dignity of their defeat.

Her body looms above him like a hill
Within whose shade a village lies at rest.
Or the first cloud so terrible and still
That bears the coming harvest in its breast.

ROY CAMPBELL

Observing The Zulu Girl

1 What is the setting for this poem?
2 What words does the poet use to create feelings of heat in the first stanza?
3 'A girl flings down her hoe'. Why is 'flings' a more effective word than, say, 'drops'?

4 ' . . . purples with the blood of ticks'. What has happened? Comment on the poet's use of 'purples'.
5 Comment on the poet's use of alliteration and assonance in the word 'electric clicks'.
6 'Tugs like a puppy'. Do you think this simile is effective? Why or why not?
7 What is the tone of the third stanza?
8 What has the poet shown us about the relationship between girl and her baby?
9 In the fourth stanza, what does the poet tell us of the history of the child's race?
10 Why does the poet compare the mother's body to a 'hill'?
11 What warning about the future does the poet give in the last two lines of the poem?
12 Do you think 'The Zulu Girl' is a suitable title for this poem? What title would you give the poem?
13 Do you think the poem could have been written from a real-life experience? Explain your viewpoint?
14 What do you think was the poet's purpose in writing this poem?

The lift man here reveals his innermost feelings towards the public as he goes about his daily duties.

The Lift Man

In uniform behold me stand,
The lovely lift at my command.
    I press the button: Pop,
And down I go below the town;
The walls rise up as I go down
    And in the basement stop.

For weeks I've worked a morning shift
On this old Waygood-Otis lift.
    And goodness, don't I love
To press the knob that shuts the gate
When customers are shouting 'Wait!'
    And soar to floors above.

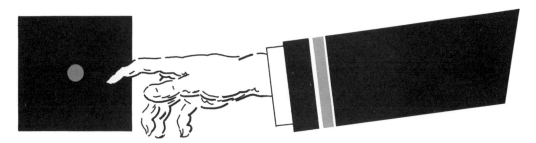

I see them from my iron cage,
Their faces looking up in rage,
   And then I call 'First floor!'
'Perfume and ladies' underwear!'
'No sir, Up only. Use the stair.'
   And up again we soar.

The second floor for kiddie goods,
And kiddie-pantz and pixie-hoods,
   The third floor, restaurant:
And here the people always try
To find one going down, so I
   Am not the lift they want.

On the roof-garden floor alone
I wait for ages on my own
   High, high above the crowds.
O let them rage and let them ring,
For I am out of everything,
   Alone among the clouds.

JOHN BETJEMAN

Understanding The Lift Man

1 'In uniform behold me stand'. What is the first impression you have of the lift man?
2 What do the words 'The lovely lift at my command' suggest about the lift man's attitude to his work?
3 What is the effect of the poet's use of the word 'Pop'?
4 How does the poet create the sensation of the lift going down?
5 Why do you think the lift man enjoys shutting the gate when customers are shouting 'Wait'?
6 Why is 'soar' a more effective word than, say, 'rise'?
7 'No sir, Up only. Use the stair'. What does the poet achieve by using dialogue in his poem?
8 What is the contrast between 'the roof-garden floor' and 'The second floor for kiddie goods'?
9 'I wait for ages on my own'. Why do you think the lift man wants to be alone?
10 'O let them rage and let them ring'. What is the lift man's attitude to the customers?
11 'Alone among the clouds'. What feelings does the lift man seem to experience here?
12 Why do you think the poet has taken an ordinary person such as a lift man and made him the subject of his poem?
13 What is your attitude to the lift man?
14 What does the poet achieve by making the lift man the speaker in the poem?

The Russian poet Yevgeny Yevtushenko presents us with a sad picture of an ageing schoolmaster whose life has lost its purpose.

Schoolmaster

The window gives onto the white trees.
The master looks out of it at the trees,
for a long time, he looks for a long time
out through the window at the trees,
breaking his chalk slowly in one hand.
And it's only the rules of long division.
And he's forgotten the rules of long division.
Imagine not remembering long division!
A mistake on the blackboard, a mistake.

We watch him with a different attention
needing no one to hint to us about it,
there's more than difference in this attention.
The schoolmaster's wife has gone away,
we do not know where she has gone to,
we do not know why she has gone,
what we know is his wife has gone away.

His clothes are neither new nor in the fashion;
wearing the suit which he always wears
and which is neither new nor in the fashion
the master goes downstairs to the cloakroom.
he fumbles in his pocket for a ticket.
'What's the matter? Where is that ticket?
Perhaps I never picked up my ticket.
Where is the thing?' Rubbing his forehead.
'Oh, here it is. I'm getting old
Don't argue auntie dear, I'm getting old.
You can't do much about getting old.'
We hear the door below creaking behind him.
The window gives onto the white trees.
The trees there are high and wonderful,
but they are not why we are looking out.
We look in silence at the schoolmaster.

He has a bent back and clumsy walk,
he moves without defences, clumsily,
worn out I ought to have said, clumsily.
Snow falling on him softly through the silence
turns him to white under the white trees.
A little longer will make him so white
we shall not see him in the whitened trees.

YEVGENY YEVTUSHENKO

Schoolmaster in Focus

1 What is the setting in the first stanza?
2 Why does the poet repeat 'for a long time'?
3 From whose point of view are we observing the schoolmaster?
4 'A mistake on the blackboard, a mistake'. Why do you think this has happened?
5 'We watch him with a different attention'. Why are the students now watching the schoolmaster with a 'different attention'?
6 'The schoolmaster's wife has gone away'. How does the narrator emphasise this fact? Why is it considered so important?
7 'His clothes are neither new nor in the fashion'. What does this show about the schoolmaster?
8 Why do you think the narrator describes the ticket incident in detail?
9 'The trees there are high and wonderful'. What contrast is there between the trees and the schoolmaster?
10 In what ways is the schoolmaster 'worn out'?
11 What does the poet achieve by the alliteration on the letter 's' in 'Snow falling on him softly through the silence'?
12 What is happening at the end of the poem?
13 What are your feelings towards the schoolmaster?
14 What is the theme of this poem?

People tend to believe that rearing children is emotionally fulfilling for a woman. Here, the poet Gwen Harwood shows the trauma associated with rearing three children.

In the Park

She sits in the park. Her clothes are out of date.
Two children whine and bicker, tug her skirt.
A third draws aimless patterns in the dirt.
Someone she loved once passes by—too late

to feign indifference to that casual nod.
'How nice,' etcetera. 'Time holds great surprises.'
From his neat head unquestionably rises
a small balloon . . . 'but for the grace of God . . .'

They stand awhile in flickering light, rehearsing
the children's names and birthdays. 'It's so sweet
to hear their chatter, watch them grow and thrive,'
she says to his departing smile. Then, nursing
the youngest child, sits staring at her feet.
To the wind she says, 'They have eaten me alive.'

GWEN HARWOOD

In the Park Questions

1 ' . . . Her clothes are out of date'. What does this indicate about the woman?
2 'Two children whine and bicker'. What is happening? Why does the poet achieve by her use of the sound words 'whine' and 'bicker'?
3 Why did the passer-by have to stop and talk to the woman?
4 'How nice'. Do you think the use of dialogue helps or hinders the impact of the poem? Explain your viewpoint.
5 How do you know that the man the woman 'loved once' is thankful he's not the father of the family?
6 ' . . . rehearsing/the children's names and birthdays'. What are the man and woman doing?
7 Why do you think the woman says, 'It's so sweet/to hear their chatter'?
8 What does the woman mean by 'They have eaten me alive'? How is the truth of this statement shown in the poem?
9 Do you think 'In the Park' is a good title for this poem? Why or why not? What would you have called this poem?
10 Rearing children is generally regarded as pleasant and enjoyable. How does the poet show the reverse of this?
11 What are your feelings towards the woman in the park?
12 What is the poet's purpose in writing this poem?

18 John Foulcher

Life Study of John Foulcher

John Foulcher was born in 1952 in the Sydney suburb of Ryde, where he spent most of his childhood and adolescence. Married with two children, he is now living south of Sydney on the edge of the Royal National Park near Bundeena. He works as an English teacher in a local secondary school.

While a student at Ryde High School during the late sixties, Foulcher began to write poetry and lyrics for some of his friends who played in rock bands. At this time, he was influenced by the lyrics of Bob Dylan, the famous American singer and songwriter. At school he developed a lifelong interest in drama.

In 1971, having completed his Higher School Certificate the previous year, John became a student at Macquarie University. Here, he not only continued to develop and hone his poetry writing craft, but also excelled in his study of English literature, completing his honours degree in 1975 with a thesis on the poetry of Robert Lowell.

The Poetry of John Foulcher

John Foulcher has now published three volumes of poetry, *Light Pressure* (1983), *Pictures from the War* (1987) and *Paperweight* (1991). Much of the subject matter of his poems arises from Foulcher's personal experiences and relationships. In *Light Pressure* Foulcher used the Australian landscape as the setting for recreating, describing and analysing recent events and developments in his life. Titles such as 'Pelicans', 'Kangaroos Near Hay', 'Dawn Sounds' and 'The Sea Days' show his experiences in a natural environment. However, Foulcher does use other scenarios. Occasionally, we are presented with scenes from the Bible as in 'Christ at Cana' or 'Elegy for Lot's Wife'. 'Martin and the Hand Grenade' takes place in a school classroom where Foulcher is the schoolteacher observer, while in 'First Morning at Home' Foulcher's role becomes that of a father reminiscing about his infant son.

In his second volume of poetry, *Pictures from the War*, Foulcher faithfully observes and analyses events of his childhood and teenage years as well as those of the present. In his poem 'Death' he involves us in his sadness and sense of loss brought about by the sudden, successive deaths of his grandparents and his father, when he himself was still only nine years old. Then, in other poems, he transports us to places like Ayer's Rock, the Olgas and Mexico City to share his recent experiences as a parent.

In *Paperweight,* his third volume of poems, Foulcher has continued to use the intensely personal approach seen in many of his earlier poems. He is the observer who describes and comments on poignant scenes from the past or present. These scenes frequently involve members of his family such as his mother, father, brother, wife and children. In poems such as 'My Mother and Harry', 'Living', 'The Day My Mother Went Back into Hospital' and 'The Whales', he movingly recreates family situations and succinctly analyses actions and relationships. Often as he acts as a participator or observer in his poems, he provides psychological insights. In 'The Sack', for example, Foulcher describes his own innermost thoughts and feelings as his son participates in a sack race at a school athletics carnival.

It is interesting that Foulcher wrote his honours thesis on the poetry of the famous American Robert Lowell, whose poem 'Skunk Hour' is included in this anthology. There are similarities in Foulcher's own poetry to that of Lowell's. Their work possesses a 'crystalline clarity' and both poets frequently use family figures, situations and relationships to create self-revelatory poetry. John Foulcher is still a very young poet, who has already achieved Australian recognition. Perhaps in the years to come he will achieve Lowell's universal acclaim.

Here is a poem from the poet's teaching experience. As he recreates the classroom scene, the poet makes us aware of the violence and horror of war.

Martin and the Hand Grenade

Martin displays the grenade, the class pauses
for history. With his father's bleak skill
Martin edges out the firing pin, indicates

the chamber where the powder went; he fingers
the serrations, bristles with the shrapnel
possibilities. Questions. No—it had limited

power: ten yards, then the spread
became too loose to catch a man's mortality.
Around the class now. And each boy holds

the small war, lifts it into the air
above the desk trenches: the dead weapon hurls
across mind fields, tears the heart ahead.

JOHN FOULCHER

Questioning Martin and the Hand Grenade

1 What is the setting of the poem?
2 What words in the first stanza suggest that the class is interested in Martin's presentation?
3 Why does the poet refer to Martin's skill as 'bleak'? From whom did Martin learn the skill of removing the firing pin?
4 What is the meaning of 'shrapnel possibilities'?
5 What is the meaning of 'too loose to catch a man's mortality'?
6 'Around the class now'. What is happening?
7 Why does the poet refer to the grenade as 'the small war'?
8 Why do you think the poet has linked the two words 'desk trenches'?
9 What do you think the poet means by 'mind fields'?
10 How has the poet suggested the destructive power of the dead grenade?
11 How do you think Martin feels towards the grenade?
12 What do you think is the attitude of the class to the grenade?
13 Why does the title of the poem, 'Martin and the Hand Grenade', attract the reader's attention?
14 How does the poet make you aware of the horror of war?

In 'A Crow That Came for the Chickens', the poet makes us aware of the continuing struggle for survival in the world of nature.

A Crow That Came for the Chickens

Suddenly, there's a disturbance in the fowlyard:
the goats are like tall mountains

about the hollow where the cock and the crow
are tangled. Dust tumbles,

the bird from the sky
on its back, wings stretched, target eyes

rimmed with blood, beak like open secateurs—
the cry that's usually heard

so slight and high, transformed
to an earth-bound bellow. I chase the hens away.

lean over this crow
that can't move. Its iron sheen

shabby with dung and husks. It threatens me
but I manage to pick it up, and I notice

how smooth it is, feel its dripping wing
and steel-sprung neck, its steel talons

around my soft hands. The chickens tinkle
in the hay. The goats settle . . .

On the verandah now, it huddles, dark
as a hole in the wood, knocks the fibro

drunkenly. I should kill it, but don't have the skill.
While I sit here writing,

it bursts with fear and isolation, its feathers
crisp as leaves on this perfect April morning.

JOHN FOULCHER

Examining A Crow That Came for the Chickens

1 How does the poet immediately gain your interest at the beginning of the poem?
2 'The goats are like tall mountains'. Why do the goats seem so large?
3 What words emphasise the cutting power of the crow's beak?
4 What contrast is there between the crow's cry in the sky and the sound it is making on the ground?
5 How does the crow react to the presence of the poet?
6 ' . . . Its iron sheen/shabby with dung and husks'. What has happened to the crow?
7 What does the poet achieve by repeating the word 'steel' in ' . . . its dripping wing/and steel-sprung neck, its steel talons'?
8 What evidence can you find to show that the crow is badly hurt?
9 How do you know that the crow is afraid?
10 Why doesn't the poet kill the crow?
11 What words show the beauty of the crow?
12 What has the poet revealed about himself in the poem?
13 What are your feelings towards the crow?
14 How has the poet shown that nature can be brutal?
15 What is the poet's purpose in this poem?

While caught in a traffic delay, Foulcher observes and comments on the negative aspects of modern living.

Summer Rain

At 4 o'clock, cars
clutter on the highway like abacus beads.
No one dares overtake.
Sunlight scrawls
through the dust and the fumes,
and shadows slap at the edge of the grass.

Somewhere ahead, there's been an accident.
One by one, the engines
stop, the cars slump into dusk.

You wrench yourself from the road,
sift the dark trees
for diversion.
Sub-division houses—teacups
of colour from television sets,

steam rising from ovens
and showers
like mist across a swampland. The cricket sound
of voices and cutlery.

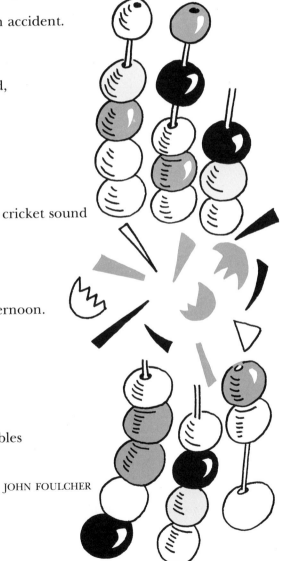

Only the children
stay outside, bruised with dirt
and school, squeezing play
from the tattered edges of the afternoon.
In the darkness, they grow
to be heroes, clash in the park
like cars on a highway,
pound out grudges
tight as steel. At last, they slacken
home forgetfully.

As the wreck is cleared, rain trembles
across the cars
and the charred, unbroken road.

JOHN FOULCHER

Appreciating Summer Rain

1 'Cars clutter on the highway like abacus beads'. What is the poet telling us about the traffic?
2 How does the poet makes us aware of the pollution created by the cars?
3 What does the poet mean by 'shadows slap at the edge of the grass'?
4 '. . . the cars slump into the dusk'. What is happening? How has the poet made the cars seem to be human?
5 What does the poet decide to do 'for diversion' while he is waiting in the traffic?
6 How is the poet able to show that the 'sub-division houses' lack privacy?
7 What does the poet mean by 'teacups/of colour from television sets'?
8 What sounds is the poet able to hear?
9 What is the poet suggesting about the children when he uses the words 'bruised with dirt/and school'?
10 What words suggest that the children's play is aggressive and violent?
11 Why do you think the poet ends the poem with the words 'the charred unbroken road'?
12 The poet has used a number of similes in this poem. Write down one of them and explain why it is successful?
13 Do you think 'Summer Rain' is a good title for this poem? Why or why not?
14 What is the poet's message in this poem?

Don Bradman is the most famous cricketer in the world. In his last innings he only needed four runs to have a test average of one hundred.

Bradman's Last Innings

Bowled for a duck, you could have asked for better . . .
From the first, through the years
of Depression, so many came to see you, forgetting

the dole queues, the homes dull with a long
democracy. And then the War, women
waiting for their Saturday oval husbands.

And peace. Padded up again, you gave people
something the world lacked: rules
to play by, winners, clear white flannels

sharp against the green turf. But it never works out,
never—four runs short of that century
average, at the last, betrayed by your own game.

JOHN FOULCHER

Evaluating Bradman's Last Innings

1 Why do you think the poet begins with the words 'Bowled for a duck'?
2 What evidence is there in the first stanza to show that Bradman was popular with the spectators?
3 In the Depression years, how were some people able to forget about their poverty?
4 What does the poet mean by 'Saturday oval husbands'?
5 What was Bradman able to give the people after World War II?
6 What is the meaning of 'betrayed by your own game'?
7 What feelings of disappointment does the poet reveal in the last stanza?
8 What is the poet's attitude to Bradman?
9 From your reading of the poem, do you think Bradman should be classed as a hero? Why or why not?
10 What does the poet achieve by using the words 'you' and 'your' throughout the poem?
11 Why do you think the poet wrote this poem?
12 Did you enjoy 'Bradman's Last Innings'? Why or why not?

Foulcher is observing in the distance the surfboard riders at Land's End attempting to gain mastery over the sea.

Land's End

Out on the sea, the surfers are spiders
in their black wetsuits, clutching their boards to them
like white moths.
The sea is tin
under the overcast light sky, the air
hangs like washing on a still day's line.

Then a large wave roars from the water—they hunt it
down, kill it, doubling back;
they fight with each other
too, black grappling hooks locked over cold iron . . .
There's a beach further down, they tell me,
you can't go near: on Sundays
they bury a cat in the sand, mow its head off—this
frees them of picnic families.

It's not so much—a little blood,
a clean beach . . .

> The day shuts tight, the moon floats up, trailing light
> over the water
> like a jellyfish—stung
> with this gold,
> the sea glides silently out.
>
> JOHN FOULCHER

In 'For the Fire', John Foulcher observes the harshness and brutality of the natural world as he gathers kindling for the fire.

For the Fire

> Outside, gathering kindling—a chopping sound
> from the forest. Its singular, human thud.
>
> No one is there, only the wind through sparse leaves
> like clockwork. Then, above me, the sound drops,
>
> chipped from a tall dead tree:
> a kookaburra hacks with its axe-blade beak
>
> tight about a lizard. I can see the reptile's mouth
> stunned open, pouting blood, its legs arched
>
> and claws clutching at air. Even now, all of its bones
> are smashed. Oblivious, the bird flays it still,
>
> knocking down twigs. I pick up these twigs
> and leave with them, the cold air congealing behind me.
>
> JOHN FOULCHER

Examining For the Fire

1 What is the poet doing at the beginning of the poem?
2 What onomatopoeic (sound) words has the poet used in the first stanza?
3 How does the poet create a feeling of suspense in the second stanza?
4 'A kookaburra hacks with its axe-blade beak'. What impression of the kookaburra do these words create?
5 ' . . . I can see the reptile's mouth/stunned open'. What has happened to the lizard?
6 What do the words 'claws clutching at air' show you about the lizard's situation?
7 What is the meaning of 'Oblivious the bird flays it still'?
8 What words convey that the weather is cold?

9 The poet leaves the scene, ignoring the kookaburra and the lizard. Why do you think he acts in this manner?
10 What are your feelings towards the kookaburra?
11 The poet has used a number of violent words in this poem. Write down two or three of them and comment on their effectiveness.
12 Why do you think the poet has called this poem 'For the Fire'?
13 The poet is an observer of this scene. What has he revealed about himself?
14 What evidence can you find in the poem to suggest it was written from a real-life experience?
15 Why do you think the poet has written this poem?

This poem analyses Harry Wood's struggle for survival and the effect it has had on him.

Harry Wood

Harry Wood worked in the mines, digging his way
out of poverty, finding
in his twenties
an empty foreman's place.

Once, he told us, he fired a man
for fooling with the ropes, and the union
went out for weeks. He held on, though, and they sank
back to the sleek coal caves
one man short,
breathing again the air invisible from rock.

And one time collapsing
the moment he started, the mine nearly took him,
he heard them say, 'Wood's gone'.
as the shovels rattled in the earth.

Now he's bought the farm,
and every year before market
he herds the steers in by himself,
pricks at their tubs of meat with a current-charged bar
until they panic
and take the long unbroken slope
creaking into the truck.

Kangaroo bones
pocked with skin and maggot bubbles of flesh
edge the house and the yard.

At night, he sits
and talks of the mines, stares at the dark window—
when he's dead,
the farm will go to his grandchildren,
and they won't be poor

as he was, and they'll have time, he believes,
for something more than survival.

JOHN FOULCHER

Analysing Harry Wood

1 What evidence is there in the first stanza of Harry Wood's struggle for survival?
2 What does the second stanza reveal about Harry Wood's character?
3 What words show the defeat of the miners?
4 'Wood's gone'. Do you think this use of dialogue helps to make the poem more successful? Why or why not?
5 ' . . . the shovels rattled in the earth'. Comment on the effectiveness of the word 'rattled'.
6 What evidence can you find to show in the fourth stanza that Harry Wood has become reasonably prosperous?
7 Why are the cattle seen as 'tubs of meat'?
8 What comments would you make about Harry's treatment of his cattle?
9 What feelings does the poet's description of Harry Wood's house and yard cause you to have?
10 What does the phrase 'stares at the dark window' reveal about Harry?
11 From your reading of the poem, what effect do you think Harry Wood's struggle for survival has had on him?
12 What evidence can you find in the poem to suggest that Foulcher wrote this poem as the result of a real-life experience?
13 What is the theme of 'Harry Wood'?
14 What are your feelings towards Harry Wood?

19 Seamus Heaney

SEAMUS
HEANEY

———

Selected Poems
1965-1975

Life and Background of Seamus Heaney

Modern Irish poet, Seamus Heaney, was born in 1939 in County Derry, part of rural Northern Ireland. Heaney is clearly a country poet, focusing mainly on the simple rhythms and experiences of his childhood and adult life in rural Northern Ireland.

Heaney recalls that his fascination with poetry began as a child with the learning of children's rhymes and chants. His primary school years were at Anahorish School where, by the time he was eleven, he had been forced, along with his school mates, to memorise whole sections of poems by writers such as Keats and Byron. He learned the whole of Keats' ode 'To Autumn' off by heart, without understanding much of it. Though much of the poetry learned was barely intelligible, there was, from time to time, a sense of satisfaction with the flow of sounds and rhythm in some of the lines, enough to stir the beginnings of his love of poetry. On the farm, he was encouraged to recite ballads for visiting guests and relations, so that his awareness of poetry included its involvement in ordinary, everyday home life.

Heaney was a good student and, although many of his friends left school early to work on their family farm, he continued his education. From the age of twelve he attended boarding school at St Columb's College, Derry. Here he was introduced to the wider world of poets which included Shakespeare, Chaucer, Wordsworth, Hopkins, Arnold and Frost. His understanding of, and love for, poetry grew and by the time he had completed high school he was capable of writing passable verse, even in Latin.

Heaney attended Queen's University in Belfast, graduating in 1961 to take up a position as a school teacher. His university studies included further exposure to the Classic poets. He found himself still fascinated by the way sounds and rhythm could appeal so directly to a reader's senses. His own response included attempts at writing poetry which was, for the most part, marked by a striving to copy the models laid down by poets of the past.

When he began teaching in 1962, he began to read the work of contemporary poets such as Ted Hughes and R. S. Thomas, the Welsh poet who was in many respects a man after Heaney's own heart, someone who wrote on rural themes. His poetry from this period on began to blend his literary education and the experience of his own life in the country.

Heaney began publishing poems with his first collection in 1966. This first volume was called *Death of a Naturalist*. It was followed by *Door into the Dark* in 1969, *Wintering Out* in 1973 and *North* in 1975. This last volume received considerable acclaim and led to his being invited to lecture at universities in Northern Ireland and the United States.

Heaney's poetry describes memories of his childhood on the farm where he lived, the local town, the people and events that made up his days growing up. He sometimes picks out events that punctuated the normal existence. Thus, in 'Death of a Naturalist' he recalls a frog plague and the change that took place in him as a result of his experience of it. In 'Mid-term Break' he recalls being brought home from boarding school to attend the funeral of a younger brother killed in an accident.

At other times he recreates for his readers rhythmic events that broke ongoing farm life into cycles and 'chunks' of experience. For example, 'Churning Day' recalls the preparations and events associated with making butter.

People are frequently central for Heaney. In 'Digging' he reflects on his father and grandfather, and sees the development of their skills take a new form in his own life. 'The Forge' recalls some of the mystery and awe surrounding the local smithy and his blacksmith shop in the eyes of the young boy.

Features of Seamus Heaney's Poetry

Rural Subject Matter
Heaney's poetry, for the most part, picks up country life as its subject matter. The farms and town life he describes are the farms and town life of his childhood, old-fashioned by our standards, simple, even humble. It is a measure of his ability as a poet that he is able to connect us meaningfully with a world that is so different to so much of our modern-day experience.

Natural, Simple Language
Heaney's choice of words is appropriate to his subject matter. He is economical, preferring simple, vivid, clear words to clever, polysyllabic language. His language

achieves the directness of effect that Heaney desires. For example, 'Digging' concludes with these words:

> Between my finger and my thumb
> The squat pen rests.
> I'll dig with it.

His use of fresh, vital images, often created through onomatopoeic words, frequently evokes a response in the reader. In the frog plague of 'Death of a Naturalist'
we encounter the frightening experience ourselves through:

>   . . . Some hopped:
> The slap and plop were obscene threats. Some sat
> Poised like mud grenades, their blunt heads farting.

Simple, Pleasing Rhythms

Heaney's poems have an unobtrusive but clear rhythm which serves as a foundation
for the sense experience the poet is seeking to craft for us. We feel it clearly in these
lines from 'Digging':

> By God, the old man could handle a spade.
> Just like his old man.

Fascinated by the trout, the poet explores its links with the world of guns.

Trout

> Hangs, a fat gun-barrel,
> deep under arched bridges
> or slips like butter down
> the throat of the river.
>
> From depths smooth-skinned as plums
> his muzzle gets bull's eye;
> picks off grass-seed and moths
> that vanish, torpedoed.
>
> Where water unravels
> over gravel-beds he
> is fired from the shallows
> white belly reporting
>
> flat; darts like a tracer-
> bullet back between stones
> and is never burnt out.
> A volley of cold blood
>
> ramrodding the current.

SEAMUS HEANEY

Fishing Further with Trout

1 The poet begins the poem strikingly with the word 'hangs'. What is the trout doing?
2 'A fat gun-barrel'. What aspect of the fish's functioning is emphasised by this description?
3 '. . . slips like butter down/the throat of the river'. What important feature of the way the trout moves through the water is captured in this image?
4 'His muzzle gets bull's eye'. What is it that the trout so accurately 'shoots'?
5 'Where water unravels'. Why does the poet use the word 'unravels' here?
6 '. . . he/is fired from the shallows.' Is 'fired' a good choice here? Why?
7 To what is his darting between stones likened? In what way is the trout different from the object he is compared with?
8 What does the phrase 'cold blood' capture about the functioning of the trout?
9 The last line stands on its own. What is the poet's purpose in finishing this way?
10 How effective is the comparison of the trout to a variety of weapons? Why?
11 How does the poet appear to feel about trout?
12 What do you see as the strengths of this poem? Give examples from the poem itself.

In this poem Heaney records an incident from the past when a plague of frogs appeared at a flax-dam. The huge number of frogs and their noise frightened the young child.

Death of a Naturalist

All year the flax-dam festered in the heart
Of the townland; green and heavy headed
Flax had rotted there, weighted down by huge sods.
Daily it sweltered in the punishing sun.
Bubbles gargled delicately, bluebottles
Wove a strong gauze of sound around the smell.
There were dragon-flies, spotted butterflies,
But best of all was the warm thick slobber
Of frogspawn that grew like clotted water
In the shade of the banks. Here, every spring
I would fill jampotfuls of the jellied
Specks to range on window-sills at home,
On shelves at school, and wait and watch until
The fattening dots burst into nimble-
Swimming tadpoles. Miss Walls would tell us how
The daddy frog was called a bullfrog
And how he croaked and how the mammy frog
Laid hundreds of little eggs and this was
Frogspawn. You could tell the weather by frogs too
For they were yellow in the sun and brown
In rain.

Then one hot day when fields were rank
With cowdung in the grass the angry frogs
Invaded the flax-dam; I ducked through hedges
To a coarse croaking that I had not heard
Before. The air was thick with a bass chorus.
Right down the dam gross-bellied frogs were cocked
On sods; their loose necks pulsed like sails. Some hopped:
The slap and plop were obscene threats. Some sat
Poised like mud grenades, their blunt heads farting.
I sickened, turned, and ran. The great slime kings
Were gathered there for vengeance and I knew
That if I dipped my hand the spawn would clutch it.

SEAMUS HEANEY

Appreciating Death of a Naturalist

As with many of Heaney's poems, 'Death of a Naturalist' recalls an incident from the poet's childhood. The poet recalls that as a young boy he had been fascinated by the flax-dam 'in the heart of the townland' near his home. In particular, the frogspawn, found so plentifully around the edges of the dam, had engrossed him. Each spring he would collect jars of it, 'like clotted water', and place them on window-sills and shelves at home and school, waiting for the eggs to develop into tadpoles and, finally, frogs. The poet's memory of this period brings into focus some pieces of information about frogs which his school teacher at the time, Miss Walls, had passed on to her class — what the male frog was called, how the female frog laid her eggs, and the fact that you could tell the weather by the changing colour of a frog. All fascinating facts for the budding young naturalist.

To this point the poem has served as a vehicle for pulling together the poet's general memories and experiences associated with the flax-dam. Now, dramatically, a specific memory is brought onto centre-stage. There is a break in the lazy, rhythmic flow of memory as the poet recalls: 'Then one hot day . . . ' On this particular day as the young boy approached the dam there seemed to be an invasion of angry frogs. 'The air was thick with a bass chorus'. Everywhere, it seemed, there were frogs making an immense din with their croaking. Overwhelmed by the sheer volume of sound, the poet is struck by a conviction that the frogs have gathered for vengeance, presumably directed at frogspawn stealers. It is too much for the young boy. Terrified, he turns and runs. For him it is the end of an era. His days of collecting frogspawn are over. The incident marks the 'death of a naturalist'.

The poem serves as an excellent example of Heaney's use of vivid, simple language to communicate directly to the reader's senses. The opening line brings a sense of ominousness, made particularly immediate to our senses by the emotive word 'festered'. We not only 'see' the decay through the descriptive language, but we feel it in the heavy vowel sounds of 'green and heavy headed/Flax has rotted there, weighted down by huge sods'. The picture is supplemented by action words such as 'sweltered' and 'gargled', each specifically teasing out other nuances of the total scene of decay. Heaney uses onomatopoeic words such as 'bubbles gargled' to suggest the life force in nature. Once again he has sensitively picked up the slower rhythm of the movement of the bubbles and captured its essence by using slower, longer words.

We are given a tiny vignette of the 'life' at this flax-dam, but, not surprisingly, it is sparse and fragile — bluebottles, dragon-flies and spotted butterflies. This leads us to another specific focus in the poem, 'the warm thick slobber/Of frogspawn' which was produced so plentifully and which fascinated the young boy. With simple, narrative skill he records how he collected the frogs' eggs, stored them and waited for them to become frogs. The alliteration of the 't' sound and the assonance of the short 'i' sound in 'the fattening dots burst into nimble-/Swimming tadpoles' appropriately brings vitality into this description of emerging life. Notice how the language used to recall the teaching of Miss Walls becomes the language of a little child: 'The daddy frog was called a bullfrog'. Again the appropriateness of the language and the skill of the poet in bringing the scene to life is noteworthy.

The day that marked a life-transition for the poet is introduced dramatically. The language picks up the mood. The frogs are 'angry' and their entry to the dam is described by the word 'invaded'. The very sound of their din is emphasised by the alliteration and onomatopoeia of 'coarse croaking'. The air is described as 'thick'. We sense the danger here. The words used to describe the frogs consist of blunt, onomatopoeic monosyllables like 'slap' and 'plop'. Danger is signalled in the assonance of the short 'o' sound as 'gross-bellied frogs were cocked/On sods'. 'Poised like mud grenades' is another image of imminent danger. Something is about to explode here. Some primitive, existential awareness enables the young boy to know that he must flee for his life or 'the great slime kings' will have their revenge.

Whereas the language of Frost appears to unfold with gentle depth, this is language that is urgent and vital. A single natural event has become a significant moment in the life of the young boy. Heaney has woven language and image together to recreate the scene in such a way that we understand. We, too, feel the horror that marks the end of the boy's preoccupation with the frogs.

The sight of his father digging takes the poet back in memory, and causes him to reflect on his grandfather's skills at digging. He recognises that his skills are different — yet perhaps there is a link.

Digging

Between my finger and my thumb
The squat pen rests; snug as a gun.

Under my window, a clean rasping sound
When the spade sinks into gravelly ground:
My father, digging. I look down

Till his straining rump among the flowerbeds
Bends low, comes up twenty years away
Stooping in rhythm through potato drills
Where he was digging.

The coarse boot nestled on the lug, the shaft
Against the inside knee was levered firmly.
He rooted out tall tops, buried the bright edge deep
To scatter new potatoes that we picked
Loving their cool hardness in our hands.

By God, the old man could handle a spade.
Just like his old man.

My grandfather cut more turf in a day
Than any other man on Toner's bog.
Once I carried him milk in a bottle
Corked sloppily with paper. He straightened up
To drink it, then fell to right away

Nicking and slicing neatly, heaving sods
Over his shoulder, going down and down
For the good turf. Digging.

The cold smell of potato mould, the squelch and slap
Of soggy peat, the curt cuts of an edge
Through living roots awaken in my head.
But I've no spade to follow men like them.

Between my finger and my thumb
The squat pen rests,
I'll dig with it.

SEAMUS HEANEY

Digging Deeper

1 What is it about his pen that reminds the poet of a gun?
2 Who does the poet see outside his window, and what is this person doing?
3 What sound is made by the spade?
4 What does the poet mean by the phrase 'comes up twenty years away'.
5 What is it that the poet recalls his father digging many years ago?
6 Why was the edge of the spade 'bright'?
7 Who used to pick up the potatoes, and how did they feel about it?
8 What bit of local fame had the poet's grandfather achieved in his digging?
9 What stands out for the poet in the memory of the time he took milk to his grandfather?

10 'Nicking and slicing neatly'. The alliteration emphasises the rhythm of the spade. Identify the alliteration in this line.

11 What is the effect of putting the single word 'digging' in a sentence on its own?

12 Memories 'through living roots' awaken in the poet's head. What smell comes back to him? What sounds come back to him?

13 'But I've no spade to follow men like them'. What feelings does the poet appear to have at this point?

14 What decision does the poet make at the end of this poem?

15 How effectively has the poet crafted this poem? What reasons do you have to support your viewpoint?

In this poem the writer recalls his earliest experience of seeing animals killed on the farm and explores the effect this had on him.

The Early Purges

I was six when I first saw kittens drown.
Dan Taggart pitched them, 'the scraggy wee shits',
Into a bucket; a frail metal sound,

Soft paws scraping like mad. But their tiny din
Was soon soused. They were slung on the snout
Of the pump and the water pumped in.

'Sure isn't it better for them now?' Dan said.
Like wet gloves they bobbed and shone till he sluiced
Them out on the dunghill, glossy and dead.

Suddenly frightened, for days I sadly hung
Round the yard, watching the three sogged remains
Turn mealy and crisp as old summer dung

Until I forgot them. But the fear came back
When Dan trapped big rats, snared rabbits, shot crows
Or, with a sickening tug, pulled old hens' necks.

Still, living displaces false sentiments
And now, when shrill pups are prodded to drown
I just shrug, 'Bloody pups'. It makes sense:

'Prevention of cruelty' talk cuts ice in town
Where they consider death unnatural,
But on well-run farms pests have to be kept down.

SEAMUS HEANEY

Looking at The Early Purges

1 What is the impact of the first line?
2 What does the word 'pitched' suggest about the way the kittens are valued?
3 'Soft paws scraping like mad'. What is happening here?
4 'They were slung on the snout/Of the pump'. Were the kittens dead or alive at this point? Give reasons for your answer.
5 'Sure isn't it better for them now?' Why would Dan think this?
6 How did the young boy feel after this first encounter with the harshness of this aspect of farm life? Find a phrase that captures his feelings.
7 How does the poet overcome these feelings? Find a quote from the poem to support your answer.
8 Of the other examples of purging pests quoted, which one seems the most emotional for the poet? Give evidence from the poem.
9 What causes 'false sentiments' to change?
10 'Bloody pups'. How does this statement signal a change in the poet's attitudes?
11 In the last stanza, what lesson of life does the poet claim to have learned?
12 What emotions are aroused in you by this poem? Why?
13 Do you think 'The Early Purges' is a good title for this poem? Why or why not?
14 Why do you think Heaney wrote this poem?

'Blackberry-picking' is dedicated to fellow poet Philip Hobsbaum. It recalls the ritual of picking blackberries, which occurred at the end of summer each year, and the pleasure and sadness that it brought to a young boy.

Blackberry-picking
For Philip Hobsbaum

Late August, given heavy rain and sun
For a full week, the blackberries would ripen.
At first, just one, a glossy purple clot
Among others, red, green, hard as a knot.
You ate that first one and its flesh was sweet
Like thickened wine: summer's blood was in it
Leaving stains upon the tongue and lust for
Picking. Then red ones inked up and that hunger
Sent us out with milk-cans, pea-tins, jam-pots
Where briars scratched and wet grass bleached our boots.
Round hayfields, cornfields and potato-drills
We trekked and picked until the cans were full,
Until the tinkling bottom had been covered
With green ones, and on top big dark blobs burned
Like a plate of eyes. Our hands were peppered
With thorn pricks, our palms sticky as Bluebeard's.

We hoarded the fresh berries in the byre.
But when the bath was filled we found a fur,
A rat-grey fungus, glutting on our cache.
The juice was stinking too. Once off the bush
The fruit fermented, the sweet flesh would turn sour.
I always felt like crying. It wasn't fair
That all the lovely canfuls smelt of rot.
Each year I hoped they'd keep, knew they would not.

SEAMUS HEANEY

'The Forge' is an account of the poet's memories of the blacksmith's workshop in his town. There was always an element of mystery about the place and the man who worked there.

The Forge

All I know is a door into the dark.
Outside, old axles and iron hoops rusting;
Inside, the hammered anvil's short-pitched ring,
The unpredictable fantail of sparks
Or hiss when a new shoe toughens in water.
The anvil must be somewhere in the centre,
Horned as a unicorn, at one end square,
Set there immoveable: an altar
Where he expends himself in shape and music.
Sometimes, leather-aproned, hairs in his nose,
He leans out on the jamb, recalls a clatter
Of hoofs where traffic is flashing in rows;
Then grunts and goes in, with a slam and flick
To beat real iron out, to work the bellows.

SEAMUS HEANEY

Peering into The Forge

1 What does the first line convey about the young boy's understanding of the blacksmith's world?
2 Identify the example of alliteration in the first line. What is the effect of this alliteration?
3 What things does the poet remember as being outside the forge?
4 What sounds were heard from within the forge? What sight does he recall from within the forge and what was noteworthy about it?
5 What is the 'music' that the blacksmith expends himself in?
6 What is there about the sound of passing traffic that reminds us this is from a bygone era?

7 'Then grunts and goes in'. What aspect of the blacksmith's personality is suggested here?
8 What aspects of this poem enable us to see that the smithy was a bit overwhelming for the poet as a young boy?
9 What are the strengths of this poem? Give reasons for your answer.
10 Why do you think the poet has written 'The Forge'?

In 'Mid-term Break', the poet relives a memory from childhood when he was called home from school because a younger brother had been killed in an accident. The poem captures the uncertain feelings of the young boy as he faces this first encounter with a family death.

Mid-term Break

I sat all morning in the college sick bay
Counting bells knelling classes to a close.
At two o'clock our neighbours drove me home.

In the porch I met my father crying—
He had always taken funerals in his stride—
And Big Jim Evans saying it was a hard blow.

The baby cooed and laughed and rocked the pram
When I came in, and I was embarrassed
By old men standing up to shake my hand

And tell me they were 'sorry for my trouble',
Whispers informed strangers I was the eldest,
Away at school, as my mother held my hand

In hers and coughed out angry tearless sighs.
At ten o'clock the ambulance arrived
With the corpse, stanched and bandaged by the nurses.

Next morning I went up into the room. Snowdrops
And candles soothed the bedside; I saw him
For the first time in six weeks. Paler now,

Wearing a poppy bruise on his left temple,
He lay in the four foot box as in his cot.
No gaudy scars, the bumper knocked him clear.

A four foot box, a foot for every year.

SEAMUS HEANEY

'Churning Day' describes the making of butter on the farm. Buttermilk, stored in large earthenware crocks, was stirred until it began to turn into chunks of butter. These lumps were fished out and put into bowls, then kneaded with small wooden butter pats into slabs of butter.

Churning Day

A thick crust, coarse-grained as limestone rough-cast,
hardened gradually on top of the four crocks
that stood, large pottery bombs, in the small pantry.
After the hot brewery of gland, cud and udder
cool porous earthenware fermented the buttermilk
for churning day, when the hooped churn was scoured
with plumping kettles and the busy scrubber
echoed daintily on the seasoned wood.
It stood then, purified, on the flagged kitchen floor.

Out came the four crocks, spilled their heavy lip
of cream, their white insides, into the sterile churn.
The staff, like a great whisky muddler fashioned
in deal wood, was plunged in, the lid fitted.
My mother took first turn, set up rhythms
that slugged and thumped for hours. Arms ached.
Hands blistered. Cheeks and clothes were spattered
with flabby milk.

Where finally gold flecks
began to dance. They poured hot water then,
sterilised a birchwood-bowl
and little corrugated butter-spades.
Their short stroke quickened, suddenly
a yellow curd was weighting the churned up white,
heavy and rich, coagulated sunlight
that they fished, dripping, in a wide tin strainer,
heaped up like gilded gravel in the bowl.

The house would stink long after churning day,
acrid as a sulphur mine. The empty crocks
were ranged along the wall again, the butter
in soft printed slabs was piled on pantry shelves.
And in the house we moved with gravid ease,
our brains turned crystals full of clean deal churns,
the plash and gurgle of the sour-breathed milk,
the pat and slap of small spades on wet lumps.

SEAMUS HEANEY

20 Emily Dickinson

Emily Dickinson's Life and Background

Emily Dickinson is recognisably the best-known woman poet of the nineteenth century United States. She is believed to have written perhaps eighteen hundred poems (many as short as four lines), although only seven are known to have been published in her lifetime, and each of these anonymously. Hundreds were sent as gifts to people she corresponded with, and we have no idea how many have been lost because of this. She appeared to have no intention of seeking publication for her poems generally, and it is almost an accident of history that some were published in 1890, four years after her death. The first definitive selection of Dickinson's poems was not published until 1955.

The knowledge we have of Dickinson's life is scant but fascinating. She was born in Amherst, Massachusetts, in 1830, and died there in 1886, at the age of fifty-five. Her family was wealthy and her father the most prominent citizen of this little town of three or four thousand people. His prominence culminated in his being elected to the United States Congress in 1852, having already served as a State Senator in 1842 and 1843. Edward Dickinson and his family shared an imposing brick house, called the Homestead, with his father, Emily's grandfather, until 1840. They moved to another house in Amherst for fifteen years, before returning to occupy the whole of the Homestead in 1855. These were the only two houses Emily ever lived in. She had a brother, Austin, and a younger sister, Lavinia, who was known to everyone as Vinnie.

Although Emily never married, biographers have generally agreed that she was in love twice. The second time, late in her life, was with a Massachusetts Supreme Court Judge, Otis Lord, who was a long-time family friend. The first time, around 1861 and 1862, is more intriguing since we are uncertain of the identity of the person. It is generally agreed that the man was already married, and a number of critics have felt that he was either the Reverend Charles Wadsworth, whom she had heard preach and who had visited her, or another married friend, Sam Bowles, to whom she sent thirty-seven poems over the years. This unfulfilled love, whatever its focus, led to a period of deep emotional heart-searching at this time, and resulted in a number of poems which have greater than usual emotional depth and intensity.

There are a number of fascinating, eccentric features of Emily Dickinson's life, for which we have only inadequate explanations. Anecdotal accounts of her life, preserved in letters by Amherst visitors, tell of a woman who, more and more, chose to dress completely in white. This peculiarity climaxed at her funeral where, following her instructions, she was buried in a white coffin, carried by six men who kept the grounds of her father's property. However, she also lived the life of a semi-recluse, progressively becoming more cut off from going out of the house and seeing people. One visitor to Amherst, Mrs Mabel Loomis Todd, who was later to be mainly responsible for editing the first selection of Emily Dickinson's poetry, wrote in a letter describing Miss Dickinson:

> I must tell you about the *character* of Amherst. It is a lady whom the people call the *Myth*. She is a sister of Mr Dickinson, & seems to be the climax of all the family oddity.

She has not been outside of her own house in fifteen years, except once to see a new church, when she crept out at night, & viewed it by moonlight. No one who calls upon her mother & sister ever see her, but she allows little children once in a great while, & one at a time, to come in, when she given them cake or candy, or some nicety, for she is very fond of little ones. But more often she lets down the sweetmeat by a string, out of a window, to them. She dresses wholly in white, & her mind is said to be perfectly wonderful.

She is also reported to have refused to see visitors at times, sending them a glass of wine, or flowers, or a poem, rather than coming to speak with them. On other occasions she is reported to have spoken to visitors only through a half-opened door. She also had the eccentric behaviour of requiring other people, usually her sister Vinnie or her mother, to address the many envelopes for the letters that she wrote. It is unclear whether she was a very aloof person, or whether her behaviour reflected an excessive shyness, or perhaps even the onset of agoraphobia or some such illness.

For all this, Emily Dickinson reveals a keen awareness of the world, and this is because she had a prolific correspondence with so many people. She is known to have written, more or less regularly, to around one hundred people. Many of these were prominent people of the world, who valued the quality of her insights, and the uniqueness of her person.

Emily Dickinson's Poetry

Dickinson's poetry is very hard to classify. Critics generally agree that the quality of her work varies greatly. She wrote on a vast number of subjects, including poems of nature, poems descriptive of varied aspects of life and death (indeed, many of her poems explore the theme of death), poems reflective of spiritual suffering, poems building from religious themes and issues, and poems exploring the world of the imagination and ideas as opposed to experiences. Because the poems were not written for publication, anthologists have found it very difficult to date them with certainty. Rarely did poems have titles, so that in most cases the given title is either supplied by an anthologist, or simply takes the first line of the poem. However, there is widespread agreement that at her best her poems have a quality of greatness.

'A Narrow Fellow in the Grass' describes some aspects of a snake, and the writer's feelings about this creature.

A Narrow Fellow in the Grass

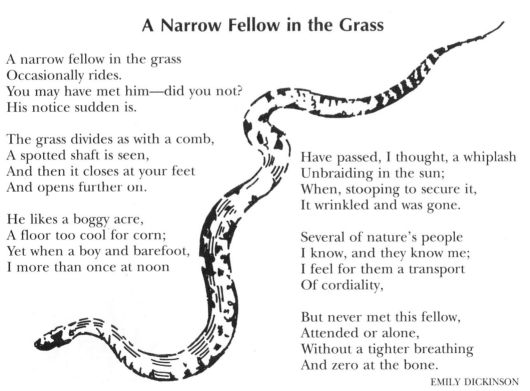

A narrow fellow in the grass
Occasionally rides.
You may have met him—did you not?
His notice sudden is.

The grass divides as with a comb,
A spotted shaft is seen,
And then it closes at your feet
And opens further on.

He likes a boggy acre,
A floor too cool for corn;
Yet when a boy and barefoot,
I more than once at noon

Have passed, I thought, a whiplash
Unbraiding in the sun;
When, stooping to secure it,
It wrinkled and was gone.

Several of nature's people
I know, and they know me;
I feel for them a transport
Of cordiality,

But never met this fellow,
Attended or alone,
Without a tighter breathing
And zero at the bone.

EMILY DICKINSON

Stepping Carefully Around A Narrow Fellow in the Grass

1 What is the effect of describing the snake as 'A narrow fellow in the grass', rather than simply 'snake'?
2 'His notice sudden is'. What does the poet mean by this line?
3 What phrase is used to describe the snake in the second stanza?
4 'A floor too cool for corn'. What are the sounds the poet is making use of here, and what is their effect?
5 The poet speaks of herself as 'a boy and barefoot'. Why do you think she speaks this way instead of as a girl?
6 ' . . . a whiplash/Unbraiding in the sun'. In what ways is this an effective description of a snake?
7 'It wrinkled and was gone'. Comment on the effect of this line.
8 What does the poet mean by 'nature's people'?
9 'I feel for them a transport/Of cordiality.' What does she mean by this line?
10 From the final stanza, how has meeting a snake always affected her physically?
11 What emotion lies behind the descriptive phrase 'And zero at the bone'?
12 The snake's existence is established by vague description, 'a narrow fellow in the grass', rather than the concrete label 'snake'. In what way is this aspect of technique appropriate to the subject matter?
13 How effectively do you think Dickinson has captured aspects of her subject? Why do you conclude this?
14 What do you think is the poet's purpose in writing this poem?

'The Spider' is a poem focusing with wonder on the beauty and intricacy of the spider's work, and its sad finish.

The Spider

The Spider holds a Silver Ball
In unperceived Hands—
And dancing softly to Himself
His yarn of Pearl—unwinds—

He plies from Nought to Nought—
In unsubstantial Trade—
Supplants our Tapestries with His—
In half the period—
An Hour to rear supreme
His continents of Light—
Then dangle from the Housewife's Broom—
His Boundaries—forgot—

EMILY DICKINSON

The Spider under the Microscope

1 What do you think the poet means by 'a Silver Ball'?
2 How effective is 'dancing softly' as a description of the spider's movements? Why?
3 Is the image 'yarn of Pearl' a good one to describe the thread that the spider weaves? Why or why not?
4 'He plies from Nought to Nought'. What do you think the poet means?
5 What is the meaning of 'Supplants our Tapestries with His'?
6 What phrase in the poem acquaints us with the fact that the spider works quickly?
7 What word from the last four lines tells us that the spider's work is superior to that of humans?
8 'Then dangle from the Housewife's Broom'. Why is the word 'dangle' forceful here?
9 What is the effect of the word 'forgot', on its own, at the poem's end?
10 What feelings do you think the poet has about the end of the spider's efforts? Why?
11 This is a simple poem. How effective would you rate it? Why?
12 What do you see as the strengths of Dickinson's poetic technique, as revealed in this poem?

The discovery of a caterpillar on her hand gives rise to the following poem. The poet recognises a kind of personal insignificance as she contemplates the caterpillar.

Caterpillar

How soft a Caterpillar steps—
I find one on my Hand
From such a velvet world it comes
Such plushes at command
Its soundless travels just arrest
My slow-terrestrial eye
Intent upon its own career
What use has it for me—

EMILY DICKINSON

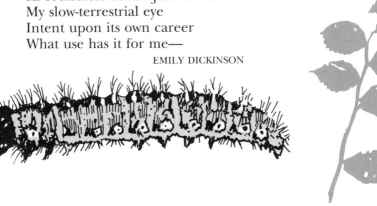

'The Bat' is a reflection on the mystery and power of the bat, and a plea for us to give thanks for his existence.

The Bat

The bat is dun, with wrinkled wings,
Like fallow article;
And not a song pervade his lips,
Or none perceptible;

His small umbrella quaintly halved
Describing in the air
An arc alike inscrutable—
Elate philosopher,

Deputed from what firmament,
Of what astute abode,
Empowered with what malignity
Auspiciously withheld.

To his adroit creator
Ascribe no less the praise—
Beneficent, believe me,
His eccentricities.

EMILY DICKINSON

'The Wind Tapped Like a Tired Man' is a descriptive poem about the wind. It shows Dickinson's ability to personify the wind in order to stir the reader's imagination.

The Wind Tapped Like a Tired Man

The wind tapped like a tired man
And like a host 'Come in'
I boldly answered. Entered then
My residence within

A rapid footless guest,
To offer whom a chair
Were as impossible as hand
A sofa to the air.

No bone had he to bind him;
His speech was like the push
Of numerous humming birds at once
From a superior bush;

His countenance a billow;
His fingers as he passed
Let go a music as of tunes
Blown tremulous in glass.

He visited still flitting,
Then like a timid man
Again he tapped. 'Twas flurriedly,
And I became alone.

EMILY DICKINSON

Tuning in to the Wind

1 Judging from the first line, how would you describe the wind's initial approach?
2 What simile tells us how the person inside felt at the outset?
3 How is the wind described in the second stanza? Comment on the effectiveness of this image.
4 'To offer whom a chair/were as impossible as hand/A sofa to the air'. Do you think this comparison is effective? Why or why not?
5 What is the effect of the alliteration of the letters 'b', 'h' and 'n' in 'No bone had he to bind him'?
6 From the poet's description, what was 'the speech' of the wind like? Comment on the effectiveness of this description.
7 'From a superior bush'. What is the meaning of 'superior' here?
8 What are the wind's 'fingers', and what is the evidence of their presence?
9 'Tunes blown tremulous in glass'. How would *you* describe the sound of the wind's fingers as he passed?
10 How is the wind's personality described in the final stanza?
11 What do you think the tapping actually is?
12 How would you describe the mood of the poem at the end?
13 The central technique used to make this poem vivid is personification. How effective do you think this is? Explain your answer.
14 What do you see as the purpose behind the writing of this poem?

An incident involving a bird becomes the focal point of this poem, which finishes in wonder at the bird's flight.

A Bird Came Down the Walk

A bird came down the walk.
He did not know I saw.
He bit an angleworm in halves
And ate the fellow raw,

And then he drank a dew
From a convenient grass,
And then hopped sidewise to the wall
To let a beetle pass.

He glanced with rapid eyes
That hurried all around;
They looked like frightened beads, I thought;
He stirred his velvet head

Like one in danger, cautious;
I offered him a crumb,
And he unrolled his feathers
And rode him softer home

Than oars divide the ocean,
Too silver for a seam,
Or butterflies off banks of noon
Leap, plashless as they swim.

EMILY DICKINSON

Examining the Bird

1 Where do you imagine the poet is when she observes this bird? Why?
2 What does the bird do that attracts the poet's attention?
3 'Raw' is an unexpected word for the poet to use. Why? What is its impact?
4 Explain where the bird got his drink from.
5 Why did the bird hop 'sidewise to the wall'?
6 Why does the bird 'glance with rapid eyes'?
7 What other evidence is there that the bird is nervous?
8 What action does the poet take and why do you think she does this?
9 What effect does this action have on the bird?
10 The poem finishes with Dickinson marvelling at the bird's flight. What aspect is she trying to capture in the word 'softer'?
11 In the final stanza, what is she comparing the flight of the bird to?
12 In the last two lines, how is she depicting the flight of butterflies?
13 What do you see as the main achievement of this poem? Why?
14 What do you learn about the character of the poet from this poem?

Dickinson found the subject of death an important one to explore. In this poem she likens its presence to a ride in a carriage.

Because I Could Not Stop for Death

Because I could not stop for Death
He kindly stopped for me.
The carriage held but just ourselves
And immortality.

We slowly drove. He knew no haste,
And I had put away
My labour and my leisure too
For his civility.

We passed the school where children strove
At recess in the ring.
We passed the fields of gazing grain;
We passed the setting sun—

Or rather, he passed us.
The dews drew quivering and chill,
For only gossamer my gown,
My tippet only tulle.

We paused before a house that seemed
A swelling of the ground.
The roof was scarcely visible,
The cornice in the ground.

Since then 'tis centuries, and yet
Feels shorter than the day
I first surmised the horses' heads
Were toward Eternity.

EMILY DICKINSON

Pausing to Look at Death

1 What is unexpected about the word 'kindly'?
2 The poet pictures her relationship with Death as like a carriage ride. What is the effect of this?
3 'We slowly drove'. What is the effect of this descriptive statement?
4 What human qualities does the poet attribute to Death?
5 What does the picture of the children striving 'at recess in the ring' contribute to the picture of the ride with Death?

6 'We passed the fields of gazing grain'. Comment on the poet's use of the word 'gazing'.
7 She corrects her description: 'Or rather, he passed us'. Who is she referring to?
8 How is she affected when the setting sun passes?
9 How does the poet picture herself as being dressed to cope with the onset of dark?
10 What significance do you see in the house 'in the ground'?
11 Carefully read the last stanza. Do you think the lady is speaking from Heaven? Or, is she still alive, conscious that she, a human being, will one day die?
12 What gives the poem a sense of foreboding at the end?
13 Is Death a 'kindly' companion or not? Refer to the poem for support.
14 Why do you think Emily Dickinson has written this poem?

Here is a very different approach to death. This poem focuses on a specific death that has occurred in a house across the road.

There's Been a Death

There's been a death in the opposite
house
As lately as today.
I know it by the numb look
Such houses have alway.

The neighbours rustle in and out;
The doctor drives away.
A window opens like a pod,
Abrupt, mechanically;

Somebody flings a mattress out.
The children hurry by;
They wonder if it died on that.
I used to, when a boy.

The minister goes stiffly in
As if the house were his
And he owned all the mourners now,
And little boys besides;

And then the milliner, and the man
Of the appalling trade
To take the measure of the house.
There'll be that dark parade

Of tassels and of coaches soon.
It's easy as a sign—
The intuition of the news
In just a country town.

EMILY DICKINSON

Looking into the Opposite House

1 What word would we tend to use instead of 'lately'?
2 What is there about the house opposite that reveals there has been a death?
3 What is the effect of the word 'rustle' to describe the neighbours' movements?
4 'Somebody flings a mattress out'. Comment on the use of the word 'flings' here.
5 What do the children wonder about the mattress?
6 Why does the poet use the word 'it' to describe the person who died?
7 How does the poet know what the children wonder?
8 What does the word 'stiffly' suggest about the way the minister feels?
9 Explain the meaning of 'As if the house were his'.
10 Who is ' . . . the man/Of the appalling trade'?
11 What do you think the poet means by 'To take the measure of the house'?
12 Why is the impending funeral procession described as 'that dark parade'?
13 What is it that is described as 'easy' at the poem's end?
14 How does the poet appear to feel about death, judging from this poem? Support your answer.
15 Do you think this poem was written from a real-life experience of the poet? Explain your viewpoint.

'We Like March' is a simple poem exploring some of the distinctive aspects of this month.

We Like March

We like March.
His shoes are purple;
He is new and high.
Makes he mud for dog and peddler;
Makes he forests dry.
Knows the adder tongue his coming
And presents her spot.
Stands the sun so close and mighty
That our minds are hot.

News is he of all the others.
Bold it were to die
With the blue birds exercising
On his British sky.

EMILY DICKINSON

In 'I Years Had Been from Home', the poet describes the fear of facing deep aspects of inner reality, drawing on the image of returning to her home.

I Years Had Been from Home

I years had been from home
And now before the door
I dared not enter, lest a face
I never saw before

Stare stolid into mine
And ask my business there—
My business but a life I left:
Was such remaining there?

I leaned upon the awe
I lingered with before.
The second life an ocean rolled
And broke against my ear.

I laughed a crumbling laugh
That I could fear a door
Who consternation compassed
And never winced before.

I fitted to the latch
My hand with trembling care,
Lest back the awful door should spring
And leave me in the floor;

Then moved my fingers off
As cautiously as glass,
And held my ears, and like a thief
Fled gasping from the house.

EMILY DICKINSON

Acknowledgements

The authors and publishers are grateful to the following for permission to reproduce copyright material:

Poems: Andre Deutsch Ltd for 'Telephone Poles' and 'Sonic Boom' by John Updike from *Telephone Poles and Other Poems*; Collins/Angus and Robertson for 'Harry Pearce' and 'On Frosty Days' by David Campbell from *Collected Poems* Copyright © Judith Campbell 1973, for 'Lady Feeding the Cats', 'Leopard Skin', 'The Brown Snake', 'The Lizards', 'Wasp', 'Wombat', 'Brindabella' and 'Crab and Cicada' by Douglas Stewart from *Selected Poems* Copyright © Margaret Stewart 1973, for 'In the Park' by Gwen Harwood from *Selected Poems* copyright © Gwen Harwood 1975, for 'Song of the Rain' by Hugh McCrae from *The Poems of Hugh McCrae* copyright © Mrs J. Hay, Mrs E. Humphreys, for 'Land's End', 'Martin and the Hand Grenade', 'Summer Rain', 'A Crow That Came for the Chickens', 'Bradman's Last Innings', 'For the Fire' and 'Harry Wood' by John Foulcher from *Light Pressure* © John Foulcher 1983, for 'Gulliver', 'Sleep', 'The Night-ride', 'Country Towns', 'Vesper-song of the Reverend Samuel Marsden', 'Wild Grapes', 'Beach Burial' and 'William Street' by Kenneth Slessor from *Selected Poems* © Paul Slessor, for 'Spring Hail' by Les Murray from *Collected Poems* © Les Murray, for 'Killed in the Street' by Mary Gilmore from *Selected Poems* © The Estate of Mary Gilmore, for 'The Two Windmills' by Nancy Cato, for 'The Peacock', 'Brother and Sisters', 'South of My Days', 'The Surfer', 'Flying-fox on Barbed Wire', 'Sanctuary', 'The Cicadas' and 'Woman to Child' by Judith Wright from *A Human Pattern* © Judith Wright 1990, for 'Magpies' by Judith Wright from *Collected Poems* © Judith Wright 1971, for 'Otters', by William Hart-Smith from *The Talking Clothes* © The Estate of William Hart-Smith; David Higham and Associates Ltd for 'The Quails' by Francis Brett Young; Mr Michael Dugan for 'To a Trainee Accountant' by Michael Dugan from *Australian Poetry Now* by Thomas W. Shapcott, Sun Books, Melbourne 1970; Estate of Robert Frost for 'A Hillside Thaw', 'After Apple-picking', 'Mending Wall', 'On a Tree Fallen across the Road', 'Stopping by Woods on a Snowy Evening', 'The Line-gang, 'Tree at My Window', 'The Road Not Taken' and 'The Wood-pile' by Robert Frost from *The Poetry of Robert Frost* edited by Edward Connery Lathem reproduced by permission of Jonathan Cape Ltd; Mr Max Fatchen for 'Signs' by Max Fatchen from *A Pocketful of Rhymes* (Omnibus/Puffin) © Max Fatchen; Jacaranda Wiley Ltd for 'Then and Now' 'Civilisation', 'Colour Bar', 'Free-dom', 'The Child Wife', 'Time Is Running Out', 'Artist Son', 'Bwalla the Hunter', 'The Last of His Tribe' and 'No More Boomerang' by Oodgeroo of the tribe Noonuccal custodian of the land Minjerribah from *My People*; Mr John Kitching for 'One Parent Family' by John Kitching from *A Fifth Poetry Book* and 'Chill, Burning Rain' by John Kitching; Longman Cheshire Pty Ltd for the poems 'Genesis', 'Homecoming', 'Life-cycle', 'Planning a Time-capsule', 'Enter without So Much as Knocking', 'Homo Suburbiensis', 'In the New Landscape' and 'Search and Destroy' by Bruce Dawe from *Sometimes Gladness*; Ms Judith Nicholls for 'Harvest Hymn' by Judith Nicholls from *Dragonsfire* by Judith Nicholls, pub. Faber © Judith Nicholls reprinted by permission of the author; Oxford University Press UK for 'Sunset' by Mbuyiseni Oswald Mtshali from

273

Sounds of a Cowhide Drum (1971) reprinted by permission of Oxford University Press; Penguin Books Ltd for 'When Gran Died' from *Cat Among the Pigeons* by Kit Wright (Viking Kestrel 1987) © Kit Wright 1984, 1987 reproduced by permission of Penguin Books Ltd, for 'A Boy's Head' by Mirosklav Holub from *Miroslav Holub: Selected Poems* translated by Ian Milner and George Theiner © Miroslav Holub 1967, translation copyright © Penguin Books 1967 and for 'Schoolmaster' by Yevgeny Yevtushenko from *Yevtushenko: Selected Poems* translated by Robin Milner-Gulland and Peter Levi © Robin Milner-Gulland and Peter Levi 1962; Peters, Fraser and Dunlop Ltd for 'Apples' by Laurie Lee from *Selected Poems*, and for 'Beatings', 'Icarus Allsorts', 'Smithereens', 'The Commission', 'Three Rusty Nails', 'My Busconductor', 'Cabbage', 'Goodbat Nightman', 'Noah's Arc' and 'Nooligan' by Roger McGough reprinted with permission; Punch for the poem 'Hey Diddle Diddle' by Paul Dehn from Punch (London) reproduced by permission of Punch; Rogers, Coleridge & White Ltd for 'The Lesson' by Edward Lucie-Smith from *A Tropical Childhood and Other Poems* (OUP 1961); Routledge for 'Starlings' by Lucy Hosegood from *Those First Affections* by Timothy Rogers; Scholastic Publications Ltd for 'He Was . . .' by John Cunliffe from *Standing on a Strawberry*; Mr Anthony Thwaite for 'Hedgehog' by Anthony Thwaite from *Poems 1953–1988*, Hutchinson 1989; University of Queensland Press for 'Letter to People About Pelicans' and 'Prosperity' by Michael Dransfield from *Collected Poems* edited by Rodney Hall; Warner Chappell Music Ltd for 'Big Yellow Taxi' by Joni Mitchell © Warner Chappell Music Ltd reproduced by permission; Faber and Faber Ltd for 'Wind', 'The Retired Colonel', 'Bayonet Charge', 'Her Husband', 'Hawk Roosting', 'Otter', 'The Jaguar', 'View of a Pig', 'Bullfrog', 'Foxhunt' from *Ted Hughes: Selected Poems* by Ted Hughes, for 'Skunk Hour' from *Selected Poems* by Robert Lowell, for 'Mushrooms', 'Insomniac', 'Blackberrying', 'Mirror', 'Cut', 'The Arrival of the Bee Box' from *Sylvia Plath, Selected Poems* edited by Ted Hughes, for 'Balloons', 'Snakecharmer', 'A Winter Ship' from *The Colossus* by Sylvia Plath, for 'Trout', 'Death of a Naturalist', 'Digging', 'The Early Purges', 'Blackberry-picking', 'The Forge', 'Mid-term Break', 'Churning Day', from *Selected Poems 1965–75* by Seamus Heaney.

Photographs, book covers: Austral International for the photographs on pp. 14, 33, 62; Australian Picture Library for the photographs on pp. 133, 225; Bettmann Archives and Newsphotos for the photographs on pp. 104, 202; Collins/Angus and Robertson Publishers for the photograph on p. 238; Herald and Weekly Times Ltd for the photograph on p. 163; International Photographic Library for the photograph on p. 173; Jacaranda Wiley Ltd for the book cover on p. 119; Longman Cheshire Pty Ltd for the book covers *Sometimes Gladness* 3rd Edition and *This Side of Silence* by Bruce Dawe and for the photograph on p. 187; Penguin Books Ltd for the book covers *Blazing Fruit* and *Robert Frost: Selected Poems*; Stock Photos for the photographs on pp. 1, 92; Sydney Morning Herald for the photographs on pp. 50, 120, 146, 214; Topham Picture Library for the photographs on pp. 77, 158, 262.

Index of Poems

Index of Poets